C000143684

The Broken String

The Broken String

The Last Words of an Extinct People

NEIL BENNUN

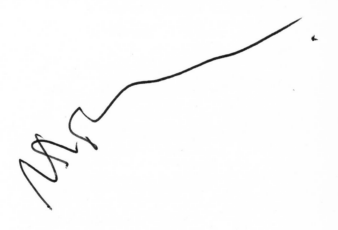

VIKING
an imprint of
PENGUIN BOOKS

VIKING

Published by the Penguin Group

Penguin Books Ltd, 80 Strand, London WC2R 0RL, England

Penguin Group (USA) Inc., 375 Hudson Street, New York, New York 10014, USA

Penguin Books Australia Ltd, 250 Camberwell Road, Camberwell, Victoria 3124, Australia

Penguin Books Canada Ltd, 10 Alcorn Avenue, Toronto, Ontario, Canada M4V 3B2

Penguin Books India (P) Ltd, 11 Community Centre, Panchsheel Park, New Delhi – 110 017, India

Penguin Group (NZ), Cnr Airborne and Rosedale Roads, Albany, Auckland 1310, New Zealand

Penguin Books (South Africa) (Pty) Ltd, 24 Sturdee Avenue, Rosebank 2196, South Africa

Penguin Books Ltd, Registered Offices: 80 Strand, London WC2R 0RL, England

www.penguin.com

First published 2004

1

Copyright © Neil Bennun, 2004

The moral right of the author has been asserted

All rights reserved
Without limiting the rights under copyright
reserved above, no part of this publication may be
reproduced, stored in or introduced into a retrieval system,
or transmitted, in any form or by any means (electronic, mechanical,
photocopying, recording or otherwise), without the prior
written permission of both the copyright owner and
the above publisher of this book

Set in 12/14.75pt Monotype Bembo
Typeset by Rowland Phototypesetting Ltd, Bury St Edmunds, Suffolk
Printed in Great Britain by Clays Ltd, St Ives plc

A CIP catalogue record for this book is available from the British Library

ISBN 0-670-91250-6

Contents

Illustrations

Section one

Section two

Illustration acknowledgements

Nos. 2, 4, 5, 6, 8, 9, 13, 14, 20, 23, 27, 28: Bleek Collection (BC151), University of Cape Town; 1, 7, 10, 15, 16, 25, 26, National Library of South Africa; 3, 18, 29: reproduced from P. Skotnes (ed.), *Miscast: Negotiating the Presence of the Bushmen*, University of Cape Town, 1996; 11, 12, 19, 24: reproduced from Miklós Szalay (ed.), *Der Mond als Schuh* (*The Moon as Shoe*), Scheidegger and Spiess, Zurich 2003; 17, the author; 21, 22, reproduced by permission of the Rock Art Research Unit, University of the Witwatersrand, South Africa.

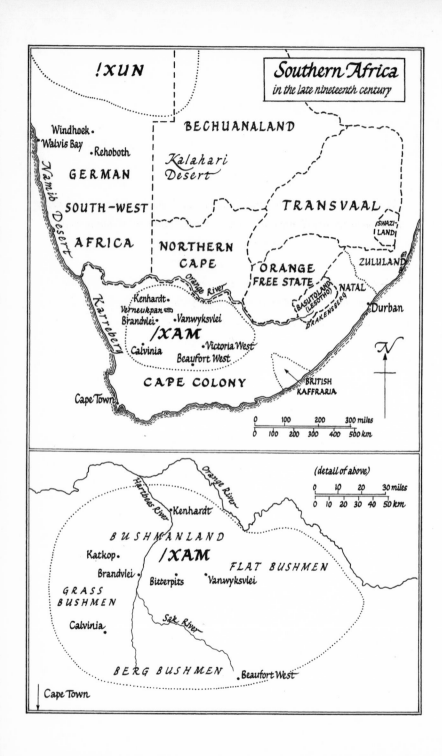

Southern Africa
in the late nineteenth century

!XUN

Windhoek·
Walvis Bay·
·Rehoboth

GERMAN

SOUTH-WEST

AFRICA

BECHUANALAND

Kalahari
Desert

Namib Desert

Karreberg

NORTHERN
CAPE

Orange River

Kenhardt·
Verneukpan
Brandvlei·
·Vanwyksvlei
/XAM
Calvinia·
·Victoria West
Beaufort West·

CAPE COLONY

Cape Town·

TRANSVAAL

SWAZI-
LAND

ORANGE
FREE STATE

ZULULAND

(BASUTOLAND
(LESOTHO)

NATAL

·Durban

DRAKENSBERG

BRITISH
KAFFRARIA

N

0   100   200   300 miles
0   100   200   300   400   500 km

(detail of above)

Orange River

Hartbees River

·Kenhardt

0   10   20   30 miles
0   10   20   30   40   50 km

BUSHMANLAND
/XAM

Katkop·

Brandvlei·

Bitterpits

·Vanwyksvlei

FLAT BUSHMEN

GRASS
BUSHMEN

Calvinia·

Sqk River

BERG BUSHMEN

·Beaufort West

Cape Town

My father used to sing that the string had broken; the string he used to hear when !Nuin-/kuïten had called forth the Rainbull. That was why things were different now.

'For things continue to be unpleasant to me; I do not hear the ringing sound in the sky I used to hear. I feel that the string has really broken, leaving me. So when I sleep I do not feel the thing which used to vibrate in me, as I lay asleep.'

At the confluence of the Senqu and the Qaqa in the highlands of Lesotho, two valleys meet to cancel each other in a broad, gravelly flat where herders bring their cattle to drink in the summer.

A bridle path leads from here into the gorge cut by the Qaqa, a swift, shallow river interrupted by boulderous moraine and low islands fastened by tall grass and the roots of cedars. Walking upstream you will pass the mouth of a cave high above the opposite bank and a steep half-acre of maize on your right; some twenty minutes later you will come to a near right-angle in the river channel at a cliff that glows spectacularly in the level evening sun, the eastern limit of a distinct space in the landscape bounded by the narrowing faces of the gorge and the flat where the rivers meet a few hundred metres downstream.

It does not take much effort to imagine away thousands of years here. It is, you might think, a magical place.

A romantic notion, of course – but this is one of the few places in the world where you might safely indulge it. This is a place that has been recognized and designated as somehow extraordinary by people who knew a thing or two about land-scape, a thing or two about magic (for want of a better term, for now) and the everyday workings of one upon the other.

About half-way between the cliff and the confluence is a long, flat screen of sandstone shielded from the worst of Lesotho's snow and hot sun by an overhang. The rock is a dark yellow-grey, paler where stretches have flaked away in sheets, the broad integrity of its smooth surface intermittently broken by moss, calcium and hearth soot. If you look carefully you will notice that someone has taken the end of a burnt stick and drawn a spate of five-bar gates on the edge of a protruding stone.

Keep looking.

Suddenly the five-bar gates are naked men about the size of your palm running from left to right across the rock. They are disproportionately tall and slender and they are running very fast; the artist has their legs at right angles to their trunks, lending them speed, their calf muscles pronounced. A few seconds later they are joined by clapping women and standing antelope and the rock face under the overhang is a long frieze full of movement and faded colour, palest where the figures are most exposed.

There is a tiny springbok on its own. There is a single man with a stick in his hand. Now there are a handful of each. It is as if a projector behind the rock is slowly finding focus. Once the eye has learned to make sense of the disposition of the faint pigments the figures arrive quickly and generally they do not come alone, although men and women on the lichened margins of the rock face come unaccompanied and take many minutes to draw themselves to the surface. You might have to wait for them.

Here is a painting of the world's largest antelope, the eland, painted in red haematite dug from Lesotho's mountain basalt and deliberately surrounded by an ochre corona. Near the running men that were five-bar gates are two taller figures with the dress and bodies of men and the hind legs and antlered heads of antelope; not far from them, flanked by half a dozen more naked men and seated women wearing *karosses* – capes – of animal skins, there is a rain animal.

It is painted in a grey-blue colour, it resembles a hippopotamus, and it stands surrounded by blue and black contours suggesting rainclouds, perhaps, or something to do with the power that belongs to clouds. Its five legs fall at a slight angle like broad columns of rain seen from a distance, which is exactly what they are.

The people who made this picture are dead and there is no one alive today who can explain it to us with first-hand experience of making rock art or the husbandry of rain creatures. The Stone Age culture that produced these artists, the language those people spoke and the eland they painted are all extinct here. None the less, we know what this hippo-like thing with rain for legs was called – !Khwa-ka xoro: the Water's Bull.[1]

We know where it lived and how it was recognized by its distinctive marks and its smell. We know its character and its habits, how it was coaxed from its home in the standing water or the river, captured and led through the sky to be slaughtered, pacified with aromatic herbs and tied fast with a thong over its black and white horns.

The rain bull, or rain animal, was a physical manifestation of !Khwa, the Water, or the Rain – and we know, too, what would happen to the young women that angered him:

!Khwa lightens, killing them; they become stars, while their appearance has changed. They become stars.

Else they would be taken to the waterpit, the Rain's home and his body on the earth, and become the water flowers known as *!kweiten.* If you were to try and pick these flowers they would disappear. They were the Water's wives.

---

[1] For a selection of /Xam names and terms together with a guide to their pronunciation see pages 386 ff.

We look at them, leaving them alone.

Someone has taken the end of a burnt stick and written 'BUSHMEN' across the running men.

In Cape Town, a thousand kilometres to the southeast of the confluence of the Qaqa and the Senqu, there is a collection of hardbacked notebooks each neatly labelled with a date, a set of initials and a number in Victorian script. !Khwa, the name of the Rain, was first recorded in one of them. Together these notebooks are a long document of the beliefs, rituals and everyday practices of the /Xam-ka !ei – an extinct branch of the indigenous people of southern Africa first known to the Dutch as Bosjemans, as Bushmen to the British and as San to South Africa's Khoe people.

A crease divides every page into two columns. On every right-hand page one column is filled with writing in /Xam – the language of the /Xam-ka !ei – and the other with an English transliteration. The facing left-hand pages contain notes and additions in /Xam and English, sometimes Dutch; there might be a note on a point of grammar or pronunciation here, a list of a someone's children, the names of a family of stars, an explanation or a clarification.

There are more than 12,000 ruled and creased pages in these notebooks. The material preserved in them offers us an insight into the culture and the cosmology of a people who did not survive the advance of European colonization north from the Cape of Good Hope into the semi-desert of the Cape interior. The individual voices that speak from the pages were among the last to remember a means of subsistence – hunting and gathering – that had allowed people like us to live in that barren region for tens of thousands of years and the ritual culture that made that lifestyle possible.

Much of what you read here appears to be very alien indeed, and calls for explanation:

The stars are also things which resemble the moon; for, they used formerly to be a person. Therefore, the star formerly sang of its elder sister; while it sang asking the time at which the //garaken flower should open; it did thus when it sang, while it questioned !Guanu, it said: 'Oh! Dost thou open?'

Many of the pages hint at the relationship between those who provided the testimony and those who recorded it:

My thoughts spoke to me, therefore, my mouth speaks to thee; I thought in the night, while I lay, I thought that I would say to thee that thou shouldst give me thread. I should sew, sewing the buttons on the jacket. The buttons which thou didst give to me; for they would be falling down for me upon the ground.

Other pages record precisely what happened to the first people of the Cape Thirstland, the southern Karoo and the mountains of Lesotho:

They bound them, they drove them, making them go to the cliff when they had driven Kki-a//ken and the other with horseback. The names of the Bushmen were as follows: 'Gert Rounabout', 'Prince Santkop' or //Kum!kan, 'Swart Klaas', Kki-a//ken or 'Stuurman'.

Myth seeps into personal history; the ancient past is populated by people from the present; recent history is described in the language of myth. This is another way of understanding the meaning of *the past*, another way of making sense of the present.

Historical document, anthropological resource and testament to an extraordinary collaboration, the notebooks offer us also a way to interpret the fragile evidence of the longest-enduring art tradition the world has ever known: the engravings and paintings on the boulders, overhangs, rock shelters and glacial pavements of southern Africa made by the /Xam-ka !ei and their relatives.

Most of the writing in these notebooks is the work of two hands. The bolder, and the scruffier by far, is that of a Prussian philologist called Wilhelm Bleek; the more careful and legible is that of his sister-in-law Lucy Lloyd, a former schoolteacher whose work over three decades filled the majority of the pages in the collection. There is a third hand to be found in the notebooks, too, completing some of the translations that Wilhelm Bleek and Lucy Lloyd left unfinished, a contribution made decades after the death of the people who began the project they called their 'Bushmen Work'.

Wilhelm Bleek and Lucy Lloyd's hands filled the notebooks and their voices pervade them but the clearest voices of all belong to five men —/A!kungta, //Kabbo, Dia!kwain, ≠Kasing and /Hang≠kass'o — and a woman called !Kweiten ta //ken, who seems to have been named for the flowers that were the Water's wives.

Kumm:

The First at Sitting People were those who first inhabited the earth

The First at Sitting People were those who first inhabited the earth. It was their children who worked with the Sun. This is why the people who inhabited the country after them say that those children made the sun ascend, feeling that their mothers had agreed together that they should throw the Sun up for them; that the Sun might warm the earth for them; that they might feel the Sun's warmth; that they might be able to sit in the Sun.

When the First at Sitting People had passed away the Flat Bushmen inhabited their ground. That is why the Flat Bushmen taught their children the stories of the First at Sitting People.

The Sun had been a man. He talked. They all talked: the other one too, the Moon. While they spoke, they used to live on the earth.

They do not talk, now that they live in the sky.

!Khwe //na s'o !kwe:

The Early Race

The beasts of prey were once people. They became beasts of prey because of the Lynx and the Anteater – they were the ones responsible. They cursed each other because of the little Springbok's doings. They cursed each other.

All things were once people.

The carrion creatures, the reptiles, the huge mammals, the primates, the antelope herds, the parasitic insects, the beasts of prey, the rodents and the birds were all men and women in the time of the !Khwe //na s'o !kwe – the First at Sitting People. They hunted game, they collected roots and seeds in their gathering bags, they cooked with pots, they married, they went to the waterpits to dip up water in ostrich shells and they lived behind thorny windbreaks in shelters of bent brushwood, just like ordinary people. They *were* people – but they were not human.

And they were not animals either.

He has feet with which he is a lion; he has hands with which he is a man. He talks. But he eats people, when he is a man, because he feels he is a lion's man. Therefore he catches people at night because he feels he is a lion's man. He is a lion, he is a man, he has hair, he is a lion, his hands are a man's.

He shines with his eyes, which are like fire. And he smells with his nose.

The First at Sitting People often ate each other, they fed their families on their own innards and they did not feel bound to keep their own shapes. This is the way things were until the Lynx and the Anteater cursed each other and brought their time to an end. Then the /Xam-ka !ei, the truly ordinary people who followed them and told their stories, inherited the newly minted semi-desert south of the Orange River from people who became real ticks, lions, rock rabbits, elephants, hyenas, lizards, hares and kudu.

For all their trunks, crooked tails and claws, the people of the Early Race wore leather on their feet, hunted with bow and arrow and fell out with their in-laws, just like the /Xam-ka !ei who came after them. The Mason Wasp hid his narrow waist from his human wife with his *kaross* and the Frog ran away from the Blue Crane by jumping across the veld – but we should not spend too much time in trying to decide whether they were animals with human characteristics or people with the features and behaviour of animals, the human ancestors of the animals they became. They were neither one nor the other, and strictly speaking nor were they *both*.

Ideas of *opposites* and *absolutes* are not always helpful in considering some of the things that the /Xam-ka !ei thought and said. Farmers brought those ideas to South Africa less than 2,000 years ago – and they were not to be forced on the /Xam people for a long time after that. Those are recent notions south of the Orange and the Limpopo.

Cursing, on the other hand, has some history there.

Destruction! You there, become a Lynx who walks about at night!

Destruction! You there, become an Anteater who walks about at night!

The spinster Anteater cursed the handsome young Lynx, he cursed her back before she had even drawn breath and then their curses became the laws that divided people and animals for good.

Before this no one had ever been quite certain who or what it was appropriate to eat or to marry; the very notions of 'animal' and 'human' had never meant a thing so it should be no surprise that the behaviour expected of the beasts of prey, the scavengers, the herbivores and the insects was negotiable. The Ticks were generally agreed to be very aggressive people and the Elephants tended to the superior. The Quaggas were family orientated and the Lions, although unpredictable, sometimes supernaturally aggressive and at other times foolish in the extreme, were by and large to be avoided at all costs.

The Baboons were awful people. Keep walking. Ignore them.

They married out of their species all the time in the days of the First at Sitting People and the consequences were always ghastly. *These people are said to have been stupid, and not to have understood things well,* an old /Xam man called //Kabbo once told a former governess called Lucy Lloyd, and he had a point.

The story of the Quagga woman and her husband the Young He-Dog is all the evidence you need that //Kabbo was right. One of the Quaggas – striped wild horses – married into the Jackals and Hyenas by taking the Young He-Dog as a spouse. She was part of the Zebra family and her husband was from a long line of reprehensible carnivores so of course the marriage was always likely to be problematic, and it certainly did not help matters that the Quagga woman gave her children pieces of her own liver to eat. She managed to keep this a secret from her husband until the Tortoise snatched a piece from her daughter and took it to the Young He-Dog's family.

The Jackals and Hyenas declared it delicious and told the young man that he had *married meat.* After a taste he had to agree. The Young He-Dog quickly decided that he would kill his wife by getting her to lie down on some bones sharpened and tipped with poison so that he and his relatives might have a feast.

The moment she lay down she knew what her husband had done. As the poison began to kill her heart she ran in desperation to a *vlei* – a shallow water pool – called Neck-Vulture to drink, and there she died, her head still in the muddied water. Her children cried as the Jackals cut her up and boiled her. The dead woman's daughter was hiding in a tree above the feast and her tears fell on the pot, cracking it.

Quaggas, wild ones, today, weep if another quagga is wounded. They cry and make a noise together if they smell the scent of blood.

Irredeemably greedy and as ugly inside as out, the Young He-Dog decided he would marry meat again (he had a taste for it now, the cannibal) and with exemplary callousness he proposed to his late wife's sister. He was pleased when her family assented to the match and he continued to be pleased until the celebration dance, when he received his comeuppance.

Many quaggas surrounded him. They trampled him to pieces, breaking his bones with their trampling. They killed him.

All of this happened a very long time ago in the parched flats and exploded hills of the region between the Orange River and the hills of the Kareeberg in what is today the Northern Cape province of South Africa. The story ends in 1878 with the extinction of the quagga, hunted out of those parched flats and exploded hills by farmers of European descent – then, or with the extinction of the language in which the story was told.

There are still wild dogs in that dry part of the world but

now they pick on the sheep that the farmers brought with them rather than their own equine wives, and of course they have not married meat since the curses of the Anteater and the Lynx.

I came from that place. I came here when I came from my place.

Oud (Old) Jantje Tooren was sat at his place, before a fire, eating a springbok that he had shot with an arrow. He was with his wife Lies, their son Witbooi and his daughter-in-law, Witbooi's wife. His daughter Sara and her husband Klein (Little) Jantje – a graceful, almost delicate man – were there too. The elder Jantje and Lies were the heads of a close family.

We can imagine that it was nearly evening, the earth was hot, and that it had not rained for nearly a year.

My wife was there; I was there; my son was there; my son's wife was there, carrying a little child on her back; my daughter was there, while she also carried a little child; my daughter's husband was there. We were like this.

It was October, spring, and the baked flats would soon be full of bleached grass and tiny desert flowers, if they were not already.

This happened ten years before the last quagga was shot for its hide. Those animals were already scarce but Oud Jantje Tooren had lived here long enough to remember migrations and massive herds.

Before he and his family had finished eating, policemen came and bound his arms. They were dressed like farmhands and they forced him into a wagon with Witbooi and Klein Jantje, both bound as securely and uncomfortably as he. Their wives climbed up after them, wanting to keep them company on the journey that they were about to begin, but the policemen ordered them out. Soon the wagon began to move.

They got out of the wagon; they walked upon their feet.

The women walked through the spring heat into the evening, east and south, heading out of Bushmanland and towards the Karoo. Witbooi's wife brought the rest of the springbok meat with her and when the wagon stopped for the night she lit a fire and roasted it. One of the policemen roasted a lamb and everybody ate.

We smoked; we lay down. The day broke; we made a fire; we smoked early in the morning.

They smoked *in the morning's mouth*, early, before the heat of the day. They liked to smoke – they were *smoking's people*, you might say.

Then, we left them, we went away to the Magistrate; while we (who were in the wagon) ran along, we were upon the road, while our wives walked along upon their feet.

The horses were too fast for Sara and Lies, carrying their belongings and their children behind their husbands through the dry heat of the Cape Thirstland. There is no shade in that part of the huge semi-desert over the mountains north of the Cape of Good Hope, only silver grass, seared bushes and sudden outcrops of black-patinated volcanic boulders. The three women could not keep up and of course the wagon did not stop for them.

We ran, leaving them, while we altogether ran, leaving them.

Eventually the wagon arrived at Victoria West, a dusty town at the bottom of a valley in the Great Karoo, a couple of streets of shuttered windows with a prison, a church, a town hall and stores supplying farmers from the region's isolated sheep farms. The magistrate, a man called Maximillian Jackson, met Oud Jantje Tooren, his son Witbooi and his son-in-law Klein Jantje. On 23 October 1869 Jackson tried them for cattle rustling and sentenced them to two years' imprisonment with hard labour.

We went to put our legs into the stocks; another white man laid another piece of wood on our legs. We slept, while our legs were in the stocks.

In the morning they got up to a breakfast of boiled mutton and they smoked. It was not too long before their wives arrived in the town, footsore after their journey from the south of the Cape Thirstland, some 150 kilometres from where the men were arrested. The two Jantjes and Witbooi began to serve out their sentences in a chain-gang building roads through the Karoo.

We came to roll stones at Victoria, while we worked at the road. We lifted stones with our chests; we rolled great stones. We worked with earth. We carried earth, while the earth was on the handbarrow. We carried earth; we loaded the wagon with earth; we pushed it. Other people walked along. We were pushing the wagon's wheels; we were pushing; we poured down the earth; we pushed it back.

One especially hot day nearly four months later they were bound behind another wagon and began a forced march towards the town of Beaufort West en route to the Cape of

Good Hope, leaving their wives behind. It rained heavily on the way.

We splashed into the water; we splashed, passing through the water in the riverbed. We walked, following the wagon, being bound, until we, being bound, came to the Breakwater. On the way, we ate sheep as we came to the Breakwater; we came and worked at it.

On 1 March 1870, the beginning of autumn, they arrived at the Breakwater Station on Cape Town's Portswood Road, a whitewashed, crenellated jail on the waterfront originally built to hold the prisoners who had laboured on the breakwater in Table Bay.

The light in Cape Town tends to the spectacular. The sun can be uncomfortably dazzling in the summer but in the evenings the trees on the brow of Signal Hill cast narrow shadows over the city and the air along the seafront glows solidly. Oud Jantje Tooren would have remarked on that; he had never seen the sea before. From his cell he could hear it and taste it.

He had come to a place of broad avenues, secret lanes and steep streets of packed red earth following the ordered grid of farm tracks and vegetable plots laid out by the Dutch East India Company early in the 1650s. Now the capital of Britain's Cape Colony, Cape Town was dusty all summer and persistently muddy until the end of spring, a polyglot town creeping into the pines on the lower slopes of Table Mountain where the sensibilities of Victorian Britain – tactical politeness, pleasure in pointlessly hierarchical societies, a veneration of the institution – had been grafted on to a society founded two centuries before by a trading corporation with its own army and laws.

Mozambique, Madagascar, Asia, Europe and the southwest of Africa met in its languages, its cuisine and its music. English, not Afrikaans, was spoken in Parliament, and the language of the Khoekhoen, the iron-age herding people the Dutch met when they arrived to plant their vegetables, was all but extinct.

On their way to the prison on the waterfront, Jantje Tooren and the men of his family passed through a city that was dilapidated, elegant, spectacular, smelly; they might have seen substantial shops and offices in the Dutch style three storeys tall, grand public buildings, shacks on the foreshore and white-washed houses with flat roofs, skirted by the ubiquitous red dust. On the lower slopes of Table Mountain there were mansions and villas occupied by the well-to-do. Everywhere shuttered windows and the glare from the whitewash lent the place a feeling of the Mediterranean. Days were punctuated by the song of the muezzin from the city's mosques and bugle calls from the barracks on the foreshore, the Castle, a place originally built to guard Dutch vegetables from the Khoekhoen.

First there was a cattle pen of stones and thornbushes, a place the Khoekhoen called //Hu!gais. Then there were vegetable plots, a barracks and a town called Kaapstad. Now there was a city called Cape Town, an unhurried, absent-minded place so quiet at night that from the saddle between Table Mountain and Lion's Head, two of the mountains and high hills bounding it, it was still possible to hear surf breaking on the beaches and rocks on the shore.

Table Bay was calm now that the breakwater had been completed, although the jail raised to hold the convicts who had built it still stood. *For human misery in the mass and over a long period I suppose there has never been anything in South Africa to match the Breakwater Prison*, someone once wrote of the Breakwater Station (although Oud Jantje Tooren, having seen what he had seen in the north, would have disagreed). It was freezing cold at night, overcrowded and brutal, *Old Newgate under our southern sun*. Prisoners left every morning in gangs, chained at the ankles and dressed in rough canvas overalls printed with arrows, to sit bareheaded on wagons bound for the quarries, railway cuttings and mountain passes about the Cape Peninsula. They would shift earth, break rocks and pick at the dusty soil until the early evening before heading back to their cells in the whitewashed castle on the harbour for supper at six and lights out at eight.

Punishment by spare diet led to outbreaks of scurvy at the prison. It was a place where you could land three days of solitary confinement, like Prisoner D202 Kabashe, for being *noisy on Sunday* – although he got off lightly compared to D6393 Jan Appie, a man who earned a day in solitary confinement for *having a dirty dishtowel* on 2 October 1888 following a caution for the same offence the previous July. Appie earned another two days in the cells on 11 February the next year for *not washing his trousers at the proper time* and two more in November for not cleaning his bedboard.

A day in the cells was still preferable to the treadmill in the yard that chopped your shins to pieces if you were too tired to continue stepping.

Oud Jantje Tooren, a gentle old man possessed of a curious gravity, did what he was told. He moved deliberately, at his own pace, and the prison staff barely noticed him. He received neither rewards nor punishments; measured and undemonstrative, none of the warders – former servicemen, policemen and sundry colonial jetsam of the unskilled sort – could possibly have guessed at the complexity of his interior world.

More than anything he wanted to go home.

Home was a place in the Cape interior that came into being at the end of the time of the First at Sitting People. The Milky Way was made in those beginningless centuries of continual creation when a young woman, frustrated to be confined in her shelter of bent branches and bushes during the rites of passage that followed her first menstruation, threw wood ash into the sky.

They must lie white along in the sky, that the stars may stand outside of the Milky Way, while the Milky Way is the Milky Way, while it used to be wood ashes

she said.

They shall sail along upon their footprints, which they, always sailing along, are following. While they feel that they are the Stars which descend.

From then on the stars descended to fetch the daybreak. She made the other stars by throwing the edible roots of the *!huing* plant into the sky; the old *!huing* roots turned into red stars, the young *!huing* roots the white ones.

The Sun and the Moon, too, first became in the time of the First at Sitting People. Before the Sun was thrown into the sky the world was cold, delicious ant chrysalids would not dry and nothing was bright. The world was lit by a diffuse grey light. An old man with light in his armpit lay before his shelter, lifting his arm every now and again to illuminate the places immediately about him.

A woman of the Early Race told her children to throw this old man into the sky. When he was asleep they crept up to him and tossed him into the air, exhorting him to stand fast. He stood, and from then on the sun was bright and round. Hunting the springbok, the ostrich and the kudu became possible and so did travelling, visiting and the exchange of *kukummi* – history, myths, news, anything told – that followed.

Kukummi, the plural of *kumm*, were very important to the /Xam-ka !ei, the men and women who inherited the Cape Thirstland from the Early Race. The exchange of *kukummi* was one of the principal reasons for visiting, and people lived to make visits.

The Sun is here, all the earth is bright; the Sun is here, the people walk while the place is light; the people perceive the bushes, they see the other people . . . They also visit each other, while they feel that the sun shines, the earth is also bright, the sun shines upon the path.

We do not know who or what was responsible for the initial creation of the universe inhabited by the people of the Early Race but we do know who brought the time to an end and provided the catalyst for the second creation, when the animals took their roles and their final shapes, the /Xam-ka !ei gained the exclusive use of human tools and the emblems of their material culture and the heavenly bodies became fixed in their orbits.

Destruction! You there, become a Lynx who walks about at night!

Destruction! You there, become an Anteater who walks about at night!

These were the curses that changed the world for good.

The Descriptions Register of the Breakwater Station is a heavy book disintegrating along its spine and held together by red ribbons. Its pages are divided into columns recording the age, marital status, religion, height, distinguishing marks and literacy of the prisoners held there. South Africans of all kinds are remembered in this book: Xhosa people, Tswana people, Zulu people, 'Dutch' people, 'English' people, Khoe people, San people.

Oud Jantje Tooren, they guessed, was fifty-five years old. He had *small eyes, wrinkled face/forehead, small wart on left side of brow*. He was four feet and nine inches tall, he was missing the top joints of both his little fingers and had a swelling on his left shoulder caused by the blow of a knobkerrie – a throwing stick. His son-in-law Klein Jantje, the prison thought, was nineteen. He was five feet tall and bore a small scar on each temple. The two Jantjes were among thirty-three men from South Africa's Northern Cape to be admitted to the prison between November 1869 and the following March.

Among the others were Simon Baai, a man of perhaps twenty years who was missing the top of the little finger on his right hand, and a composed eighteen-year-old called Klaas Stoffel. Stoffel, who was just under five feet tall, was admitted on the same day as 4629 Jack, a man of perhaps sixty years with a *small withered face, first joint little finger left hand off*. Many were friends and many were related by marriage or by blood, like 4644 Willem Streep, about twenty-seven, tattooed on his breast and missing his right little finger from the top joint, admitted with his little brother Klaas.

In all, nine of them were missing at least one joint from their little fingers while all but two – 4434 David Hoesar and 4435 Klaas Katkop – were serving sentences for *receiving stolen goods*. Hoesar and Katkop had shot a man.

Klaas Katkop was just over five feet tall. He had a *double tooth* on his front upper jaw and his left wrist was fractured; we do not know how it happened, but we can guess as to why. He was a man from a dusty little *dorp* in the Hantam

Karoo called Calvinia, it is recorded; he was married, he was about thirty-seven, he practised no religion at all and he was illiterate. His brother-in-law David Hoesar, likewise, practised no religion. He was about twenty-five, he could neither read nor write and he was also married. Both men had been sentenced to five years of hard labour for culpable homicide.

Another book records the punishments and rewards that the men from the Northern Cape earned as their weeks in captivity turned into months and years. Oud Jantje's son-in-law Klein Jantje was given a reward of six shillings for good work at school in November 1870; 4634 Coos Plaatjie was given three hours of labour for *disobedience* on 21 March 1871.

The dates of their releases or their deaths are recorded here, too; 4621 Albert Baardman died in June 1871 at the age of about twenty and Jack, the old man with the small withered face, died only a few weeks after his admission.

David Hoesar, the killer, was given three hours of labour for *disobedience* a few months after his incarceration and he spent two days *in the cells* at the end of May 1871 for having *dagga* – cannabis – in his possession. He was a gentle, sweet-natured man with a large curved scar on his right cheek who had learned to use all the force it took to defend himself.

Inked at a right-angle to the ruled lines of the column *Native Place*, to save the prison official the effort of repetition, are the words *Bushmans land*. Oud Jantje Tooren and his native place had other names but none were recorded in the Descriptions Register of the Breakwater Station because none of the guards or officials there could pronounce them or write them down. All thirty-three of the prisoners from the Northern Cape incarcerated at the Breakwater knew Oud Jantje Tooren as //Kabbo. 'Bushmans land' had been known as /Xam-ka !au for as long as the language of the /Xam-ka !ei had been spoken there.

/Xam-ka !au means 'the dust of the /Xam'. A thousand kilometres west of its source in the highlands of Lesotho and some six hundred kilometres north of the Breakwater Station, the Senqu, now known as the Orange River, becomes the border of South Africa and Namibia at the dry confluence of the Cape Thirstland and the southern Kalahari. To the north of the river are mineral fields, red sand dunes and the bright mountains of the Richtersveld; to the south are the parched flats, dry watercourses and densely black volcanic boulders of the Northern Cape: /Xam-ka !au.

The red of the soil there is one of the dominant tones in an immense landscape of countless different yellows, browns and burnt greens, the colours of its thorny scrub and bushes, sporadic grass and stark copses of quiver trees like miniature baobabs. Good rains at the end of winter bring temporary miles of spectacularly reflective silver grass but drought is the rule and the *leegtes* and *vleis* of the Cape Thirstland – its watercourses and pans – are persistently dry, its springs prized. Water has been prized in this place since it was first occupied by people like us more than 100,000 years ago.

The thirty-two men from the Northern Cape held with //Kabbo at the Breakwater were direct descendants of those nameless founding settlers and, whatever their ancestors might have called themselves, the /Xam-ka !ei had been there for tens of thousands of years, a hunting and gathering people who used stone technology. Their surviving relatives in South Africa, Namibia, Botswana and Angola are the most ancient people in the world, genetically speaking, and the closest relatives of the first people to leave Africa to colonize the planet. They were the first people there and they were the oldest people in the world.

When the Dutch came to the Cape of Good Hope with the intention of staying for good the first thing they did was to plant a vegetable garden; twenty years later they had taken the whole of the Cape Peninsula. The long-settled iron-age herding people the Dutch found on the Cape – themselves relatives of the /Xam-ka !ei – called themselves Khoekhoen, meaning 'People People', but the European newcomers called them Hottentots, an insulting term with a meaning that no one has ever satisfactorily explained.

The Khoekhoen, to whom cattle were wealth, called the Stone Age hunting and gathering people of the mountains and the desiccated Cape interior San, an insulting term meaning 'cattleless'. The Dutch, when they eventually encountered the San, called them Bosjemans, which translates to Bushmen in English but was originally an insulting term meaning something like 'homeless, godless, shiftless and purposeless'.

Two hundred years after the Dutch East India Company founded a town on the Cape of Good Hope at a cattle kraal called //Hu!gais, the traditional hunting and gathering lifestyle of the first people of South Africa had become impossible. By the mid-1800s there was nothing anyone could have done to halt the cultural and linguistic extinction of South Africa's San or Bushmen people.

No one had ever written down what the /Xam-ka !ei called themselves.

!gam ke ≠ei yan	the Bushmen
ge hin //hion	eat the cattle
ka xoro	of the Boers;
//hun gan /keye	the Boers take
ge hin //hion	the children of
yan /hanken	the Bushmen

Dr Wilhelm Bleek lived in Mowbray, a peaceful village of some fifty houses on either side of the wide, oak-lined road from Cape Town to the old village of Rondebosch. Once you had learned to ignore the magnificent views of the Hottentots Holland mountains on the other side of the Cape Flats and the waves of vapour that broke every day on Devil's Peak the place was a thoroughly English idyll of haycarts, dappled shade, meadows and horse troughs. Simply passing through was enough to make English settlers homesick. Born in the Prussian capital of Bonn, thin, angular of face and extravagantly bearded, Wilhelm Bleek was an Anglophile of note. He liked Mowbray very much.

Mowbray's English character was not its only advantage, or so Wilhelm's wife Jemima believed. Separated from Cape Town by Devil's Peak and the curve of the mountain, the village was comparatively cool in the summer and spared the worst of the vicious southeasterly wind that forced the city-dwellers to close their shutters in the middle of the day and sit in a hot gloom to keep out the red dust whipped up from the roads. And nor were the bad airs of the ditches lining the city's thoroughfares such a present problem to someone whose health was as poor as her husband's.

When the couple first met in the autumn of 1861 he was a thirty-four-year-old retired explorer, fluent in half a dozen African languages and already very ill. Tuberculosis had made him an old man when he was barely out of his twenties. The Bleeks had moved to Mowbray from their little house on Cape Town's New Street in the spring of 1869. With their limited means it would have been impossible for them to have rented a house of comparable size in the city itself. There were wheatfields and pasture about their new place, a large, rustic building in the Cape Dutch style called The Hill, thatched, gabled and whitewashed with a large garden and creepers on the *stoep*. A good place to raise children.

mama kan /an	my mother
ibo kan /an	my father
n!ga kan /an	my brother
n//kapa kan /an	my sister

It was February 1871, the height of summer. The couple shared their home with two of Jemima's sisters, Julia and Lucy Lloyd, and two daughters, Mabel, who was a year old, and Edith, aged seven. Jemima was pregnant again, having lost her infant son Ernst the previous summer.

Jemima's marriage to the eccentric Prussian linguist nine years before had allowed the Lloyd sisters to put a thousand miles between themselves and their father, the Reverend William Henry Cynric Lloyd, an erratic, bankrupt, religious fundamentalist who treated strangers with endless charity and who threw Jemima and Lucy out of his house when they refused to allow him to spend the money they had inherited from their late mother.

Upon William Lloyd's appointment as Colonial Chaplain in 1848 the Lloyds left Norbury, a village in Staffordshire, to sail for Durban, a partially erected sandbath of a town on the sub-tropical coast of Natal, a colony that may as well have been in the Indies or the Americas as far as most British people knew or cared. Frances, Lucy, Jemima and Julia, the four daughters left to the Reverend Lloyd by his late wife, were neither consulted nor considered before their father bought the tickets for the month-long voyage by steamer to Cape Town and the short, uncomfortable journey from there to Port Natal on the Indian Ocean.

It was certainly not their father's calling to be a missionary that took the Lloyd sisters and the Reverend's second wife Ellen to Natal but the £300 a year that came with the position of Colonial Chaplain and the man's desire to escape from his creditors.

xoro g'/ei	heart of ox
a k'/ei	thy heart

Their time in Natal and the behaviour of the Reverend William were to affect Jemima and Lucy Lloyd deeply for the rest of their lives. Before her marriage, Jemima had even found it impossible to call her future husband Wilhelm since the name was too close to her father's, which had become

so dreadfully associated in my mind with many more than painful times, and scenes in our lives; and has been so desecrated to my ear by being used as it has been by his poor often mad wife – I mean the present Mrs Lloyd.

It was not until she went to Bonn to meet her fiancé's family that she felt comfortable using his name, although for the most part, on account of his full bottom lip, his long hair and his beard, she called him Lion.

The lion goes, for he goes above in the heaven. Therefore he stands firmly above in the sky. He is a lion who talks, he eats people, he talks. He is a lion, he is a man, he has hair, he is a lion, his hands are a man's.

The sisters prized their intellectual independence and they would be taken advantage of by no one. Lucy, who had learned to value herself and her gifts so little, would have to wait until the last year of her life for her exceptional achievements to be recognized.

Lucy Lloyd came to the Cape Colony from her home in Natal to help Wilhelm Bleek arrange his marriage to Jemima and moved in with the two of them soon afterwards; a third sister, Julia, followed her in a matter of weeks. Now they lived together at the end of a long, hedge-lined lane in a humbly decorated, hospitable house, comfortably but sparely. They were not rich. They were careful of their candles and the fire in the winter: threats to the hundreds of manuscripts and books in Wilhelm's library, a collection of essays, papers, printer's proofs, grammars, vocabularies, dictionaries and philological studies of languages from every continent – Sanskrit, the Kasi language of Lower Assam, Arabic, Aramaic, Berber, Ancient Greek, Egyptian hieroglyphics, Basque, Maori and Chinese.

With the publication of the first part of his *Comparative Grammar of South African Languages*, the work that was to lay the foundation for every subsequent study of southern African languages, Bleek's reputation as the world's greatest expert on the subject had been secured. On his shelves was material dealing with Tswana, Zulu, Xhosa, Nama and Sesotho, too, among dozens of other languages spoken south of the Sahara.

There were no books in his library dedicated to the language of the people the Khoekhoen called San and the colonists called Bosjemans or Bushmen. None had ever been written. Missionaries had given up on them and the Boers were more concerned with prosecuting their genocide than recording their language for the attentions of linguists. They were yellow-skinned vermin, addicted to theft, too lazy or stupid to cultivate or work for food, incapable even of understanding the simple precepts of Christianity. They had no idea of the spiritual, so no practices of worship; they ate disgusting creatures and their language sounded like the chatter of baboons.

No one was shy about saying this.

> The stars are
> different
> they are many
> they are thus they
> are red
> yet they are cold
>
> for they have star children
>
> Thus they are many
>
> for they
> have star
> children
> many truly
> thus they are cold
> for
> they all run in the sky

As the summer of 1871 was about to turn Jemima was pregnant for the fourth time and Oud Jantje Tooren, //Kabbo, was at the Breakwater, serving the sixteenth month of his sentence.

Until recently Lucy Lloyd had found regular work as a governess and Jemima Bleek had stayed at home to look after

Edith and Mabel and manage the household. Now Lucy, troubled by ill health for some time, stayed at The Hill to assist her brother-in-law in the research he regularly brought home from the South African Public Library.

Every weekday Wilhelm Bleek took the train from Mowbray Station to the terminus at Cape Town. From there he made the short walk to his place of work in the library at the bottom of the gardens planted to provide greens for the scurvied Indiamen of the Dutch East India Company two centuries before. In the high-ceilinged, shuttered Grey Room overlooking the flowers, lawns and shade the Company's vegetable plots had become, he worked as the curator of Sir George Grey's famous collection.

At enormous personal expense and over many years, Sir George Grey (Bleek's patron and friend, the former governor of the Cape Colony and now the governor of New Zealand) had assembled a collection of some of the greatest printed and illuminated treasures of European literature. Since 1856 Bleek had been employed to catalogue the Old World texts it contained and to search out and collect material in languages from all parts of the colonized world to add to it. African languages and literature were his main obsession, however, and in the years he had spent working at the library he had written hundreds of letters, cultivating contacts with missionaries, officials and travellers in every part of the continent. He corresponded with David Livingstone and took tea with the famous missionary Robert Moffat when the man was in town.

Now the Grey Collection boasted more African folktales, legends, songs and miscellaneous linguistic material in African languages than the British Library. The preservation of the disappearing 'literature', as Bleek called it, of the indigenous peoples of the colonized world was his cause. Bleek believed that the true purpose of the science of linguistics was the *discovery of the process of human development*, since through its study *the original skeleton of the entire history of human development is laid bare*. His approach to philology – originally the study of ancient texts – was essentially archaeological.

Grammar, vocabulary and phonology are the invisible tide-marks of empires, migration, trade and intermarriage; when a linguist compares related languages, he or she becomes a historian. This was already taken for granted. Bleek, however, had a further abiding fascination with the idea that syntax and grammar offered solutions to the mysteries of the origin and the development of speech itself.

A language implied a particular *mode of thought*, he wrote, a way of making sense of the world – so every language was an image of the culture that produced it. The study of ancient languages was a kind of long-distance anthropology and to examine those *living* languages that preserved ancient forms of syntax and phonology, and the myths, folklore and other traditional material belonging to them, was to study nothing less than the history of the human mind. His first, cursory, examinations of the language of the Bushmen had suggested that it might preserve something particularly ancient. It was immensely frustrating that so little had ever been written down.

Hopefully anticipating progress in the young science of linguistics, Bleek was determined to preserve as much as he could of the world's fragile and fast-disappearing oral material threatened by disease, massacre and the missionaries. Unfortunately it was plain that his time was short. Now he was coughing up blood after every serious cold. He would be dead before his work was finished and he could only guess how long he had.

| xoro tsotsoki | ox lungs; |
| m-n tsotsoki kan tang | my lungs are sore |

At the end of his day at the library he would walk back to the terminus, catch the train back to Mowbray and walk home to The Hill to eat with his family, play with his daughters and write his letters and papers. If he were feeling strong he would go to bed late. He had to be terribly careful with his health now because he had an enormous amount to do before he died. He adored his children and the thought of leaving them fatherless was painful to him.

On 16 February 1871, //Kabbo, a convicted cattle rustler from the Northern Cape known to the prison authorities as Oud Jantje Tooren, came to the door of The Hill. After more than a year spent in the oppressive heat and uncomfortable cold of Victoria West and the Breakwater Station he had been released. Although he would never be shackled to a gang again //Kabbo was still a prisoner in the eyes of the colonial government and work was still expected of him – but he was exchanging prison walls for a furnished shed in a colonial garden and his labour was to be less exhausting than breaking rocks and picking at the peninsula's red earth to make roads.

Wilhelm, who had already met him at the Breakwater (where the old man had been photographed, naked, staring at the lens resentfully with a measuring stick in his hand) had arranged his release. //Kabbo was to become his teacher.

He would have taken off his canvas prison overalls and put on softer clothes given him by the Bleeks; he would have been fed properly for the first time in months and then shown to the building in the garden where he was to see out the remainder of his sentence. Waiting to meet //Kabbo were Bleek, the Lloyd sisters and a young man whom he had last seen at the Breakwater before the spring: 4636 Klaas Stoffel. //Kabbo knew him as /A!kungta. They had been admitted to the Breakwater on the same day.

According to his entry in the prison's Description Register /A!kungta was about eighteen years old, married, and just under five feet tall. He had a mole on his left temple and several more on his right cheek and he was serving a two-year sentence for receiving stolen goods. Apparently he had been caught eating part of an ox. Hunger had made criminals out of all of the /Xam men at the Breakwater.

> I shall drink the water.
> I am hungry.
> He sits, cannot speak for hunger, cannot stand up.

On 23 August, a Wednesday, Wilhelm Bleek had written to the governor of the Cape Colony, Sir Henry Barkly, asking permission to receive one of the /Xam prisoners at the Breakwater into his new house in Mowbray. Barkly granted it. The prison chaplain, Reverend Fisk, recommended Klaas Stoffel, *the best behaved Bushman boy*, and on the Tuesday of the following week /A!kungta left the Breakwater for a locked room at The Hill to begin the work that //Kabbo had now come to continue.

A note in the very last column of the young man's entry reads *Detached to Dr Bleak on 29 August 70*. /A!kungta's work began the very afternoon he arrived.

In the Special Collections archive of the University of Cape Town is a fat hardbacked book of 337 ruled pages. The parchment-coloured cover is marked with candle wax and a

ring the size of a wineglass; the bottom right-hand corner is
discoloured by fingermarks. On its thick spine is embossed
BUSHMAN MS 1866–1871.

Bleek had interviewed two /Xam men held at the Breakwater in the 1860s but the awful conditions of the prison and
the resentment of the prisoners had not made for a productive
encounter and he had realized then that if he wanted to begin
a systematic study of the /Xam language he would have to
travel to the Northern Cape, impossible given the state of his
health, or find a way to work with /Xam speakers outside the
walls of a jail. This had been at the back of his mind when he
first saw the spare rooms and garden of The Hill.

Two flaps of paper fold out from the inside cover of the
book where they have been glued. On one is pencilled

*no beard, Adam Klienhardt, . . . had one, some Bushmen have, some not,
his father had a large beard, was a Koranna, his mother a real Bushman;
her brother had no beard; but his brothers (her sons) have much beard . . .
The Hill Bushmen have much beard.*

Another scrap opposite folds out to reveal translations of
simple /Xam words to do with parts of the body and family.
Then there are simple sentences:

*give bread.
Give bread that I might . . . eat.
give meat that I might . . .*

This book had already been used in the Bleek household
for the teaching and learning of language. The first six pages
are filled with a long German–English translation exercise in
tiny, neat, handwriting:

the Pussycat runs into snow the little dog runs him after
oh pussycat lift thou back then

These words, written in the course of a lesson, are very
different from those in the bold, hurried scrawl that fill the
book from its seventh page. Here the student, a consumptive
graduate of the University of Bonn, is twice as old as the
teacher, an illiterate teenager whose hunger drove him to jail.

The eland, the springbok and the quagga are sifted from
digits, features of the face and the names of the stars as translations of words for limbs, tools and food give way to phrases
and then sentences. In a matter of pages, simple vocabulary
leads to qualifications concerning possession, the plural and
singular and size or the passive and active forms of verbs. Then,
towards the middle of the book, there is a brief interpolation of
German homework marked *very good* in pencil.

On 20 July 1871 Bleek took down

one Dutchman has many sheep;
the Dutchmen have much cattle;

the Bushmen run away with them
(the cattle)

If you were learning the language of the indigenous hunting
and gathering people of South Africa in the second half of the
nineteenth century, the first words and sentences you learned
were to do with hunger, dispossession and crime.

The notebook's pages are creased down the middle, forming
columns. On every right-hand page there is a transcription
in /Xam in one column and an English translation in the other.
The left-hand pages are filled with clarifications, genealogies,
notes on how to form the clicks in the mouth, the correct

pronunciation of words and relevant points of grammar. As Bleek's ear became more practised and he refined the application of the orthography he was using to transcribe the clicks, the *!gam* of *!gam ke ≠kei* became *!kam* and then */xam*; it was some weeks before he arrived at */Xam-ka !ei*.

/A!kungta arrived at The Hill on 29 August 1870 and began to provide information about his language and his people that very day. All of it was recorded – but none by Wilhelm Bleek.

There is another notebook in the archives, a handwritten pamphlet of twenty pages, the first of which is filled with a large alphabet in a neat Victorian hand. The writer had been a teacher and it was once a schoolbook. Folded inside the front cover is a piece of paper headed *1st Bushman (L.) got at Breakwater* and a simple vocabulary:

gun, small, the pipe is here, cough, he coughs, walk, crawl, roll, sit, lie, sleep, hold, beat, scratch, shake, water, horse, neck, butterfly

The notebook itself begins:

Got at Breakwater and much of it I can even now see is very wrong, but I keep it partly for use, and partly for the curiosity of the 1st attempt at hearing this difficult language.

The L in *1st Bushman (L.)* stands for Lloyd. This was Wilhelm Bleek's sister-in-law Lucy, a woman with no formal training in linguistics, or indeed any university education. From the moment they began what they would come to call their 'Bushman Work' with the arrival of the /Xam-speaking prisoners at the Breakwater interviewed and photographed within a matter of weeks of their admission, Wilhelm Bleek and Lucy Lloyd worked in collaboration.

By November 1870, three months after /A!kungta's arrival, Lucy was writing down sentences:

the old Bushman loses a thing which sitting, gets up and goes in search of it, all the while it is there, close by where he had been sitting
I think it is a cat
(of a noise heard on the garden bed under the window)
thou thought it a dog
I think he is angry with thee

and soon, like Bleek, she was recording more complex material, setting down songs and fragments of myths:

The old Woman sings; goes singing along; sings as she goes; the old woman sings as she goes along about the Hyena –

> 'The old she Hyena,
> The old she Hyena,
> Was carrying off the old Woman from the old hut;
> The old woman in this manner,
> She sprang aside,
> She arose,
> She beat the Hyena.
> The Hyena, herself,
> The Hyena killed the Hyena.'

and notes:

[The Hyena] killed herself, by casting herself violently upon the pointed rock on which she had intended to cast the old Woman who was upon her back; but the old Woman sprang aside and saved herself.

The old Woman, who was unable to walk, lay in an old, deserted hut. Before her sons left her, they had closed the circle of the hut, as well as the door opening, with sticks from the other huts . . . They had left a fire for her, and had fetched more dry wood. They were obliged to leave her behind, as they were all starving, and she was too weak to go with them to seek food at some other place.

When /A!kungta arrived he spoke no English, and of course the European linguists spoke no /Xam, so the three began their work together by communicating in Afrikaans, the one language they had in common.

Bleek drafted in his seven-year-old daughter Edith to help him differentiate conditions such as plural and dual. There was a lot of pointing, standing, sitting and jumping in the course of the lessons, which mainly took place on the *stoep* and in the drawing room. /Xam vocabulary Bleek and Lloyd learned in the course of trips to the zoo, the public gardens and the museum. Edith's picture books proved useful, too.

Wilhelm Bleek and Lucy Lloyd had thought /A!kungta consumptive when he first arrived, although his bad chest did not stop him smoking. He was terribly thin and although his health quickly improved his lungs were to trouble him throughout his stay; Bleek could sympathize. Married to Ka, whose Afrikaans name was Marie, /A!kungta was a 'Flat Bushman' from an extremely flat part of /Xam-ka !au situated between the Verneukpan – the Deception Pan, named for its mirages – and the Hartbees River, a tributary of the Orange. His genealogy was recorded as far back as his great grand-parents, and we know that his parents were !Haken/ya and /Toaken-ang. His maternal grandmother was called ≠Xammi;

her father was Jio'a!e *whom the lion grasped at night*. He had
been arrested with his brother Yarrisho, who was still held at
the Breakwater.

At first A!kungta stayed inside the house, guarded by an
invalided constable armed with a gun. This was more for the
benefit of the Cape Town prison authorities than for the safety
of the Bleeks, who immediately recognized that the young
/Xam man was too ill to have attempted an escape and thought
it an unnecessary expense. The constable cost them £19 5s.
in *food, beverages &c.* for the five months he sat outside
/A!kungta's door. By the time of //Kabbo's arrival the young
/Xam man was already living in the furnished shed in the
garden.

When he was strong enough /A!kungta was paid to do light
tasks around the house; Bleek had been awarded a government
grant of £100 a year for his project and was careful to specify
in his accounts that he had paid the /Xam man from his own
purse. /A!kungta saved the wages he earned in the garden to
buy a violin which *he played by ear with a talent that would have
graced a better instrument*, Edith Bleek was to remember. She was
also to remember him as a poor gardener, perhaps unsurprising
since the /Xam people had no tradition of agriculture at all.

As well as trousers, shoes and a dark greatcoat, /A!kungta
was given a flannel shirt which he turned into a waistcoat
by removing the sleeves. He was immensely proud of it, but
his skill on the violin and his idiosyncratic dress sense were
not enough to stop the servants at The Hill mocking him.
Everyone knew Bushmen by repute; they were uncivilizable
people who went everywhere naked and barefoot. Eventually
/A!kungta had enough of being reminded.

I was born in shoes!, he shouted.

It was not easy for him, separated from his brother and the
other /Xam-speaking men still held at the Breakwater. Life

was better in Mowbray than it had been in prison but he was
as far from home as he had ever been.

With his sentence due to expire in March he would have
no reason at all to stay where he was. In mid-summer 1871
Bleek gained permission for another /Xam man to come to
The Hill and /A!kungta was joined in that hot February by
4628 Oud Jantje Tooren, who had now spent nearly a year at
the Breakwater after his months at Victoria West working out
his sentence for stealing the Steenkamp's cattle. /A!kungta's
contribution to the Bushman Work was to introduce Wilhelm
Bleek and Lucy Lloyd to the /Xam language, allowing them
to begin the study that was to last them the rest of their
lives. //Kabbo then showed them a cultural profundity that
the popular consensus of the time could not admit.

Before long, to incomprehension from the academic community in Africa and Europe, Bleek put aside his work on
the second part of his *Comparative Grammar of South African
Languages* to have more time to concentrate on what he was
learning from //Kabbo and /A!kungta. It was not only that
he believed the work to be of the greatest importance to
science, the material capable of solving otherwise unanswer-
able questions about the origin of language and the deep
history of mankind; in all the years he had spent collecting the
'literature' of the world's indigenous peoples he had never
heard or read anything like the testimony his /Xam informants
were giving him.

Within a very few days of //Kabbo's arrival at The Hill,
the notion that the indigenous people of the Northern Cape
had no sense of the spiritual, no religion, and no literature
of their own was exploded for good: but their work, they
discovered, was urgent. There was horror in it.

They could not record the stories, beliefs and rituals that

fascinated them so much without recording how those stories, beliefs and rituals were being beaten to death on the farms and murdered in the dry veld a few days by wagon to the north. If Bleek should live to be sixty he would outlast the culture and the language he was documenting.

What life would be like in /Xam-ka !au before the coming of the herders and farmers was settled in the very last days of the First at Sitting People with the reciprocal curses of a spinster Anteater and a handsome young Lynx.

This is what happened.

The Anteater was a person. She was one of the Early Race.

Every day the Anteater with no husband and no children sat beside the mouth of her hole, offering a handful of the dry ant chrysalids she kept in her bag to every Springbok mother that passed by with a female child. Everyone loves ant chrysalids, of course. They are absolutely delicious once they have been spread out to dry in the sun, so you would think that everyone would have taken some – but no one did. The price was too high.

'Is that a girl or a boy?' the Anteater asked every Springbok mother that came near with her child. All the Springbok mothers knew well enough to answer that it was a boy because they knew just as well what the Anteater wanted: a girl to bring up as her own. The ants were bait.

One day the Anteater asked her question to a dozen Springbok mothers one after the other and they all said the same thing. *It is a male child.*

Another Springbok yet comes, she is stupid. The Anteater asks her, she speaks: 'It is a female child.' Then the Anteater says 'Bring her, that I may look at her.'

The Springbok woman brought her daughter over to the Anteater. Her name was !Khoukau.

She was a springbok. She was a person.

!Khoukau hid under her mother's *kaross*, frightened, but the Anteater was kind and nice. She shared her delicious ant chrysalids and made small talk. Eventually the Springbok mother trusted the friendly Anteater enough to let her hold her daughter, the easier for her to feed her.

Then the mother screams, screams from the heart, for the Anteater has sprung and put the child into the hole.

'Go home!' called the Anteater from her burrow. 'You may as well go home now, because I'm never giving my daughter up!' And eventually the Springbok returned home, weeping as she went.

Her husband was furious with her. 'How could you be so stupid!' he shouted. 'Everybody knows about the Anteater!'

He was so angry he clove her foot.

After many years !Khoukau grew into a beautiful woman and quite forgot her real mother and her antelope family. Out dipping up water one day she caught the eye of a handsome suitor, a young Lynx, who fell so in love with her that he decided he would marry her whatever the cost. While the Anteater was out collecting food he crept into the hole where she lived and explained to her that she was under no obligation to stay with the old woman at all; he told her that she was a

Springbok, not an Anteater, and that the woman she thought of as her mother had stolen her from her real family.

Eventually he managed to convince her, and the next day, when the Anteater was going along the dry riverbed on her way to dip up water, !Khoukau left with the Lynx to be his wife.

All would have gone well for the two were it not for the Partridge, who flew and told the Anteater that the Lynx had taken her !Khoukau away.

My daughter, my daughter, my daughter! A bad man has carried off my child from me!

As !Khoukau and the Lynx walked, the Springbok woman noticed something. *The ground is trembling!* she said, but the Lynx kept walking. *The ground is trembling!* she said again; again the Lynx continued to walk. She said it a third time and finally the Lynx stopped. Before long they saw what was making the ground tremble. It was the Anteater, burrowing frantically towards them, leaving a mound of raised earth in her wake.

Thinking fast, the Lynx dug a hole and set a snare made from his bowstring. When the Anteater found herself caught she was so angry that she succeeded in changing creation.

The Anteater said: Destruction! You there, become a Lynx who walks about at night! Springbok! Stand! You must eat bushes. Lynx, stand! You must eat springbok which eat the bushes. Lynx shall be the one which must eat springbok.

(It seems obvious to *us* that this is as things should be, but the First Bushmen were stupid and did not understand things well. Besides, we have the benefit of hindsight.)

Now he could not possibly marry his fiancée. Instead he

would have to eat her. Heartbroken and furious he cursed the Anteater back.

The Lynx said: Destruction! You there, become an Anteater who walks about at night!

It had been said – and the arbitrary balance of the world was upset for good. The Lynx visited !Khoukau's family to explain how everything had changed and the Springboks agreed to eat bushes while the beasts of prey hunted them. Soon a parliament was convened, attended by all the people of the Early Race, where the Anteater explained the new laws. She told them not only who should eat what, or who, but *how*.

The jackal eats the mouse, while a greedy one he is; he eats the shrew, while a greedy one he is. He eats the striped mouse. The jackal eats people; the hyena eats people; the lion eats people, while they are ugly; they go about by night, while they smell with their nose; they look with their eyes which resemble fire; therefore they go about by night; therefore they go seeking for people by night, that they may kill people; that they may eat the people by night; while they remain beasts of prey, which are different.

The animals acquired their shapes and their habits that day. Before, !Khoukau had been a Springbok woman. *She was a springbok, she was a person.* After this moment she went on four legs, a doe. From then on things were different for the herbivores, the parasites and the carnivores too.

They speak, for they feel that they are becoming beasts of prey. Then, Springbok has horns, the Hyena has hair, then the Hyena eats Springbok. He used to talk, because he was a man; now he feels he is a cunning hyena.

The porcupine marries a porcupine. The mongoose eats puff-adders, ground-squirrels and mice. The hyena eats ostrich's eggs at night. The leopard hunts springbok with dignity; the hyena is a coward. The hyrax eats mountain bushes, and jackals eat the hyrax, striped mice, shrews and gerbils.

That was the day that the behaviour and culture of human beings was decided. From then on people caught springbok to eat, just like the lynxes. The Anteater told people that they should eat meat cooked on the fire and boil things in pots; they should drink water from the shells of ostrich eggs while the lynxes, the leopards and the cheetahs ate raw meat. From then on people, called /Xam-ka !ei, wore the skins of leopards and cheetahs and made shoes of gemsbok skin, quagga skin, hartebeest skin, wildebeest skin, kudu skin and eland skin. They ate the meat of the kudu, the zebra, the quagga, the eland, the elephant, the cheetah, the lynx, the leopard, the steenbok, the duiker, the hyena, the blue crane, the cat, the ostrich, the porcupine, the ground-squirrel, the great hare, the striped mouse and – poor, foolish woman – the Anteater.

When the Mason Wasp took off the *kaross* he always wore to hide his narrow waist from his wife he became a mason wasp.

The Elephants put down their hunting bags and became elephants.

The Meerkats put out their cooking fires and dug burrows fit for meerkats.

At the end of the ancient time, people became people and animals became animals, although of course there were hangovers. The quagga and the hare were never to be entirely non-human. Quaggas would always smell like the people they used to be and the hare's thighs, which still look so much like ours, were always thrown away because to eat them would be cannibalism.

But, being animals, the hare and the quagga have never had *manners*. Animals do not follow the rituals of food sharing, marriage, rites of passage – or any of the other habits that first secured the survival and the happiness of people who hunted and gathered in Africa's most difficult places. It was *custom* that divided animals and people at the end of the time of the Early Race. Animals do not observe any customs apart from one, and that is the custom of remaining animal.

Although the Anteater's laws brought an end to immortality and the transformatory free-for-all of the first creation, replacing them with recognizable physical laws and heavenly bodies, something more than the smell of the quagga and the shape of the hare's thighs persisted. The /Xam-ka !ei did not necessarily think of time as a series of successive events and so it was possible to reach the past in the dry watercourses, *kloofs* and tawny flats of /Xam-ka !au. There were ways to reach the places where the dead lived. //Kabbo, for one, knew them.

Two powerful beings survived the passing of the Anteater's laws. They were supernatural entities considered during specific rituals such as the burning of springbok horns, the casting of fragrant leaves on still water and the care you took to hide your arrowhead from the wind once you had shot an eland.

One of these supernatural entities was !Khwa, whose name translates as both 'rain' and 'water'. The other was /Kaggen, whose name translates as 'Mantis'.

A mantis is a green creature that holds its forelegs up as if it is praying, an insect of the family *Mantidae*. /Kaggen was, and was not, one of these. He was an old man who created the moon on the first of all nights when he threw a shoe red with the dust of /Xam-ka !au into the sky. All his possessions spoke and responded to his call. He gave the gemsbok its pale colour by giving it pale liquid honey to eat and the hartebeest its red colour by feeding it the comb of young bees; he gave the places of /Xam-ka !au their names. He sat between the horns of his favourite animal, the eland, the colour of dark wasps' honey.

He gave the parti-coloured springbok the red cells of young bees with the insects still moving in their combs. When you chew these little bees they are as white as milk in your mouth, as everyone knows.

/Kaggen was the creator of the /Xam-ka !ei.

We who are Bushmen were once springbok, and the Mantis shot us, and we really cried like a little child. Then the Mantis said we should become a person, become people, because we really cried.

He brought fire, clothes and tools to human beings through the power of his dreams alone.

The old man was also *gloriously* selfish, uncannily socially inept and one of the most spectacular cowards of world myth. Bested in fights with ticks, birds or meerkats he would then try to fight the people who offered him help. He once turned himself into an antelope carcass and allowed himself to be butchered as part of a particularly committed seduction technique. Put your tongue against your top teeth and quickly withdraw it with a loud suck: the first sound in /Kaggen's name, represented by a /, is a sound of disapproval.

Being entirely amoral, unprincipled and deaf to advice unless he had been beaten to within an inch of his life, his stories are uniquely useful lessons in bad manners, boastfulness and immaturity. They were stories of a man who has *never grown up*, who *does not behave like an adult*. He was extremely funny.

Creator, trickster, pathetic fool and tragic hero, the Mantis was a trial to his family and he loved the eland beyond all measure.

Kumm:

/Kaggen, the Eland, the Meerkats and the Moon

/Kaggen put /Kwammang-a's shoe into the waterpool.

The Mantis put /Kwammang-a's shoe in a place where reeds stand in water. We know this much. He either found it or stole it. /Kwammang-a was /Kaggen's son-in-law.

Then /Kwammang-a missed the shoe. He asked his wife about it.

His wife said to him: 'I do not know.' !Xo was his wife.

!Xo, /Kaggen's adopted daughter, was the Porcupine.

/Kwammang-a missed the shoe, but he was silent.

It wasn't a shoe for long. At the waterpool it became an eland.
The waterpool was alive. It was where the Rain lived on earth; his body. The living went through the waterpool to get to the past and the dead came through it to reach the present. /Kaggen made his eland here, at a place of resurrection and transformation, and he was very pleased indeed with what he had done.

He went away, then came back again, came up and looked. He turned away again, for he saw that the eland was still small.

It may have been small but it was so beautiful that he was almost moved to tears.

Now, it was /Kaggen's job to bring his family honey from the bees' and wasps' nests he knew out in the veld. He'd cut the honey with his stone knife and take it back home in his hartebeest-skin gathering bag for everyone to share. Because he liked honey he didn't mind the effort, so his family, it is probably fair to say, had become used to eating good, rich honey. *Fat* honey, as the /Xam-ka !ei put it.

'Fat' was a euphemism and a metaphor, an excellent word to do with meat, and sex, and things generally good and rich. There was real power in animal fat of both the magical and the calorific kind. /Kaggen's eland looked as if it would be a very fat creature indeed.

Overnight the Mantis stopped bringing the good fat honey home and his family very quickly began to miss it. The reason, of course, was his beautiful eland. Once he had filled his bag with freshly cut and deliciously moist honey, /Kaggen went to the water and called his little creature from where it stood hiding in the reeds. It trotted out to eat the honey the old man had put on a flat stone with a little hollow in the middle.

The eland went back into the reeds, so that he could stand in the middle of the reeds when he had eaten the food. He went to stand in the reeds.

Having given the best, fattest stuff to this new beast, /Kaggen went home with the dry, lean honey he had left over. History does not record which excuses or diversionary tactics he used when he presented it to his family, but we do know that the next day he did exactly the same thing: he went into the hunting ground, filled his bag with honey, put the best on a stone dish on the edge of a waterpool and called his eland from the reeds. He sang to it as he rubbed it with honey. Then he went home with the crusty, lean stuff. Supper.

It was three days before the Mantis came back to see his eland. Imagine him in the meantime visiting relatives or family friends (the Elephants, say) and embarrassing /Kwammang-a by telling hugely inappropriate stories to the children or trying to steal all their dinner and then picking a fight with the biggest Elephant there. Otherwise you might imagine him disappearing into the hunting ground to be beaten to within an inch of his life by one of the Ground-squirrels and whining all night about his injuries.

It was morning when /Kaggen came back to the water with his hartebeest-skin bag full after a visit to the veld-hives.

He called the eland, and the eland rose and came forth, and the ground resounded as he came.

'Resounded' because the eland was now as big as an ox, now the largest antelope in the world, the fattest creature in what was to become /Xam-ka !au. It was magnificent, dark and splendid. /Kaggen sang for joy.

> *Ah, a person is here!*
> */Kwammang-a's shoe's piece!*
> *My eldest son's shoe's piece!*
> */Kwammang-a's shoe's piece!*
> *My eldest son's shoe's piece!*

He fed him all the honey he had and went home.

Not for the first time /Kaggen's family ran out of patience with the old man and decided that they should try to discover how he was deceiving them. His deceptions were transparent at the best of times and it was more than suspicious that the honey should dry up at precisely the same moment he became unaccountably smug and began to spend equally unaccountable hours in the veld cutting such awful, dry, stuff for them. Or came home with nothing at all. While the old man *wasn't listening*, which was /Kaggen's default method of familial inter-action unless he was hungry or in pain, /Kaggen's grandson /Ni, the Mongoose (better known as the Ichneumon), was instructed by his father /Kwammang-a to follow Grandfather out into the hunting ground to discover where his time and honey were going.

The Ichneumon went out after /Kaggen, who left for the honeyspots with predictably suspicious nonchalance, squint-ing at the low sun, perhaps pretending he couldn't remember the words to a song about bees, and practically twitching with the most ill-concealed excitement. It wasn't long before he saw /Kaggen cut good fat honey, fill his hartebeest-skin bag, skip off towards the water, put the honey on the stone and call his eland, which ran massively from the reeds to eat.

As it fed, /Kaggen sang for joy. He wept as he ran his hands over the huge, beautiful creature he had made, which basked in the water as /Ni watched.

/Ni didn't go home to tell his family what he had seen (according to one version of the story, although according to another he went home and told /Kwammang-a, who knocked the creature down and began to cut it up almost as soon as he knew it existed). No, /Ni went to see his cousins the Meerkats at their house and told *them* instead. He told them that he had seen his grandfather filling his hartebeest-skin bag with lovely honey that he took to the water to put on a flat stone with a hollow in the middle for a creature living in the reeds, singing all the while.

The Meerkats were all ears. They wanted to know how /Kaggen called the creature to him; they wanted to know exactly how to find the waterpool; they wanted to know exactly what the creature was. /Ni answered the first question easily, because he had heard everything; he answered the second by promising to show them the water himself; he couldn't quite answer the third question since it was a new kind of animal altogether. *The thing is black*, he said. *It is large.*

Trouble coming.

Foraging the next day, /Kaggen found the honey dry. What had happened?

It seemed as if the eland's blood was coming out. 'What is making the honey lean? It is not always like this. The honey is not always like this, for it is always fat. It seems as if /a has come to me.'

/A is a word that meant 'fight', or 'curse', or 'harm'. When /Kaggen said that */a* had come to him, he meant that it was touching him: he felt it inside. Why did it feel *as if the eland's blood was coming out*? Why was it that he only felt it when he found the honey dry?

There are connections between things that cannot possibly be connected and messages in the movement of insects, the direction and the temperature of the wind, the behaviour of kudu and the moisture of honey. The world is full of signs. Almost everything is telling you something.

With a touch of desperation, perhaps, he went to find more honey. And that honey was dry too. He put on his quiver and strode elandwards, his arrows rattling. /Kaggen rattled everywhere he went.

He went to see for himself because he felt his body. That his body was not right.

'A feeling of foreboding', you might say, experienced as a

physical sensation but almost specific enough to be read like a letter.[1]

And he went. He had no honey. He put down the quiver. He reached the flat stone. He called the eland.

The eland didn't come. He called it again and again; still it didn't appear.

'Why is it that I do not always wait so long when I call here? Why am I now calling for a long time? The eland will not come out. The fight must have been true, and it entered me.'

When he saw the blood on the stone dish he put down his quiver and he wept.

/Kaggen turned back because of it. He wept.

He picked up his quiver again and rattled along the spoor of his wounded eland, weeping as he went. He ran along a little bank where he saw the Ichneumon in the company of a party of Meerkats. On the earth was his eland, and they were butchering it and cooking its flesh on hot stones. Without his permission.

The first thing /Kaggen did was to put his quiver over his head so that his arms were free and he could easily reach his arrows with one hand. The second thing he did was to plant his foot solidly on the dust, aim an arrow at a Meerkat, and loose it off.

[1] //Kabbo said *a presentiment is a thing which we feel when something is happening at another place. A presentiment is also like a dream which we dream. Sometimes when we are alone our body starts at some place. It seems as if something were there which our body made us dread.*

He wanted to fight the eland's fight.

Meaning: the eland's battle was his battle. Meaning also: angry, he wanted to fight against the eland's potency, released by the Meerkats when they cut it open.

/*A* does not only mean 'fight', 'curse' and 'harm' but 'a concentration of power'. Created in the waterpool, a potent place, by a man who could change the world by dreaming it changed, and steeped with honey, one of the most potent substances it was possible to obtain, the creature was as powerful as it was beautiful – powerful, indeed, because it *was* so beautiful. By killing it and butchering it the Meerkats had released this potency. They were sitting in the powerful smell of its cut fat, a smell very much like honey, with its flesh cooking on fired stones, and the eland's /*a* was theirs.

So /Kaggen loosed off an arrow.

And the arrow came back. The arrow passed over his head, and he ducked. The Meerkats continued to cut up the cooked meat, feeding themselves. They knew that these arrows would not kill them. So they continued at their ease.

The eland's /*a* was powerful.

Then /Kaggen said: 'There is still an arrow here, standing in the quiver, with which I will shoot you. It will hit you.'

/Kaggen put his arrow to the bowstring and let it go, and once again it reached the laughing Meerkats only to turn in the air and bear down on the old man, who would have had his head pierced had he not ducked. Realizing that eventually he'd be the death of himself, he put his quiver down, produced his knobkerrie and ran full tilt at the mocking butchers.

*He ran, coming up. And he asked the Meerkats why they were doing what
they were doing, and why they had killed his eland.*

For an answer the Meerkats took the knobkerrie from the
old man and beat him with it. Some of them took hold of his
legs while the others took turns to hit him. Then they threw
him on his own eland's horns. They told him to go and get
wood for their fire.

Beaten, humiliated and heartbroken, he went to fetch the
wood. Suddenly he saw his eland's bitter gall bladder hanging
on a bush where the murderers had thrown it. /Kaggen broke
it open and darkness spilled out. It was night.

The gall told the Mantis he should leap into the dark.

/Kaggen leapt into the dark. He couldn't see. He took off his
shoe and threw it into the sky.

'I am /Kaggen. This shoe will be the moon and shine in the dark.'

It shone with the red colour of /Xam-ka !au, *the dust
of the /Xam*, since Kaggen hadn't shaken the dust from it.
Something to see by in the night.

*The sun is white because it is hot. The stars are red because they are cool.
The Mantis said: the sun goes out first, the moon follows the sun; it comes
at night for it is cold.*

The Mantis spoke thus.

*So the moon shines in the dark. Thus the moon is cold, because it is a
shoe. It is skin, therefore it is cold. In sunlight people go to drink. Because
of the sun people thirst, and so they drink. The moon being here, they warm
themselves by the fire and they sleep.*

So the moon shines at night. In sunlight men hunt the springboks, when it is warm; men shoot the springboks when the sun is warm.

All the earth is light. All the places are light. All the people hunt.

Another version of the story has /Kaggen using a feather to wipe the night from his eyes. He threw it into the sky where it shone for ever because it took some of his sight with it into the black air. He punished the Meerkats by dreaming their possessions away.

The Meerkats don't cry with tears: they cry with their thoughts they think so much about it.

Another version still has the first herds and hunters created on the same day: imagine /Kaggen bearing down on the quaking butchers and spattering drops of eland blood from their cooking pot on the ground. Every drop became a herd of buck and ran off, angry and afraid.

'If you want to eat that nice flesh now, you'll have to hunt for it. You spoiled the eland. Go and hunt.'

/Kaggen:

The Mantis

When a man is lying asleep, starving (//Kabbo told Lucy Lloyd) /Kaggen *comes and puts it into his thoughts to steal a beast.* The man refuses, but /Kaggen *puts his thoughts together with the Bushman's thoughts and turns around the Bushman's thoughts.* He goes and steals the beast.

/Kaggen can be *by you* without you seeing him, he said.

//Kabbo was punished for stealing a beast and he was starving when he stole it.

When //Kabbo arrived at The Hill in the summer of 1871, Wilhelm Bleek and Lucy Lloyd's knowledge of his language was well advanced. They had hoped that by taking in an older man they would be able to learn more of the beliefs and oral traditions of the /Xam-ka !ei too, and they were right.

//Kabbo was from the same region of /Xam-ka !au as /A!kungta, a so-called Flat Bushman from the plains south of the young town of Kenhardt. He had three names: Jantje Tooren, the Dutch name by which he was known to the Breakwater and to the farmers in his part of /Xam-ka !au, and two /Xam names, //Kabbo, meaning 'Dream', and /Uhi-ddoro, meaning 'Smoking Tinderbox'.

Like Cape Town, and //Kabbo, and practically everything else in South Africa, the Mantis had three names too. Most often his family called him /Kaggen, of course, and from time to time he called himself 'Tinderbox', but he also had a third name he produced when gloating was called for, a name we will come to later.

It was not coincidental that /Kaggen and //Kabbo shared the name 'Tinderbox'. //Kabbo's son-in-law /Hang≠kass'o said that //Kabbo was a */kaggen-ka !kwi*, a phrase which means 'a mantis's man'. //Kabbo *had mantises*, he said.

'Tinderbox' was a name that belonged to a person with very special abilities. Like /Kaggen, //Kabbo was a *!gi:xa*, a word Bleek and Lloyd translated as 'sorcerer', and he was not the only member of his family to possess what most of us would consider to be impossible skills. He came from a long line of sorcerers (*!gi:ten*): his grandmother ≠Giri, for example, was a *!gi:xa* too, a woman who had *made springbok come and helped sick people* before she was eventually killed by a lion.

There were many different types of *!gi:ten* in /Xam bands. Healers, people with a measure of control over game animals and those who could influence the weather were the most common. When //Kabbo's son-in-law said that //Kabbo *had mantises* he meant that he derived his power from a powerful animal, the mantis. This insect was not the only animal whose power was available to the *!gi:ten* of the /Xam-ka !au, however. In the same way that //Kabbo was a *mantis's man*, the healer called Give Me The Arrow There might *have lions*; an old man known as Springbok's Holder, gifted at bringing the rain, might be a *springbok's man*; the woman called Smell Ashes, who could bring antelope looking for the hunter, might *have kudu*.

//Kabbo was a *!gi:xa* of the rain. His mantises helped him with the weather. From his three names and the barest details of his family we can glimpse some of the historical, cultural and spiritual forces that still operated on the /Xam-ka !ei in the late 1800s.

/Tottono, the first husband of his grandmother ≠Giri, had been killed by a rhinoceros.

The rhinoceros sleeps under the thick bush, he runs out, he runs at the man, he runs after the man, he pierces the man with his horns.

≠Giri's second husband, a man called /To/na, had died of starvation, while //Kabbo's father /Ku/ya had died when he was young. /Ku/ya's sons were brought up by /Ku/ya's brother //A/khain:yan, a man with very white hair whom the Boers had known as Oud Bastard.

//A/khain:yan has Bitterpits and //A/khain:yan has the Vulture's House, he has a small hill and //A/khain:yan has (a forest), he has Brinkkop, he has large trees along a watercourse, he has small green shrubs. I have the Great Brinkkop.

A *brinkkop*, which simply meant 'brown hill', was one of the steep mounds of brown to densely black dolerite boulders that rise abruptly from the plains of /Xam-ka !au. They were places to spot game, but they could be powerful places, too. Rain-makers were known as *brinkkops' men*.

//Kabbo was married to his first cousin !Kwabba-ang, with whom he had a son, //Goo-ka-!kui – 'Smoke's Man', still at the Breakwater – and a daughter, Suobba-//kein. Known as Sara to the settlers, Suobba-//kein was married to Klein Jantje, known in /Xam as /Hang≠kass'o, who was still imprisoned down on the waterfront with Smoke's Man.

He also had an adopted daughter, Betje, born to his elder brother. She was now grown.

She married, leaving me; she, who came to me by travelling a long distance; because I was the one who feeding, brought her up. Her father was not the one who fed her. For her father died, leaving her.

//Kabbo's brother had been murdered as he slept beside his

wife. He had been away from home for five nights and his
murderer had fed Betje, still a baby, while he was gone; she
cried constantly, missing him, and the murderer was so angry
about her crying and her father's long absence that when
//Kabbo's brother returned he killed him in his sleep with an
assegai bought in Wittberg, so //Kabbo remembered.

Betje's mother died of an illness while she was staying with
one of her sisters, herself too ill to bury anyone. When
//Kabbo heard news that they were sick he set off at once,
fearing for his young niece's life should her mother die before
he got there. He arrived to discover his sister-in-law's bones
gnawed by jackals and made a shelter for the night near by.
That night Betje's aunt saw his fire from a distance and came
to him to put the little girl into his care for good.

//Kabbo was a solemn man. Like many of the /Xam-ka !ei
he was fair skinned, a colour the first settlers often described
as yellow. His face was heavily wrinkled and he walked with
a gentle stoop. One of Bleek's friends used to call him The
Philosopher on account of his gently sad, meditative air. The
name by which he was best known – Dream – was apposite
for a number of reasons; there was an otherworldly air
about him that many of those who knew him commented on,
but he was also a man who put his dreams to some kind of
practical use.

He had been in the house for a month when Bleek wrote to
Sir George Grey in Auckland:

One of my wife's sisters, of whom two are staying with us, is already further
advanced in the practical knowledge of [the /Xam] *language than myself,*
and as she has a far quicker ear I shall have to trust to her observation in

many ways. She is of course able to devote more time to this study than I can.

Lloyd, whose ill health prevented her from teaching, had plenty of time to devote to the Bushman Work and recorded testimony throughout the week on the *stoep* and in the garden at The Hill while her brother-in-law spent his days at the library considering how the languages of sub-Saharan Africa and Polynesia were related, gathering *traditionary literature* and (somewhat half-heartedly) compiling the Catalogue of the Grey Collection. For the most part he worked with //Kabbo and /A!kungta in the evenings and at the weekends. When Wilhelm and Jemima Bleek left Mowbray for their annual summer visit to Kalk Bay, a picturesque fishing village on the road that ran along the False Bay shore towards Cape Point, Lloyd stayed in the shadow of Devil's Peak at The Hill to record *kukummi*.

An important word. *Kukummi*, the plural of *kumm*, were stories, myths, news, history – anything told.

Even when //Kabbo spoke at length there was a compellingly oblique, almost poetic, quality to his testimony. It meandered. Dictating *kukummi* over several days he would disregard the rules of traditional narration the better to explore tangents and explanations that often became fully fledged *kukummi* of their own. His stories, navigated by annotations and dates on the left-hand pages, began to weave themselves across several books.

He quickly understood that Bleek and Lloyd were offering him the opportunity to record some of the *kukummi* that would otherwise disappear for good along with his people and that by continuing his teaching something could be preserved. It pleased him very much that the things he was relating would be recorded in books. //Kabbo would have other more personal reasons for staying at The Hill once his sentence had expired, but this was very important to him.

It was an unlikely collaboration. In 1871 the greater part of the oral traditions, beliefs and practices of a threatened people, extraordinary things that would otherwise have gone entirely unrecorded and unacknowledged, were narrated by an old man from a long line of hunters, sorcerers, artists and story-tellers; the work had been initiated by a German scholar and humanist with an astonishing gift for languages and would not have been possible without the methodical, painstaking labour of a former governess born and christened in a village in Staffordshire not far from the Welsh border.

A town founded on a crescent of evil white sand shot through by creeks and surrounded by swamps, Durban was barely twenty years old when the Lloyds arrived from the Cape Colony at the end of their six-month journey from England. Its future buildings were plotted by posts and string and several of the thoroughfares, marked out and named even though they led nowhere, were lined with nothing but bushes and tree stumps. Even though the family had spent five months in Cape Town, a place with the distinct air of a frontier town about it for all its dilapidated sophistication and two hundred years of history, Durban was something very like the end of the world.

It was still possible to see crocodiles in the rivers about the town and elephants on the open patches of ground in the forested hills of Berea when the Lloyds arrived in June 1849 (although the elephants' days were numbered). In the Market Square, where the Reverend Lloyd's church would be built, there were wild date and vegetable ivory palms and banana trees. After dark hyenas scavenged for scraps.

The family's first home, a short walk from the beach, was a thatched parsonage something like an old farmhouse on a marshy street directly opposite the Post Office. A hide store with a saddlery, a billiard room, a store for yellow-wood planks, a chemist and *a shanty of the mining camp class* were close at hand.

Lucy, the second eldest of the children left to the new Colonial Chaplain by the late Mrs Lloyd, was sixteen years old. We do not know if she had wanted to leave the village of Norbury for Britain's African colonies but we can be quite certain that she, like her three full sisters and the three children now born to her stepmother Ellen, had not had any say in the matter. The Reverend William Henry Cynric Lloyd was not keen on discussion. His children thought him a tyrant. A bearded and ostensibly avuncular man, the Reverend Lloyd's parishioners in Norbury, to whom he had ministered for twenty-two years, considered him *a friend and a brother*. In Durban he would be noted for his charity and his support for new emigrants, his *ambling way of speech* and his *habit of making much of trifles, which are pleasantly original.*

His daughters, who had been shuffled around the family of his late wife for their education as a money-saving measure, had an entirely different perspective on the man. Jemima thought him a hypocrite and an actor and came to consider herself and her sisters *fatherless* and *orphaned*.

Within weeks of his arrival the new Colonial Chaplain attained a kind of affectionate notoriety as the priest who always needed a loan and who would shoot your animals with deadly precision if you were to allow them to come too near his house. The traditions and institutions of provincial Britain had already begun to evolve peculiar shapes in Durban's sub-tropical fecundity and the Reverend Lloyd found he could exercise his eccentricities there with impunity. He did so at the cost of his family's happiness and ease, the sanity of his second wife and the respect of his daughters.

It was his financial incompetence that had caused him to seek a new start in Natal and in 1851, barely two years after his arrival, he was forced to sign his salary over to his creditors. Nothing very much had changed. Frances and Lucy Lloyd, the eldest of his daughters at twenty and sixteen years, found themselves the breadwinners of an increasingly large family: Ellen, the second Mrs Lloyd, was to bear another thirteen children in all. All the sisters had benefited from schooling in continental Europe, fortunately, and Lucy spoke French and Italian fluently. She found work as a governess, eventually teaching at the Government School.

Ellen Lloyd was deeply unhappy in southern Africa and fought with her husband constantly. Often she did not seem rational at all.

Sometime before 12 May 1854 the Lloyds moved from the parsonage near the beach to The Glebe, a collection of tents and wattle-and-daub buildings surrounded by large sub-tropical trees. On that day in May The Glebe burned to the ground; the fire took quickly and there was no water at hand to put it out. William Lloyd was out of Natal, either in Britain or in the Cape Colony, but his children and his neighbours managed to save their clothes and some of their furniture.

After the fire the Reverend Lloyd's famous generosity and reputation for charity were undiminished, even though every-one knew the man was bankrupt. His wife began to slide into mental illness and the atmosphere in the household, already difficult, became positively toxic. Ellen became so ill that she could not take care even of her children; her husband, incapable of managing the household's finances, was of little help. Frances, Lucy, Jemima and Julia Lloyd ran the house, provided for their little stepbrothers and sisters and nursed their stepmother, whose condition eventually deteriorated to the point that she faced *confinement*.

One Sunday, a year after the Lloyds' disaster, John William Colenso, the new bishop of Natal, arrived in Durban from Liverpool aboard the *Jane Maurice*. He was an unorthodox 'broad church' priest with excellent Zulu whose efforts to understand the cultural practices of the people he had come to convert would lead him to question the literal truth of the Old Testament. Naturally the Reverend Lloyd – who accepted the Bible with *a child's implicit faith* – would come to despise him.

With Colenso was a vigorous, clumsy Prussian man of twenty-eight who had come to Southern Africa to help the bishop compile his *Zulu Grammar* and to begin a career as a linguist-explorer in the homesteads of Natal and independent Zululand, the state across the Thukela River to the young colony's north. Wilhelm Bleek PhD waded to the shore, took a wagon to the town with the bishop and struggled through Durban's notorious sand to the Royal Hotel, a thatched building not far from The Glebe. Later he went to St Paul's where he heard one of Lloyd's sermons.

Two days after that Dr Bleek left for Pietermaritzburg with the bishop and his party without having been introduced to any of the Reverend William Henry Cynric Lloyd's daughters.

What are you, Wilhelm? What are you? Wilhelm Bleek's grandmother would ask him.

Ich bin ein kleines scheusal, he would announce, having been tutored. *I am a little monster.*

She was fond of him but there was no denying that he was an unattractive child.

Bleek survived a scaly infancy, poorly and afflicted by *eruptions* of the skin, to grow into the strongest and clumsiest of the nine children born to the aristocratic Augusta Bleek and her husband Friedrich, celebrated Professor of Theology at the University of Bonn. He grew up in a house with a large garden bounded by a fragment of the old city wall where he made gunpowder with his brother Phillip and his sister Auta. There he read everything he could, from Homer to travellers' journals; a particular favourite of his was Le Vaillant's *Travels Into the Interior Parts of Africa By Way of the Cape of Good Hope*, a book with a brief vocabulary of 'Hottentot'. He knew about the Khoekhoen of the Cape before he was sixteen.

The eldest child in an intellectually fertile environment, Bleek was raised to think independently. It was a family trait. His father, whom he *venerated*, had made his reputation as an unorthodox biblical scholar with the publication of a commentary on the Old Testament a year after the birth of his little monster; his cousin was the naturalist Ernst Haekel, one of the first exponents of Darwinism; the family counted theologians, poets and statesmen amongst their friends.

At the age of eighteen he gained entrance to the Philological Seminary at the University of Bonn with an essay on the etymology of ancient Greek synonyms, written, as was customary, in Latin. From the moment he understood the basic precepts of philology Wilhelm Bleek was fascinated by the idea that what was the most ancient was the least corrupted and he began his undergraduate years studying the works of Homer in an attempt to *restore as far as possible the oldest form in which these poems existed.*

He always liked to set himself the most extravagant goals. Although he did not always attain them he made important discoveries on the way that invariably fed his next consuming enthusiasm. He was passionate about his work.

Under the tutelage of the Egyptologist, philologist and palaeographer Karl Lepsius at the University of Berlin, Bleek abandoned Greek and Latin texts for Sanskrit, Arabic, Aramaic and ancient Egyptian. Soon after that he first encountered the phonologically and grammatically curious languages of Africa south of the Sahara, comparatively unknown to European linguists and regarded by many as barely fit for study.

Bleek, determined to discover what relation these languages bore to those of Europe and the Middle East, set about learning one. He settled on Tswana, a language spoken in what is today Botswana and the north of South Africa, when the Church Missionary Society in London sent him a copy of *Evangilia Hotasa Mahuku a Molemo a Kuariloenq Ki Luka*, a translation of the Gospel of Luke. He knew nothing about the language at all (*for anything that I knew to the contrary, it might have been spoken near the Atlas Mountains*, he later wrote) but Tswana became his obsession. His sloping scrawl filled entire notebooks of carefully folded pages with tables and lists of words as he sifted suffixes and prefixes from the roots of the nouns, unravelling grammar and vocabulary through painstaking comparison of translations of the Bible in different languages.

In 1850 he discovered the language of the Khoekhoen – the iron-age herding people who lost the Cape Peninsula to the Dutch – and the direction his linguistic career was to take was decided once and for all. The clicks in the Khoe, Zulu, Xhosa and SeSotho languages of southern Africa spoke of great antiquity, he believed, and nothing interested him more than age and origins.

Before long he was the world's greatest expert on the

languages of southern Africa. His thesis, submitted in August 1851, was the first comprehensive linguistic survey of those languages and many of its findings are taken for granted today. In it Bleek compared Zulu, SeSotho, Xhosa, Tswana and Herero with Nama, Koranna, ancient Egyptian, Hebrew, German and Aramaic in an attempt to prove that the Khoe dialects best preserved the most ancient features of a language once spoken throughout the African continent, the parent tongue of the Indo-European languages. If his conclusion remains controversial, the evidence he discovered to substantiate it demonstrated for the first time how the languages of southern Africa were related to each other – and they were not barbarous, savage languages as far he was concerned. Indeed, his achievements were predicated on the idea that there was no such thing as a *savage tongue* at all.

His personal library included texts from places as far afield as Senegal, Zanzibar, Namaqualand and Mozambique, but he still had yet to set foot in Africa.

Three years after the publication of his thesis and soon after the publication of his essay 'On the Origin of Language', intended as *a first chapter in a history of the development of language* (there would be no second chapter), he had his opportunity. With the help of Baron von Bunsen, the Prussian ambassador to Britain and a Bleek family friend, the British Admiralty appointed an impossibly excited Wilhelm Bleek the Third Officer on an expedition to chart the major rivers of the Congo: the Niger and the Tsadda.

Charged with the expedition's ethnological and philological research Bleek set sail from Plymouth for West Africa on the *Forerunner*, a mail steamer, in the last week of May 1854. With him was Dr William Balfour Baikie, author of *A Manual of Natural History for the use of Travellers; being a description of the Animal and Vegetable Kingdoms (with remarks on the practical study of geology and meteorology)*, a physician, naturalist and linguist appointed the expedition's second-in-command, and Baikie's assistant, a young zoologist called Dalton. The expedition was to be led by a man called John Beecroft, the governor of a volcanic island colony some twenty miles off the Niger delta, Fernando Po.

A naturalist and an explorer of great experience and famous fortitude, Beecroft had a kind of tree-dwelling hyrax named after him and knew *every creek up every river in the Gulf of Guinea*. As well as his having *made the highest ascent of the Kwarra achieved by any of its explorers* he had already survived two ill-fated expeditions up the Niger and was regarded as the perfect man to lead the expedition. Bleek, Dalton and Baikie were to meet Beecroft at Fernando Po and embark for the interior aboard the *Pleiad*, a 100-foot schooner fitted with a library and a brass chandelier and armed to the gunwales with sabres, pistols, two four-pound cannon and a weighty twelve-pounder between the fore-hold and the fore-cabin. Baikie took a supply of quinine along as a preventative measure against fever.

The orders given by the British Admiralty to the distinguished crew of the *Pleiad* were to chart the Tsadda, one of the Niger's principal tributaries, from Dágbo as far east as possible and to *afford assistance* to the missing German explorer Dr Barth, one of Bleek's heroes, if they should discover his whereabouts. They should also load up on goods such as palm oil with the aim of opening trade with the people of the interior. The first attempt at the expedition had been made in 1832 by the explorers Laird and Oldfield and had claimed the lives of all but nine of the forty-nine Europeans aboard: it was not going to be an easy journey.

Notwithstanding the very real dangers of fever, violence and shipwreck, Bleek further intended that, if he did not succeed in discovering the whereabouts of Barth, he would continue into the African interior from the source of the Niger and attempt to meet the famous explorer Dr Vogel, thought to be somewhere south of Ethiopia.

According to Baikie's journal, he, Dalton and Bleek got on very well and passed the time in conversation, Baikie periodically making an attempt to *waylay some rare pelagian voyager* or trying his hand at *intercepting some crepuscular pteropod* with his nets but succeeding only in catching *some minute tunicaries and acelphs*. Bleek was seasick.

It was intensely hot as the *Forerunner* approached Freetown, the picturesque coastal capital of Sierra Leone, to take on coals. Bleek's first steps on the African continent were portentously delayed: there was a hot tension in the air, the clouds low, and after sunset a tropical storm broke that lashed the steamer into the early hours. Too dangerous to launch the dinghy that night, it was not until the next morning that he was able to walk Freetown's ordered streets. In Sierra Leone he met the famous explorer R. A. Oldfield and he bought a black oilskin travelling bag.

Once he had caught malaria he made his way back to the steamer.

When they arrived at Accra on the Gold Coast, Bleek desperately hoping to recover from the fever that came over him on the *Forerunner*, the party discovered that Beecroft had died, his *once iron frame* having *sunk under the combined inroads of climate and disease*. His death meant that Baikie was now in charge and at the very end of the month-long voyage from Plymouth to Fernando Po he invalided Bleek, *his health being evidently unsuited for a tropical African climate, especially as it had already considerably suffered.*

This gentleman was, as might have been expected, much disappointed, and left us with great reluctance, wrote Baikie. The journey to Fernando Po had taken thirty-two days. Bleek stayed on dry land for four days before he caught a steamer back to England.

To the discomfort of sixty days at sea, all the attendant seasickness and bad food, a debilitating fever and the crushing disappointment of having to return home without having even seen the mouth of the river that was to have led him into the African continent, Bleek suffered the crowning bad fortune of a near-shipwreck off Madeira on the return passage.

In the Grey Collection is a copy of the Sierra Leone *Almanac* for 1854, inscribed *Dr Bleek with the best wishes and kind regards of R. A. Oldfield*, given him on 12 June 1854, its yellow pages spotted with tropical mould, one of only six texts that Bleek brought back with him.

Wilhelm Bleek had been back in London for barely a month when he was contacted by John William Colenso, an Anglican priest recently ordained the bishop of Natal. A linguist, mathematician and theological radical, Colenso had been appointed after a short correspondence by the conservative bishop of Cape Town, Robert Gray, who had mistaken him for an establishment minister with a declared interest in missionary work. An improbably petty man, Gray later made good on his error by seeing Colenso tried for heresy.

In London the new bishop of Natal offered Bleek the opportunity to come back to Africa to help him to compile his *Zulu Grammar*. The linguist agreed on the instant. He had lost his first opportunity to study West African languages *in situ* but this was even better: Zulu, Xhosa, Tswana and 'Hottentot', the languages of southern Africa, were his speciality, tongues that fascinated him above all others.

Just how far his researches had already taken him was made very clear when he addressed the Philological Society in London shortly before his departure. There he presented a paper in which he described connections between certain African languages separated by great geographical distances. Within two years he would have a name for this family of languages spoken from Cameroon to Kenya and as far south as British Kaffraria, south of Natal: Bantù. No other linguist in the world possessed both the breadth of his practical knowledge and the sophistication of his analyses of African languages, yet he was still to spend a week in any part of the African mainland.

He left for Natal from Liverpool aboard an overcrowded, rat-infested steamer, the *Jane Maurice*, with the bishop's party on 15 March 1855, a week after his twenty-eighth birthday, and sighted the colony on a misty Saturday morning in May after a voyage of seventy-three days. It was the month in which the Reverend Lloyd moved his congregation from a store on the corner of Aliwal Street to St Paul's Church, an unfinished brick building with sheets of calico for windowpanes.

Soon after their arrival the party began their five-day journey to Pietermaritzburg in a caravan of five wagons, each drawn by a team of twelve oxen. Avoiding waystations, the missionaries and the linguist slept under canvas aboard the wagons and barbecued improvised beef kebabs in an open fire.

Bleek was chasing after his horse, collecting *inganekwane* – oral material – and doing the first anthropological fieldwork in history in the homesteads in the foothills of the Drakensberg at about the time that William Henry Cynric Lloyd threw his daughter Lucy out of his house, apparently frustrated that she would not allow him to spend her inheritance. It was June 1856. She was twenty-one.

The world is a harsh place, it does not owe you a thing and there is no disguising or explaining this. There is no purpose behind your most frustrating reversals and you can count on nothing, not even failure, since creation can be as generous as it is remorseless and pitiless.

That is why the creator is a trickster; that is why he is remembered in the hunt.

/Kaggen does not love us if we kill an eland.

When you have shot an eland and you are looking for your arrow you do not cross the creature's tracks. The poisoned bone or quartz of your shallow arrowhead is not intended to stick and when you find the shaft lying on the ground you do not pick it up with your fingers without a thought, as if it had missed, but with a leaf and another arrow. You hide it from the wind as you move it to your quiver so that the wind sees neither it nor the eland's hairs stuck to it. This is the wind that blows when you have made a kill – it is easily read and */Kaggen does not love us if we kill an eland.*

Once you have put your arrow into your quiver you walk back to the camp slowly and quietly. Tell yourself that there is nothing remarkable about anything you see and take as little notice of the things about you as you can. If you become excited about anything, and you get your blood up, you will get the eland's blood up too. The two of you have a connection, now that the animal has been poisoned by your arrow, and you want to keep life out of the dying creature. The poison is working its way through the animal as you walk home and you must regard everything about you almost as if you were afraid. If you do not, the eland will not look at the world as if it were afraid either.

For the poison is killing its heart, it does not know that it is afraid.

Stand quietly opposite the bent branches of your shelter when you reach the camp until the men see that you have returned and come to speak to you. They should come on their own, without any of the children of the camp, to ask you why you do not go inside. (The children are full of noise and life best kept from the animal you have shot.) You reply quietly, as if you were in pain, that you have pricked your foot on a bush, and that you must sit down. One of the older men will tell the others that they should open your quiver and examine your arrows. They will carefully pull them from your quiver and examine every shaft and arrowhead for hair fixed there by blood.

When they find it they will know you have shot an eland. If it is your first you are leaving childhood behind; your first eland kill makes you a hunter, a man. The men will build you a shelter somewhere near the camp, away from the noise of the children, and you should lie there as if you were sick. You do not belong in the camp where there are boys and men because you are neither one nor the other.

You do not urinate. If you do, the animal you have shot will piss too and you want the eland to keep its bladder shut so that the poison can continue to churn through its heart.

Someone will sleep in there with you, looking after the

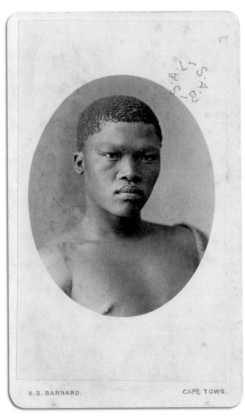

1: /A!kungta, also known as Klaas Stoffel, the first of Bleek and Lloyd's /Xam 'teachers' to be released from the Breakwater Station into their house in Mowbray, *c.* 1870.

2: Lucy and Jemima Lloyd's father
William Henry Cynric Lloyd,
Durban, *c.* 1860.

3: Lucy Lloyd shortly after her
sister's marriage in 1862.

4: Wilhelm Bleek in the front garden of The Hill, between
October 1869 and February 1875.

5: Wilhelm and Jemima Bleek in the garden of The
Hill with Edith, Mabel and Margie, *c.* 1872.

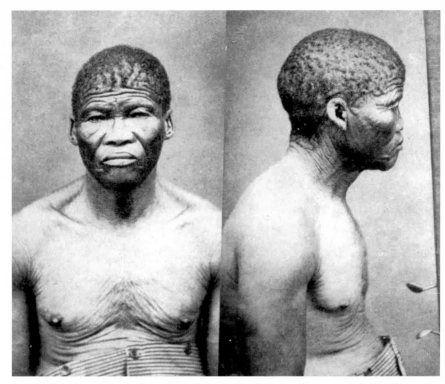

6: The second of Bleek and Lloyd's /Xam 'teachers', //Kabbo (Oud Jantje Tooren) while still a prisoner at the Breakwater Station, *c.* 1870.

7: A group of /Xam men in the yard of the Breakwater Station, a picture from a series of photographs taken on behalf of Wilhelm Bleek in the summer of 1870/71.

8: Dia!kwain, the 'gentle' man imprisoned at the Breakwater for culpable homicide who stayed in Mowbray between June 1874 and March 1876. He holds his flute and offers his brass ring to the camera.

9: *I shall have wings, I shall fly when I am green, I shall be a little green thing.* Dia!kwain's drawing of /kaggen gwai, a male mantis, March 1875.

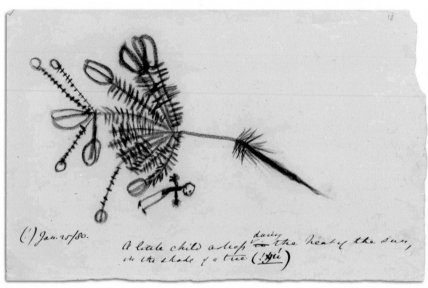

10: *A little child, asleep during the heat of the sun, in the shade of a tree.* One of many pencil drawings made by !Nanni during his stay at Charlton House, January 1880.

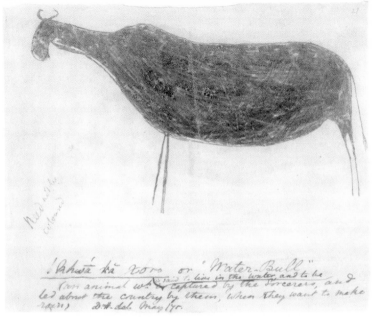

!Kahusá ká xoro or "Water-Bull"
(an animal which said to live in the water, and to be
captured by the sorcerers, and
led about the country by them, when they want to make
rain.) D.A.dah May /yr.

11: *An animal which is said to live in the water, and to be
captured by the sorcerers, and led about the country by them, when they
want to make it rain.* The Rain Bull, !Khwa ka xoro, drawn by
Dia!kwain in May 1875.

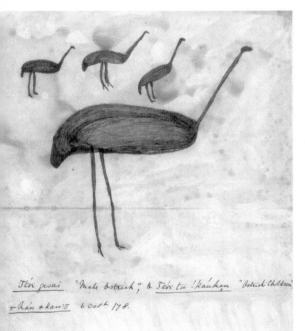

Jǔri pwai "Male Ostrich"; & Jǔri tu !Kauku "Ostrich Children"
+han +han's 6 Oct 178.

12: *The Bushman,
when an ostrich is
coming and is
scratching the back of
its neck with its foot,
feels the tapping in the
lower part of the back
of his own neck; at the
same place where the
ostrich is scratching.*
Male ostrich and
'ostrich children'
drawn by
/Hang≠kass'o in
October 1878.

13: Wilhelm Bleek, apparently in better health, *c.* 1875.

fire. By now /Kaggen will have struck the dying creature on the horn to try and get it moving, to put some life back into it. If he has no luck he will follow your spoor back to your shelter where he will come to see whether your bowstring is taut, to see if it was you that shot his eland. Once he has checked the tension of the bowstring, /Kaggen will come to pinch the inside of your ear, trying to rouse you, in order to get the eland on its feet.

For the Eland is quite stiff, because it feels it is going to die, because poison is that which kills an Eland, the poison with which the man has shot it, which comes wet off the shaft. Poison attacks a thing's arteries; it takes hold of a thing's heart's arteries, it bites at a thing's heart, killing it.

/Kaggen might make the sound of a puff-adder to try and frighten you onto your feet, or he might come as a louse and bite you. Wriggle uncomfortably but don't kill it. It is as if death is sitting on the eland, and that is where you want death to stay. You know to be careful of /Kaggen because you know very well that he is thinking

the man will kill the louse, its blood will be on his hands, with which he grasped the arrow when he shot the eland; the blood will enter the arrow and cool the poison.

There is plenty of life in your blood. Do not let it save the eland you have shot.

Now the man in the shelter with you should see you struggling with /Kaggen and he should make up the fire to drive the Mantis away. It could be an uncomfortable night.

In the morning you will take the other men to the place where you shot the animal and they will track it from there; you should return home unless you want the meat to be poor and lean. They will walk carefully to one side of the eland's spoor, making sure that they do not cross it, until they find the carcass. Then, while the others wait close by, looking away so that their gaze does not make the meat lean, one of the men will approach it. He should come to the animal so that it is between him and the sun, because his shadow will also make it lean.

If you want to help the men butcher the animal you have shot you will have to wait until they have cut out the heart. This is because of your scent. /Kaggen is with the eland as it lies dying and if he smells you there he will take it as a provocation and make *certain* that the meat will be lean.

Like the Meerkats, those greedy men who killed the first eland on the day that hunting was invented, you have killed the animal without permission. Your first eland kill recreates you as a hunter, a man, and there will be celebration and ritual – but do not expect /Kaggen to be watching the dances with happiness in his heart.

It would have been a scandal in Staffordshire, the Reverend Lloyd's casting out of his second-eldest daughter Lucy, but Natal was a very long way from Norbury.

All we know for certain is that the Reverend Lloyd was bankrupt and his daughters were not. Lucy refused to help her father. We can safely imagine an angry peroration on the obligations of a good Christian daughter, forcefully and articulately rejected. The Lloyd sisters had been forced to read a *heavy Psalm* or a chapter every day for years and Lucy had learned enough from the teachings of Jesus of Nazareth to know that her father was a hypocrite. Independence had been forced on her in Natal by an incapable stepmother and an incompetent father; now she discovered that she did not share her father's idea of what it meant to be either a Christian or a daughter.

She left her father's house a woman certain only of her own mind but equally convinced that that mind was worth nothing, thinking herself *ugly, stupid* and *unmarriageable*. She was both terrified and contemptuous of life; she was never going to have the opportunity to use her unique gifts because she would never have the opportunity to discover what they were.

Lucy Lloyd moved to a farm owned by a family called Middleton. There were coffee and sugar plantations of some 160 acres belonging to Middletons at Buffel's Bosch in Pinetown, today the Durban suburb of Shalcross, and it is probable that this was where she went. Although parted from her sister Jemima, who thought of her as her *second self*, she at least had the advantage of real independence and a life away from her father and the poisonous atmosphere of the family home.

Exploiting the laws of hospitality as applied to men of the cloth, her father habitually descended on the farms around Durban for unannounced refreshment stops, tying his horse and staying for supper, but it is very likely that he would have avoided the Middleton estate from the moment his daughter arrived there. The estrangement seems to have been serious.

Eighteen months after her eviction Lucy Lloyd became engaged to the well-travelled and sweet-natured George Wooly, the son of a rector from Derbyshire. She had not asked her father's permission, since she believed it would have *implied obedience*, and that would have been hypocritical of her: she detested hypocrisy utterly and besides, if he would not be a father to her then she was not obliged to behave like a daughter. None the less, the Reverend Lloyd was furious when he found out.

She missed the advice her mother could have given her

then. Even in old age she would regret that she had had no one to turn to as her life began to unravel as it now did. Jemima wrote to Wilhelm before their marriage:

A family who lived on a neighbouring farm had given her a home with them, which both her independence and gratitude (of both which qualities she has I think rather more than a common share) concurred to make her repay by her services to the best of her power – and so well did she succeed that she became invaluable to them; and they being unfortunately very selfish people, and especially the woman, who was most clever too – they managed to sow distrust and pain between her and poor George; feeling if she married him that of course they must lose her aid –. Oh it was such a thing – such a diabolical thing to do – I think – so heartlessly cruel. And there she was poor girl, away from all of us, who, tho' not nearly so sensible as she is, yet might have helped her by just our love and empathy – and without any mother to guide her – just at the mercy of these wretched Middletons.

You can fancy how easy it was for them to make all her intercourse with poor George most uncomfortable, and nearly impossible by their disagreeable speeches; for she is very sensitive at all times; and of course on such a subject so difficultly placed, would be doubly so and being able thus to prevent all possibility of quiet explanation and clearing up of things, the game was in their own hands – as a clever woman like Mrs Middleton could easily under the guise of disinterested friendship, which she knew only too well how to simulate at times – say things first to George and then to Lucy about each other, which must end in mistrust.

Lucy Lloyd broke off the engagement, depressed to the point of incapacity.

Early in the summer of 1860 the Reverend Lloyd made another speech and threw Jemima out of his house, apparently for the same reasons he had Lucy, hoping that they would return to England together. They did not. The two set up home together in Durban and asked their elder sister Frances to move in with them, much to the disapproval of Durban's more high-minded citizens. They were proudly unconventional, socially and religiously, and became very well-regarded by the family of Colenso, the bishop of Natal.

The Lloyd sisters were *highly esteemed by those who know them best*, wrote Colenso's wife Frances in a letter, adding that their mother had been *a woman of fortune, so her children are independent, but they have been admirable daughters, and as their father is a little cracked about money it has not always been easy to be so.*

It took Lucy Lloyd until she was in her thirties to make peace with her former fiancé, but in October 1860, before she had quite had the opportunity to explain herself, he died.

Pity /Kaggen's family.

'Good manners', chief of which were your obligations to your parents and your children, were first invented tens of thousands of years ago to ensure the survival of extended families of hunters and gatherers in environments as difficult as the deserts, plains and forests of eastern and central Africa. All cultures have 'manners' of some kind and all are fossilized forms of identical obligations. Most start at the dinner table. Every polite thank-you note was once a way of telling someone you would not let them die of thirst if you were sitting on a spring in a drought; we have been hunters and gatherers for more than nine-tenths of our history as a species and we are not likely to lose the ritual inheritance easily.

/Kaggen did not have any manners. Either he knew none of the rules of food sharing, visiting and gift giving or he let his appetites override them, and if he did not get his way he would sulk or bend the laws of physics. The only people capable of keeping the old man in check were his family, a very curious lot who suffered him surprisingly gracefully.

/Kaggen was married to /Huntu!katt!katten, the Hyrax or Rock Rabbit, known in South Africa as the Dassie. With her he had a daughter called Ywe-/nan-//kaintu and two sons, !Gaunu-ts'axau, !Gaunu's Eye (named for the great star who sang the names of the stars), and /Kaggen-opwa, the Young Mantis.

The old man's sister was the Blue Crane and he was a protective uncle to her child, a little springbok called Kattau.

His adopted daughter !Xo was the Porcupine. Her real father, //Khai-hemm, was known as the All Devourer, and with good reason – he ate everything he came across and the touch of his tongue burned you. You knew he was coming when you saw the bushes on the ridge disappear, and you knew he had arrived when his shadow surrounded you; his shadow was as thick as smoke. It *was* smoke. He was a bushfire.

!Xo was married to /Kwammang-a, who was visible in the rainbow. He may even have been the rainbow itself, it is difficult to tell, and there is no one we can ask to make sure. At any rate, both he and /Kaggen could be seen in the rainbow, *yellow above and red below*. /Kaggen was the yellow and /Kwammang-a the red.

/Kwammang-a and !Xo gave /Kaggen two grandchildren, a mongoose called /Ni, known as the Ichneumon, and Young /Kwammang-a.

Visits are perhaps the most trying times of all for /Kaggen's family because the old man will insist on coming whenever /Kwammang-a and /Ni set off to see their relations, and although they know full well what the consequences will be there is nothing anyone can do to stop him tagging along.

They tell him he will be scared when they go to visit the Lions and suddenly the Lions are his old friends; they tell him it is too far for him when they go to visit the Proteles and suddenly /Kaggen has to go everywhere with /Kwammang-a and keep him company at all times. Apart from anything, it is tremendously embarrassing for /Kwammang-a to take his father-in-law to visit his people.

/Kaggen is horribly greedy and he will attempt to terrify or eat the children of the family he is visiting. Exchanges like these made /Kwammang-a's heart sink:

/Kwammang-a said: 'Oh, /Ni, let's go to the Lions' house, that they may roast Quagga's meat for us!'

  /Ni said: 'We will do so.' He agreed with him.

  /Kaggen said: 'Let us do so.' For /Kaggen also agreed.

/Kwammang-a, you will notice, was talking to /Ni.

No one *invites* /Kaggen, or asks him along anywhere – ever. It is just that when arrangements like these are being made then his terrible hearing is spontaneously fantastic. And if he is out on his own, he does not need an invitation anywhere.

/Kwammang-a is brave, socially adept, and fulfils his obligations to his family without comment or flourish. At strangers' houses he will sit quietly, only speaking to obtain stories or news, *kukummi*. /Kaggen, on the other hand, is a terrible coward who will play with children as if he were an infant himself before telling them filthy and inappropriate stories.

Frequently beaten by the animals he finds in the veld, Meerkats one day, Ticks the next, /Kaggen likes to turn ignominious flight into victorious gloating when, suddenly winged and feathered to avoid a more serious beating, he will drop everything and make his transformed ascent to the accompaniment of one or the other of his catchphrases, both adaptable to the severity of his bruises or burns. As he calls his hartebeest-skin *kaross* and bag, his *hartebeest's children*, his quiver and his stick to follow him, he will cry *Ha! My name is /Kaggen! No one equals me!*

If he has won a fight he will ascend as he proclaims his glorious third name, the special name he uses for himself on the surprisingly frequent occasions when he is able to have a good gloat: *My name is Penis! The man has* done *it!* he will declare to the barren veld.

If he cannot flee on the wing for any reason, he will just run away very fast. He is entirely shameless.

Instead of my high German boots from the court-shoemaker of Prince Albert, I should have worn veld-shoes of lion or hyena-skin, with but one spur, wrote Bleek, sitting on the pressed mud and cow-dung floor of a rondavel in the highlands of Zululand. It was July 1856 and he had yet to meet the Mantis in person. Although he had been a year and one month in southern Africa, his exploring had only just begun.

I should have worn a blue flannel bush-shirt, instead of my once-fashionable brown cloth jacket; the waistcoat I should have left at home. It would have been quite stylish just to wear a shirt and trousers. As I am wearing two of the latter, linen ones on top of flannels, I am indulging in unusual excesses, and socks are an unheard-of luxury. The striped cotton shirt is more in keeping with the prevailing fashion.

Accompanied by a Natalian Zulu man called Nongalasa and porters from Natal and Zululand picked up en route, he carried with him his bedding, comprising a large blanket and an old coverlet which served as a mattress, an old blue coat

more than ten years old, his superfluous waistcoat, a snow-beret
which doubled as a nightcap, a scarf, a pair of rubber galoshes
and a horse blanket incorporated into his bedding during
nights when his horse was untethered, which was rare since it
was constantly running away from him. For a pillow he used
unnamed *surplus garments, of which I have a large stock.*

He also had with him soap, coffee, tea, sugar, salt, cutlery,
a heavy iron kettle, a folding stool, his rifle, *a cast-iron pot, a
little tin mincer, a tin jug with lid as a milk-jug which, when I have
guests, may be used as coffee-pot or teapot, and a tin dish serving at
the same time as a washing up basin or a dinner platter (you cannot
be fussy out here).*

In addition to his substantial personal effects he also brought
with him trade goods and presents which he kept in the black
oilcloth travelling bag bought during his ill-starred stop-off in
Sierra Leone. Most importantly of all, he had with him his
leather writing case and his books: a Zulu dictionary, a Xhosa
grammar and dictionary, an unnamed Zulu text, a copy of the
New Testament and Sir Francis Galton's *The Art of Travel,
or Shifts and Contrivances Available in Wild Countries*, an illustrated survival guide for travellers, missionaries, emigrants and
soldiers with advice on traps, water, fire and horse husbandry.

He was aware he was not dressed *in the style of the country*
and he did not care. If anything he found it useful. He was
always at pains to make sure that it was understood that he
was neither *u Mfundisi*, a missionary, nor a trader. He was
prepared to pay for his food and his accommodation with the
red material and glass beads he had with him and all he wanted
from his visits were grammar, vocabulary and myth.

Neither trader nor missionary, what he was, in fact, was an
anthropologist, probably the very first.

After sixteen months spent collecting Zulu *traditionary literature* in isolated homesteads across Natal, Bleek had crossed the

Thukela River from the British colony into independent Zululand in the winter of 1856. His goal was kwaNodwengu, the royal homestead of King Mpande, supreme ruler of the Zulus and successor to the great chief Shaka kaSezangakhona. Bleek arrived at Mpande's court after a month-long journey through Zululand's mild uplands having collected enough material to complete a book and having had frequent cause to consult the chapters relating to horse husbandry in Sir Francis's travelogue. His mount, a clever creature that had had its tail bitten off by a cow belonging to a missionary called Schreuder, was an aggressively independent animal.

He spent six weeks in the royal homestead, attending beer-drinking parties, taking snuff and periodically retrieving his horse before he finally met the king himself, huge and gouty, and then made his way back to Natal. He arrived in Durban in the second week of September and almost immediately rode out to a new mission station on the Umlazi River in the company of a Mrs Robertson, 'magistrate for the Natives', and the newly promoted Archdeacon William Henry Cynric Lloyd.

During the journey Bleek, who had begun the introduction to his 'On the Origin of Language' by arguing that there was no such thing as a divine plan and that we should not speak of a heavenly *purpose* in creation, rather a *process* that could be explained by science, succeeded in convincing Lloyd that he was an altogether godless individual.

Shortly afterwards he left Natal for Cape Town and an audience with the morally curious governor of the Cape Colony, Sir George Grey, whom he had first met in London. His intention now was to seek funding from the governor for a journey into the north of the southern African subcontinent and he hoped that Grey, who had few qualms about lavishing government funds on any project, mission or scheme that might cause him to be remembered as an enlightened humani-

tarian and gifted intellect, would be able to help him. Grey
was a linguist of note with a declared fascination for 'native'
folklore and language; Bleek had run out of money.

He arrived in Table Bay on 1 November 1856 after another
near-shipwreck.

Sir George Grey did not fund Bleek's further explorations
into the African interior but he did appoint him Government
Translator on a salary of £250 a year and employed him in a
private capacity to catalogue and to augment his growing
library of texts gathered from the colonized world. He possessed a trove of literature from the first peoples of Africa,
Polynesia, New Zealand, Australia and the Americas begun in
the course of the mortal fiasco that was his exploration of
northern Australia two decades earlier.

The governor greatly admired Bleek's prodigious facility
with languages and hoped to increase his own reputation
for erudition through association. Bleek in turn admired his
patron's dedication to collecting the rarest and even the slightest piece of literature he could find even if it meant paying
hundreds of pounds for a pamphlet of barely a dozen leaves.
Now he had a measure of security and the opportunity to seek
out exactly the kind of literature that most fascinated him,
which he could pay for with someone else's money. Capti-
vated by his new patron's famous charisma he was to remain
grateful to Grey for the rest of his life, often praising his
humanity, his energy, his learning and his gifts as a statesman.

They grew to be friends, although Bleek depended on Sir
George's largesse and influence for his financial security for
years to come, even after Grey left the Cape for New Zealand
in 1862. It was an unequal friendship. Grey needed praise but
he did not need Bleek.

By December 1858 there were over 350 books in the Zulu,
Xhosa, Tswana and Khoe languages alone and more than 150

texts from New Zealand in Grey's collection. The catalogues
of the texts from New Zealand and Australia were ready for
the printers, pending the arrival of some important manuscripts, and Bleek was readying himself to tackle texts from
Madagascar, the islands of the Indian Ocean, Polynesia and
Papua. After that there were Arabic, Ethiopian and Native
American texts to address. All this literature remains in the
South African library system today. Most of it, including
twenty volumes of Maori manuscripts, remains unpublished
and untranslated.

If it were not for the confidence afforded him by this
intellectual prosperity and financial security Bleek would not
have begun to consider beginning work on his *Comparative
Grammar of South African Languages*, a typically ambitious
labour that he intended to run to three volumes.

Bleek established himself in Cape Town. He threw himself
into his own linguistic work, visiting Robben Island and the
prisons on the mainland to interview speakers of indigenous
South African languages and publishing papers and translations. For the first time he even succeeded in interviewing
Bushmen, speakers of an all but unknown language that had
fascinated him for years. He still had to collect a single story
of the /Xam-ka !ei, however. All he had managed to record
were a few /Xam words and phrases, enough to convince him
that the language of the Bushmen and the language of the
'Hottentots' were as different as English and Latin and that
the Bushmen's was the older. None the less, his first four years
in Cape Town he could consider a success – but we used to
be springbok and the man who shot us is above morals and
has not owed us a thing since he made us stand up.

A typical Mantis story might go something like this.

/Kaggen is out walking in the veld (walking, visiting and hearing *kukummi* being preferable to hunting or otherwise providing for his family) when the old man sees a creature of some kind. It might be a cat singing to itself about how the Lynx insulted him for being a slower runner. It might be !Gwe!kweitentu, the desert Will o' the Wisp, a man with his eyes between his toes.

Singing cat or man with a curious head is provocation enough for /Kaggen, who will make a few lunges with his knobkerrie before he has his head broken, confused by the idiosyncratic fighting techniques of his adversary. He effects his escape by growing feathers and flying away, or by running very fast, having left his hartebeest-skin *kaross* and quiver, his stick and his arrows behind. At a safe distance he will call them, and they fly to him. Covered in blood and unsteady on his feet, /Kaggen will then return home to his family who throw up their hands and roll their eyes at his predictably damaged state. As /Kaggen basks in self-pity his wife /Huntu!-katt!katten might ask 'Who was it this time? Mice? Meerkats? Ticks?'

When he finally explains who it was that beat him up, his son-in-law glowering in silent but ill-concealed contempt, it falls on his grandson /Ni to coax out the full story. When the facts are known, /Ni tells Grandfather what everybody knows: how to beat the person using a little rudimentary knowledge of their habits.

After a night spent writhing noisily in pain, /Kaggen returns to the veld for his revenge, and wins. He is anything but magnanimous in victory, claiming he always knew what he had to do, even when he was so obviously pleased with himself that his adversary could tell by his walk alone that someone had supplied him with tips.

On his victorious return home, the Mantis gloats to his family about his singular prowess as a fighter. /Ni, who is always the one to admonish the old man, lecture him on the rules of appropriate behaviour or tell him what his family thinks of him, will then say something on the lines of:

'O /Kaggen, you are foolish, you are deceitful. I taught you; I, a child, taught you, a grown-up man. You are foolish, you are cunning, you are deceitful.' Thus they talked there. The women laughed.

/Ni said: 'You agree with me; is not /Kaggen foolish and deceitful?'

Mrs Roesch was a woman of Dutch descent, although her hair and her eyes were black enough to arouse suspicions in those Victorian Britons with an eye for the inevitable genetic interventions of the colonies. She might greet the new arrival at her boarding house in Adderley Street with a plate of fresh oranges and later offer advice on the dangers of drinking tea offered to good Christian folk by the Cape's Muslims, whom she believed administered maddening poisons that might take effect years after they were drunk or unspeakable love potions that explained why so many Christian women converted to Islam in order to marry Malay husbands. Apparently it had not crossed her mind that the Church forbade mixed marriages.

Her place had very high ceilings and ill-matching furniture and some of the doors began three inches above the floor, but it was very clean throughout and everyone who stayed there thought that the dinners were sublime.

Jemima Lloyd and Wilhelm Bleek, who met while staying at that establishment in March 1861, both agreed on that.

The Reverend Lloyd's second-youngest daughter was in

Cape Town waiting for the *Celt* to steam her to Britain, a place she now found difficult to refer to as home, intending to see family she had not seen for twelve years and to take specialist medical advice on the neuralgia she had recently begun to suffer in her hands and face caused by the stress of life in Natal. It was the beginning of autumn on the Cape when the two met. Then the southeasterly wind that shredded the gardens of the Dutch East India Company two centuries before begins to soften, taking with it the aridity of the Cape summer.

A German, Dr Bleek by name, has just come to stay here, wrote Jemima to Frances in Durban on the 21st. *He is in bad health. A curious but very intelligent face.* A strong, almost leonine face with a small nose and a very full bottom lip.

He was once at Natal. I believe he is engaged under Sir George Grey's auspices in compiling different native dictionaries and grammars . . . they say this is a very clever man.

He was clean-shaven, missing one or two teeth, thin; he was courteous and poor and tuberculosis had brought his career as an explorer to an end for good. Now his explorations were linguistic and he travelled from grammar to grammar. Jemima, slight and symmetrical of face, wore a centre-parting and a skirt over crinoline hoops, on first appearances a some-what shy woman with archetypically fragile Victorian nerves. This was deceptive. She had been brave enough to claim for herself some of the social freedoms offered by colonial society and had come to view the world in a manner that owed little to her father's conservatism. Fresh from the frontier and liberated from the notice of both family and the scandal-mongers of the provinces, she and her travelling companion Emma Fisher enjoyed the freedom they found on the Cape.

They made a splash at Mrs Roesch's and basked in the mild notoriety that followed.

Like her elder sister Lucy she was a mixture of awkward insecurity and very certain convictions, a woman who had grown to detest the artifices and pretensions of 'society' but none the less very much wanted to be liked and respected. She believed herself a *moral coward*, without principle when it mattered, a weakness inherited from her father.

Generally unshockable and with an eye for the unconventional, Bleek was delighted to have someone in the house more interesting than the harbour official Captain Jamison and the pallid Captain Hill to talk to.

Jemima, who could be rudely forthright in conversation with those for whom she had no respect and found herself tongue-tied with those whom she admired, found, it seems, that Wilhelm brought out the best in her. At any rate, during the month the two spent at Mrs Roesch's, we know that their conversation included wild, funny, speculations about the character of Captain Spencer – who was to captain the *Celt* to Southampton – and the spiritually limiting nature of orthodox Christianity.

Bleek, who had come to believe that his poverty and the poor state of his health virtually precluded any hope of marriage, had met someone who trusted her own mind and whose unconventional opinions were compatible with his own.

When Jemima Lloyd boarded the *Celt* for Southampton on Sunday 21 April, Bleek, normally careful to the point of obsession, came aboard to wish her *bon voyage* wearing only his thin summer coat on a windy day. Jemima was glad he had come to wish her farewell, but she was certainly worried about his health and was concerned to see him shivering.

Wilhelm Bleek was already in love with Jemima Lloyd by

the time the *Celt* set off for the north. She had promised to write him a letter before the *Celt* reached St Helena, an island a few days north of the Cape, and on a calm day as the steamer drew near she began it. Apologizing for the ugliness of her handwriting, she described the passage of the *Celt*, the improving state of her health and the other passengers, whom she thought very pleasant if uninspiring. She missed him. *You don't know how many times I've been wishing for a talk with you,* she wrote. She hoped he would not find her note 'tiresome' and signed off *Goodbye dear Friend. Believe me very sincerely, Jemima.*

This was the beginning of a courtship preserved in an epistolary time-lapse that saw Wilhelm Bleek heartbroken and elated by turns every six weeks.

It took at least five weeks for every letter from the Cape to reach Britain and to be forwarded to Jemima touring the southeast and northwest of England, and five weeks at the least for her reply to reach the Cape. Bleek wrote replies to letters he had not yet received and received letters that either made him wish he had been bolder or convinced him that his presumption had ruined everything. Jemima was steadier, and not until the end of the year would she dare to admit to herself that she had anything to lose.

Bleek began his first reply in a familiar but polite fashion, gossiping in a gently deteriorating copperplate script about the other residents at Mrs Roesch's before turning to philology and theology and outlining his proposal for a *Union* of free-thinking people dedicated to the pursuit of an understanding of God that rejected scripture and doctrine. At one point he even wrote in Greek.

Great religious truths are indeed impressed upon the mind by every sincere contemplation of our intimate and indissoluble connection with the whole of

our race; − we must feel strongly how only by this connection and in
consequence of it we are human beings, and how by furthering the advance
of the great organism of humankind, we have the only possibility of raising
ourselves

he explained. Admirable, and ahead of its time, but this was
not conventional loving talk. Fortunately it was the only way
that Jemima Bleek would ever be won. She quite simply
believed that she had only met one genuinely honest man in
her life.

Their correspondence quickly recalled the familiarity the
two had known in Cape Town, and Jemima wrote honestly
and candidly. As much as she was enjoying the company of
her old friends and family, she wrote, *still the old pain of having*
to take care not to shock or pain them to some degree spoils all −
making me feel so caged.

Oh I long to be back at Natal for that with all its faults and drawbacks one
has freedom there. Perhaps you will say it's my own fault for that he who
will may be free anywhere. But to do that one must not be a moral coward
as I am − and I long for the place where even a coward may be free − and I
can at Natal.

Wilhelm, cautious not to frighten the woman he loved
from replying, addressed Jemima as his *Dear sister* from the off,
cleverly hinting for her to send him her photograph and subtly
asking if there were anyone who might be one day closer to
her than a brother. He moved from Mrs Roesch's, whom he
had grown to dislike, to a place called Granite Lodge where
he paid less rent for a bigger room. He was very lonely.

Well these dreadful prospects of many years of spiritual and mental fasting
make me sometimes very savage . . . making me wish that slavery was a

lawful institution, and that I was allowed to buy my dear sister as a slave, to keep her all for myself. But then I am afraid I should never be able to pay the price for a jewel so much valued as she is; and if I had it I should not be able to set it in proper fittings. But I see already your face thoroughly shocked at this . . . and must therefore implore you not to read the preceding last sentences, or if you have already read them to forget them altogether, except you should like to hear them, what indeed cannot well be supposed.

If I had the least spirit of chevalerée in me I should have altered the proposition altogether and have supposed myself a humble slave, who craved to be bought by a master or a mistress he liked. But then you see there would not have been much difficulty about it, as I would have been rather a drug in any decent slave market and could, therefore, be had very cheap, though it might be said that it was not worth having at all. As to my own predilection I should certainly prefer being a slave to being a slave owner.

Every time a steamer put into Table Bay a flag was raised on Lion's Rump, the hill overlooking the Breakwater Station and the harbour. Bleek could see it from his bed and by September the first thing he did when he woke up was to check to see it was flying. This is clearly the behaviour of someone in love and in September he was brave enough to tell her, signing his letter . . . *let me always hear good news from yourself, my dear friend, and believe love, W.H.I.B.*

In his more reflective moments he realized it was hopeless. Who would possibly agree to marry a penniless consumptive with an uncertain future? Manfully, he resisted the urge to tell her his feelings.

Oh! dearest Jemmy, my love, my treasure, the desire of my heart, my constant thought and dream by day and by night — do you really return a little the love which I feel for you? Oh! do tell me this! Let my hope of this be not quite disappointed and I shall be comforted in the loneliness which to share with me I have not the heart to propose it you now.

Yes my dear, dear friend, I do love you. I can't at all adequately tell you what your dear letter giving me the right is to me

she replied, going on to discuss practical matters such as her eventual return to the Cape, the state of her finances and how to make the announcement of their engagement. She was sorry only that she could not consult her dead mother, since her father had by *turning us out of his house of course forfeited all a father's claims of this kind.*

She warned him that there was madness in her family and he warned her that he would probably be dead before her, to which she replied

And as to your only other doubt about our union darling, I mean your dread that it might so be that you have to leave me sorrowing and lonely in this world if you are summonsed from it first, I think we may trustingly leave that to our heavenly father's hands.

I feel none but He can take you from me – and as I believe He is perfect love and wisdom that it will not be until or unless He sees it's the real best for us both – and dreadful as it would be to me to lose you darling – bitter beyond all words – yet I know that he who dealt the blow would give me the power to bear it – and even then my darling, whenever that hour does come, it will not be really losing you – I mean not in its full bitterness, like losing you from my soul.

She signed the letter *Jemima (wife).*

Of all the people in South Africa his daughter could have chosen as a husband, the Reverend William Henry Cynric Lloyd believed, Bleek was the very worst. When Bleek wrote

to him to tell him that he intended to marry his daughter the priest was apoplectic.

The Prussian linguist, who exchanged corespondence with Darwin, was one of Bishop Colenso's most outspoken supporters. Lloyd hated Colenso, who publicly and famously questioned the historical accuracy of the Old Testament, but Bleek did not stop there. He thought that Jesus of Nazareth was a charismatic individual who had been deified over centuries for nakedly political reasons, and although he preferred not to advertise his religious beliefs he would never deny them.

Jemima Lloyd, the daughter of a man who believed in the Bible with *a child's implicit faith*, was to marry someone known to be an atheist.

William Lloyd replied to Bleek's letter only to express his astonishment that a man who knew himself to be a disbeliever in God's Holy Word could propose to a member of his family and demanded to know if it were really true that Bleek did not believe in the Ever Blessed and Eternal Trinity.

Bleek's supremely tactful reply gave the impression of a man genuinely sorry for the upset he had caused, but the letters he exchanged with Jemima tell a different story. There was nothing William Lloyd could have done to prevent the marriage. Wilhelm Bleek had written out of courtesy and pity alone; a zealous bankrupt with a reputation for callousness to his family would not be allowed to come between him and his happiness.

Jemima came back to Cape Town in November 1862. She had not seen Bleek for more than a year and a half. Two weeks later, after an exchange of increasingly short and illegible notes sent between Mrs Roesch's, where Jemima Lloyd was staying, and Wilhelm Bleek's hotel, the two were married in

St George's Cathedral next door to the library. Mrs Roesch provided the flowers.

Three weeks before her sister's return to Africa, Lucy Lloyd came to Cape Town from Natal aboard the *Waldensian* to help Wilhelm with the preparations for the wedding. A storm blew the vessel into the breakers near Cape Aghullas, the southernmost point of Africa. All of the 121 passengers aboard, including a group of famous minstrels, were ferried ashore aboard fishing boats. She managed to save the two blue glass vases she had intended as wedding presents by bringing them ashore in her lap, later finding another intended gift – a set of the works of Sir Walter Scott – washed ashore in their water-proof packaging.

When he heard the news of the steamer's wreck, Bleek wanted to jump in a carriage and go to Lucy's assistance at once, but he was too ill. When the two first met on a cold, gusty spring day in Cape Town he looked so terrible that she was too upset to give an account of her experience.

Jemima and Wilhelm asked Lucy to move in with the two of them and she agreed, although she came close to changing her mind when Wilhelm wrote her a note questioning her Uncle Marmaduke's capacity to act as one of Jemima's trustees by alluding to some *inconsistency of behaviour*. Jemima tactfully brought her around a matter of hours before the wedding and they moved into a house near the Botanical Gardens with six rooms for the family and another for an American man of African ancestry who had been the first cook aboard the *Waldensian* until its shipwreck had left him without a job.

Lucy Lloyd never went back to Natal and it seems that she saw her father no more than twice in the following seventeen years, the first time when he came to Mowbray to visit his grandchildren. Lucy and Jemima both left Natal with the kind of cynicism born of constant disappointment, an unshakeable sense of loyalty to those they believed deserving of it and a life-long hostility to stupid, weak or duplicitous men.

/Kaggen shrugs off descriptions like *stupid, weak* and *duplicitous*, although he certainly could be all of those things – as well as creative, unpredictably generous, even family-orientated. He would do anything for his sister the Blue Crane, for example.

For her he would even climb into an elephant's arse. We know this categorically, because he did, in order to retrieve her daughter.

You can tell a story about /Kaggen and fall about laughing at the old man's exemplary stupidity but there are other times when it is vital to be discreet. He has some influence in the day-to-day lives of everyone in your camp, especially the hunters.

A trickster has to do with the hunt because of its inexplicable contingencies, its unpredictability, its frustrations and its un-expected successes. The creator, too, is a trickster because tricksters are above morals and responsibilities. /Kaggen had this in common with 'creation', of course, which was sporadi-cally bountiful, certainly very beautiful, often ironic and funny, but plainly above any kind of responsibility to anyone.

If arrows missed, people died of hunger. If the rains failed people died of hunger and thirst. The explanations and com-forts offered by religions founded by agriculturalist societies only serve to prove that you have to get very comfortable indeed before you earn gods with good manners. It had always been like this for the /Xam-ka !ei.

Two lions, !Gu and !Hauë ta ≠hou, 'Mat' and 'Belt', were a double-act from the time of the Early Race, comic and carnivorous. Mat, the clever one, was the first of the two to hit upon the idea of eating human flesh. He was eating a woman and Belt was really not that interested in joining him. *Taste! Her flesh is like the ostrich*, !Gu told him.

We have these two to thank for showing us that /Kaggen was capable of acting out of more than self-interest. This is how the story went.

The Blue Crane's friend was the Frog. The Frog was a person; her husband was a person; the Blue Crane was a person. They were people of the Early Race.

/Kaggen's sister the Blue Crane had picked a very bad day indeed to visit her friend the Frog. The Frog was not speaking to her husband, who was sitting in a sulk, ignoring them both. When a beetle flew past his nose he found the excuse he needed to leave the house and he hopped after it, heading off into the veld. The Blue Crane, who was quite unlike her brother in that she was a generous sort of character far more capable of imagining the feelings of others, immediately took it upon herself to bring him back and jumped up to chase him.

Missing him every time she made a grab for him, the Blue Crane found the Frog very difficult to catch. Eventually she lost sight both of him and of his tracks and began to scour the ground for signs of him. She searched and searched; she walked and walked. When she found his spoor it led her under a flat rock where he had hidden from her a long time before. She continued to search for him; she looked everywhere.

And she grew lean while she was searching there. Grief made her grow lean; she became bones.

As she was searching, wasting away, !Gu and !Hauë ta ≠hou – Mat and Belt – heard her. The two Lions stalked her by the sound of her crying until they caught sight of her. Then they killed her and ate her. *Finish her all up*, !Gu told his stupid friend. *Don't let any of this person's bones spring out of your mouth.*

Naturally that was exactly what happened a few moments later when the Blue Crane's breastbone jumped out of Belt's mouth and landed somewhere near by. It was a big bone and so they looked everywhere for it but eventually they got bored and wandered off to find someone else to eat.

Soon /Kaggen missed his sister and went to find her – but the only spoor he saw was lion spoor. He knew what it meant and so he followed the lion tracks to the place where she had become food; there he searched the ground until he found the bone that had sprung out of !Hauë ta ≠hou's mouth. He picked it up and carried it to a *vlei*, where, like the shoe that became an eland, he put it in the water and left it.

Then he headed off home.

The next day he came back and saw his sister. She was tiny, and when she saw him she jumped into the water with a splash, scared. /Kaggen turned round and went back to the shelters. When he came back the next day, he came as quietly as he could so as not to startle her. She was sitting in the sun and he saw that she had grown; he turned back and went home without frightening her.

While the Blue Crane sat basking, he went to make things, clothes which he meant to give to the Blue Crane, when she grew up.

He came back the next day and saw her still sitting happily

in the sun. Now she was a little girl and he turned back, leaving her in peace. When he left for the camp for the waterpit the next day he took with him the clothes he had made and crept up to his sister as quietly as he could. When he caught hold of her she tried to leap back into the waterpit and escape him, but he held her fast and rubbed his powerful sweat over her face, making her smell his scent. He told her

I am your brother. I am the Tinderbox, your elder brother. Stop struggling and sit.

She sat. He gave her the cap he had made for her, wrapped her in a skin petticoat and put a *kaross* over her shoulders. His sweat and the clothes made her a person again.

Then he took the Blue Crane with him; they returned home.

Kumm:

How the approach of a commando is foretold by the mist

While the people are still coming to attack us, when they are still making for us, in the morning, the mist — our mist — sits. They shoot at us in the mist. We make cloud, our blood is smoking, while the people shoot at us in the mist.

That is why we make cloud before the people have come to us. Therefore, the people who know exclaim, they say: '/A appears to be coming to us today.'

My father used to tell me that it seemed as if I did not know that our mist sat there when /a was coming. The people fought us in the mist. And, when the people had finished fighting with us, and they went away, leaving us, after they had fought us, and gone, the mist went too, because it felt that our blood had flowed out.

That is why our mist went. It felt that our blood, which had been making clouds of smoke, had poured out.

/A meant 'war', 'harm', 'a curse'. It also meant 'a concentration of magical power'. A 'commando' was a party of men armed for the purpose of killing Bushmen.

K'au:

Commando

The General Commando of 1774, some two hundred farmers and soldiers divided into three mounted companies, was the first to comb the frontier country with the explicit aim of making it safe for settlers from the threat of its indigenes.

Many hundreds of people died that year as the Afrikaner colony sought to secure the land and labour it required, and only one of those deaths was European. Dozens of official and informal parties were mustered in the following years and people continued to die for decades. The San of the Cape interior fought back with such vehemence that it became a commonplace that they preferred death to defeat – but arrows and throwing sticks proved to be no match for gunpowder and rifle balls. The men were killed without mercy while the women and children were captured and forced to labour on the ranches founded on the region's migration paths and springs.

!gam ke ≠ei yan	the Bushmen
ge hin //hion	eat the cattle
ka xoro	of the Boers;
//hun gan / keye	the Boers take
!gam ke ≠kei	the children of
yan /hanken	the Bushmen

Farmers always need more land. This is an historical constant. They invented wealth and perfected the idea of property and have measured them ever since in stock, hectares and sons who need land of their own. Generally the first thing those sons do when they arrive where hunting and gathering people live is to kill them.

Farmers are landowners who see people, hunters and gatherers, with no understanding of property or the value of land or anything worth the description 'religion'; they seize unworked, apparently unwanted soil and then use deadly force to protect their wealth and the fruit of their labour; they build beside springs and rivers and they hunt for profit rather than subsistence.

There were once migrations of springbok across the Cape Thirstland so huge that it was dangerous to be caught before them, flash floods of animals and processions so vast that the air was thick with dust all the way to the horizon.

The springbok resemble the water of the sea. They come in numbers to this place, the springbok cover it. Therefore the Boer's gun-powder becomes exhausted, that and the balls.

In about 1500 the Khoekhoen first arrived on the better-watered fringes of /Xam-ka !au with their cattle and sheep, having crossed the Orange River upstream a few centuries before. Until they acquired domesticated animals about 2,000 years ago they had been a hunting and gathering people like those they now called San, to whom they were closely related; it had taken them centuries to reach /Xam-ka !au from the north of Botswana, where they originated.

This was the very first time in 100,000 years of human settlement that a lifestyle other than hunting and gathering had been practised in the region and doubtless there was some friction along the Orange River, since to herders livestock are wealth but to hunters they are protein, for eating and for sharing. If the arrival of domesticated animals brought a degree of tension to the fringes of the area, worse was to follow. The Khoekhoen had neither guns nor the idea that land itself could be valuable.

Some two hundred years later, in the late 1600s, Khoe people from the Cape of Good Hope threatened by the infant Dutch colony founded on the shore of Table Bay began to move north. Soon after, from 1739, the ancient hunting and gathering populations and the more recently arrived Khoekhoen were joined by the colonists from the Cape Peninsula themselves: the *trekboers*.

Khoe people herding in the plains, mountains and huge valleys immediately north of the Cape of Good Hope lost their herds and their land in less than thirty years. Then the settlers took their Merino sheep, animals resilient enough to survive in the sparsest grazing, north towards the Orange.

Today it is difficult to imagine migrations in the Northern Cape of any kind at all. The Boers shot the eland, the springbok and the quaggas with industry as they moved further and further into /Xam-ka !au for the grazing and standing water available after the rains. Their stock ate out both the seasonal pasture of the wild herds and the fragile *veldkos*, the roots, seeds, larvae and tubers gathered every day by the San. Food became harder to find as the settlers built permanent home-steads and appropriated water sources used by hunting and gathering populations since the land's first occupation.

San bands, traditionally of about fourteen people, began to join together in order to resist. Some retreated north and others fought with the most extraordinary bravery and selflessness. Before the San of the region understood quite how much the settlers valued their livestock, they had taken their animals to eat: that is what animals had always been *for*. As the frontier became bloodier and more dangerous they took the settlers' animals with the aim of hurting the Boers financially. Under cover of darkness the /Xam-ka !ei and their southerly neighbours the Swy-ei began to drive stock off towards the hills to be slaughtered and hobbled, a tactic the Boers thought barbaric. They killed shepherds and farmers, too, and finally the settlers' anger became focused and organized.

In the last decades of the 1700s, when the quasi-military commando companies were sent in, massacre began in earnest. The explicit aim was the complete subjugation, or the final eradication, of the hunting and gathering people of the Cape interior. Resisters were to be fought and killed and survivors divided amongst the settlers for their labour. The Bosjemans were considered vermin, their lives valueless. Men, women and children were killed for sport.

A kind of murderous anarchy obtained south of the Orange River for the first half of the nineteenth century as /Xam people armed by resisting Khoekhoen and with rifles stolen from the Boers fought for their land. It was an unequal fight.

They surrounded the place during the night, spying the Bushmen's fires. At daybreak the firing commenced, and it lasted until the sun was up a little way. The commando party loaded and fired, and reloaded many times until they had finished . . . The women threw up their arms, crying for mercy, but no mercy was shown them. Great sin was perpetrated that day.

In 1847, when the British Cape Colony officially annexed all the land south of the last few hundred kilometres of the Orange River, the 'war' on the /Xam-ka !ei was all but won. European people, the remnants of the Khoe people and the so-called Bastards or Basters, people of mixed African and

European ancestry, were given equal grazing rights and government decree 'disappeared' everybody else.

It proved even easier to shoot people who did not actually exist. The commandos continued to hunt for families and bands of 'wild' /Xam, who became trespassers simply by hunting game or gathering *veldkos*. /Xam men and women could either take employment in the service of the Basters and the Boers in conditions no better than slavery, they could stay in the veld and try and eke out an existence hunting and gathering, stealing stock and hiding from the commandos, or they could simply starve.

The arrests of //Kabbo, /A!kungta and /Hang≠kass'o in 1869 were occasioned by some of the last acts of resistance of the ancient population of the Northern Cape. Of all the people who came to stay at the Bleeks', only //Kabbo, perhaps, was old enough to remember the time when the violence was still only a threat.

Ruyter was brought up by white men, he died while he was with the white men. The Boer had been beating him about herding the sheep, that he had not herded the sheep well. Therefore the Boer was beating him with the strap which lies under the oxen's necks. That was the strap the Boer beat him with, when the Boer had bound him upon the wagon. The Boer beat him as he lay bound upon the wagon. He beat him, as he lay bound upon the wagon.

And when the Boers thought they had done beating him, a Boer unloosed him; when the Boer was unloosing him, he fainted. People came to lift him, because the Boer had beaten him very badly. He told the other people that he was in pain, that it felt as if the Boer had beaten him to death. It did not seem as if he would live.

He had looked after the sheep, he told the people that it felt as if he

should not be long where he was, because of pain which he felt in his body.
He told the other people that the middle of his body ached badly, he was the
one who walked, although he ached, where his body felt like that.

For, the Boer not only beat him, but when the Boer was beating him, he
trampled on him while he was beating him. Therefore he felt that it seemed
as if the Boer had trampled, breaking his body's middle.

This happened that beating was the one he died of.

In the first 100,000 years of human settlement in Southern
Africa, the first people of the Northern Cape had not built a
single permanent structure. They did not 'own' their land and
they did not 'use' it. Unlike the ancestor-worshipping Zulu
people, who could be brought to comprehend the tenets of
Christianity, Bushmen were incorrigibly brutish people who
worshipped the praying mantis and boasted for their single
ritual an unsettling circular dance that ended in fighting and
fits. Their genocide was almost a duty.

European settlers embarked on that course believing and
arguing that the Bosjemans were less than human and citing
as evidence their inability to recognize the worth of land, the
apparent invisibility of their culture and their bestial ignorance
of the spiritual.

The truth was that not only did the /Xam-ka !ei have a
profoundly sophisticated understanding of the 'value of land'
and a conception of 'the spiritual' but the two ideas penetrated
each utterly. They did not distinguish between the material
and the spiritual at all, at least not in any way that can be easily
understood without some kind of explanation. Their culture
was invisible to the settlers not only because genocide is
simpler when you dehumanize the people you want rid of but

because it was so fundamentally alien to Europeans from generations of bakers, millers and farmers.

The settlers were seizing land that defined the spiritual, ritual and everyday practices of the people that first lived there, a people who, without an understanding of history as a chain of successive events, incorporated the slaughter into their myth.

It was an assault on a way of making sense of the world. The /Xam-ka !ei did not fight for their land because it was all they had to lose but because it was all there *was* to lose. The violence was genuinely spiritual.

We make cloud, our blood is smoking, while the people shoot at us in the mist. That is why we make cloud before the people have come to us. Therefore, the people who know exclaim, they say: '/A appears to be coming to us today.'

Kumm:

//Kabbo's journey in the railway train (from Mowbray to Cape Town and back)

I have said to you that the train (fire wagon) is nice. I sat nicely in the train. We two sat in it, I and a black man.

A woman seized my arm; she drew me inside, because I should have fallen, therefore she drew me in. I sat beside a black man; his face was black; his mouth was also black; for they are black.

The black man then asked me: 'Where do you come from?' I said to the black man: 'I come from this place.' The black man asked me: 'What is its name?' I said to the black man: 'My place is the Bitterpits.'

//Xara-//kam:

The Bitterpits

Off an improbably level gravel road connecting two dry Northern Cape towns separated by 150 kilometres of bleached grass and scorched bushes is a turn for a potholed track that leads into a sheep farm of 6,000 hectares. If you follow the track for some fourteen kilometres you will arrive at a farmhouse within sight of an isolated volcanic plug, the only hill for many hours' walk in any direction. It is a steep scramble to the top but the views from there are spectacular. Before sheep replaced the herds south of the Orange River it must have been a tremendously useful place for a hunter to spot game.

The flat summit is strewn with boulders of dolerite cracked into carapacial shapes like monumental sculptures and patinated a dense black by the atmosphere and the sun. It must be one of the most uncanny landscapes anywhere in the world, and it has been recognized as a particularly 'powerful' place already.

There is still game to be seen here.

With a stone stylus someone has cut through the black patina on a near-spherical boulder to engrave two elephants, shaped with foreshortening and then almost entirely filled in with scratches, two hands tall and nearly five from head to tail. There is an ostrich and another elephant near by, both larger than a hand, and eland everywhere, engraved with the greatest care and filled in with aligned scratches, their dewlaps and their hanging fat detailed with deep grooves. Some are only properly visible in the morning and evening when the light catches them at certain angles. The smallest is perhaps two hands from nose to tail. The largest is huge, nearly five.

All of the animals depicted here were considered particularly rich in *!gi*, the /Xam word for potency or power. Everyone had a measure of *!gi*. All animals had it to a greater or lesser degree; animals and people were connected by 'threads' of it. Certain places, it seems, were either steeped in it or were good sites in which to conjure it. Many people were skilled in using their *!gi* to specific purposes; //Kabbo was one.

From the top of this hill it is possible to see the bungalows where the owners of the farm and the farmhand live, a wind-mill pumping water, a few outhouses and trees. Near by is a circular tank made from plastered bricks and filled with water pumped slowly from the deep waterpit to which it is adjacent, dug long before sheep here outnumbered eland.

This place was known in /Xam as //Xara-//kam, in English the Bitterpits, and it was once //Kabbo's place. By the time of his arrest and trial there were already *strangers* here, Boers who had taken advantage of the water to found a sheep farm.

The old waterpit that gave the Bitterpits its name is covered by a sheet of corrugated zinc sheeting held down by a rusted oil drum and a piece of stone. It is a deep cistern surrounded by bushes and a simple wire fence to keep away the sheep. Water that collects here is pumped into a circular tank made from plastered bricks a few metres in diameter and about five feet high, into which it drips through a narrow pipe that also serves as the entrance to a bees' nest. The surface of the dark water, brackish and slightly bitter, is covered with their bodies.

In the winter of 1871, four months after //Kabbo's release, the transcription sessions continued in the house and, when

it was warm enough, in the garden, where //Kabbo and
/A!kungta now worked together.

We are all well, still studying with main and might Bushmen,
Wilhelm Bleek wrote to Sir George in New Zealand, *but in
fear of losing our Bushmen soon, as they are very homesick, and our
researches for their wives have yet turned out failures. Another two
years would make us complete scholars. We have now, I suppose,
nearly four thousand columns in this language.*

//Kabbo talked constantly about his wife !Kwabba-ang,
whom he had not seen for two years. Her Dutch name was
Lies, the Dutch form of Lisa, but he could not pronounce the
L and called her his 'Oude Nies'. Edith, who was now nine,
remembered this for the rest of her life.

Lloyd and Bleek had been trying to find !Kwabba-ang and
/A!kungta's wife Ka from the moment the men had arrived
at The Hill from the Breakwater, believing that if they were
happy in Mowbray they might stay once they had served their
sentence. They were also very keen to record testimony
from women, since there were of course none at the prison.
Unfortunately their efforts had come to nothing.

When //Kabbo's son-in-law Klein Jantje – /Hang≠kass'o
– was released from the Breakwater Station at the end of his
sentence, they believed they had their best chance to find
them.

He came straight from the prison to The Hill on 22 June
1871 and stayed there until the end of July, recuperating
from his term of hard labour. If Lloyd and Bleek asked
//Kabbo's son-in-law what he knew, they wrote none of it
down. Bleek, at least, had other things on his mind: the day
after /Hang≠kass'o's arrival Jemima gave birth to twin girls,
Margaret and Hermine. Neither baby was very strong but
Hermine worried her parents very much.

Lloyd and Bleek asked /Hang≠kass'o if he would return to /

Xam-ka !au to find his wife Sara and Oude Lies, hoping that
both women would return with him in order that the extended
family might live together in Mowbray. /Hang≠kass'o agreed
and was equipped with food, a pair of Bleek's old trousers, a
letter addressed *To Whom it May Concern* for his assistance and
instructions to contact the magistrates of Beaufort West and
Victoria West who would provide food and transport for the
party for their return journey to the Cape. With £4 1s. 6d.
for travel expenses he set off for Victoria West, where the
women were thought to be staying.

Three weeks after he left, Hermine died and was buried
beside the infant Ernst Bleek at the cemetery in the nearby
village of Wynberg.

Almost three months passed with no word from the
north. //Kabbo continued to teach Wilhelm and Lucy the
/Xam language, and both he and /A!kungta continued their
work about the house, waiting for Oude Lies, Sara and
/Hang≠kass'o. //Kabbo thought his chores *woman's work*: he
was digging in the garden, like a woman with her stick
weighted with a bored stone, foraging for *veldkos* in the baked
soil of /Xam-ka !au. Digging was not a job for men. Every
day that passed with no news from /Hang≠kass'o was more
difficult for him.

Translated from /Xam-ka !au to the city on the Cape
Peninsula in which he found himself, the spiritual imperatives
of home continued to work on //Kabbo. Simply describing
the events of his working day he cast light on the world-view
of the San people of the Cape Thirstland.

One morning he told Lucy Lloyd of a dream he had had
the previous night.

I dreamed of a lion which talked, he began. The lion spoke to
its friends.

I was listening. I saw them. They were black. Their feet resembled the lion.
Their legs were many. They had hair. Their tails were long. I was afraid,
startled awake. I did look for I was startled awake. I did earnestly looking
lie. Their tails were topped with black hair. They were shod with hair.
Going, they said to their fellows that they would find the springbok by
following their spoor. I was startled awake. I saw the springbok spoor, while
the lions talked to their fellows about it. I saw the springbok and the tracks
they had left. I was startled awake.

He slept again and dreamed of his wife !Kwabba–ang hundreds of kilometres north in /Xam-ka !au; she asked him for
tobacco. He gave her a pipe and she asked him *What pipe is*
this? He replied that he had bought it, and that the magistrate
had brought him to stay at a *white man's house.*

She did say to me that I did not return to her. She asked if I did still work;
that I had not returned to her. I said to her that I did not work; for I have
been teaching here. She said to me that she had seen springbok. She did not
eat springbok. I told her that I had been waiting to get her. /Hang≠kass'o
was to have brought her to me. I said so, I talked to her.
  The cow did knock (with its horns) in the house.

The cow tethered in the garden woke him up, interrupting
their conversation.
  He went back to sleep, but when the cow knocked on the
walls a second time he got out of bed. It was morning,
/A!kungta was milking the cow and //Kabbo had been talking
to his distant wife in his sleep.
  /A!kungta untethered the cow and brought milk into the
main house.

He shall wash the milk's pail, while I get into my trousers. I shall drink
coffee. I do take the broom; I shall sweep the stoep nicely. I shall put down

the broom and go to the cow's house, I shall take the rake and clean the path, while I work clear away little pieces of wood from my house; that my house may be nice. That I may walking go over ground which is nice; otherwise I shall fall down in the darkness when I come to eat . . . for, I also work for the cow, in the darkness; when the place is dark. Night is darkness.

I bring water for the cow when I cannot see the ground well. That the cow may drink, in the darkness. That the cow may be full of the darkness's milk, while the cow does sleep, the house inside; while she stands fastened. For, she did eat green grass, which was wet, she may drink, putting in water.

So //Kabbo continued his 'woman's work'. He remained living in the Bleeks' garden, homesick, missing his wife and his place, making journeys of the spirit to visit both.

In February 1872 Wilhelm and Jemima set off for Kalk Bay on their annual summer retreat to the cool of the False Bay coast; /A!kungta went with them. He held collection bottles as the three combed the shore for specimens of marine life for Wilhelm to send abroad to his cousin, the naturalist Ernst Haekel. Among their many finds was a previously unclassified kind of sponge which Haekel named after his cousin.

Soon after their return //Kabbo helped Wilhelm Bleek to make a map showing the young towns of Kenhardt in the north, Vanwyksvlei in the south and the places in between, recording the lost names of the springs and *vleis* of the part of the Northern Cape where his relatives and the other prisoners at the Breakwater were living at the time of their arrests. //Xara–//kam, the Bitterpits, his place, was in the centre. The pencil lines connecting these springs, *vleis* and farms are marked with the time it took to walk from one to another; the line joining Rietfontein in the north with Haarfontein, known to //Kabbo as ≠Oa:xa, for example, reads *15 days (a sheep path).*

Here at Haarfontein, //Kabbo's son //Goo-ka-!kui – Smoke's Man – once saw the wind. Lloyd recorded:

The young wind blows, because the young wind feels that his parents used to blow; for, they are wind. So they blew. For the people did not tell me about the wind's parents; for they merely spoke of the young wind.

In the past the wind's son was a person. He became a bird. And he flies; while he does not walk as he used to; for, he flies, and he lives in the mountain. So he flies. He used to be a man. Therefore, he formerly rolled a ball; he shot; while he felt that he was a person. He became a bird; hence, he flies and he inhabits a mountain's hole.

'Smoke's Man' was the one who spoke to me about the wind.[1]

'Smoke's Man' saw the wind at Haarfontein's mountain. Therefore, he threw a stone at the wind; while he believed it to be a bird called the !kuerre-!kuerre. And the wind blew hard, on account of it. Therefore, the wind did not gently blow; the wind took up the dust, because he had thrown a stone at the wind. The wind took up the dust, while the wind thought to fly away. The wind went into a mountain hole, and the wind blew hard; the wind did not blow gently. And 'Smoke's Man', being afraid, went home; he went to sit under the house's bushes[2] *instead of watching the sheep.*

/Xam-ka !au was a place where magic, so to speak, was taken for granted. The spiritual and material tessellated directly in

---

[1] *'Witbooi Tooren' son of //Kabbo and !Kwabba-ang (Oude Lies). /Hang≠kass'o used to teach Witbooi springbok hunting; being grown up when the latter was still a child, //Kabbo told Lloyd.*

[2] *I.e. the bushes broken off and used to make a shelter for the mat hut,* said //Kabbo.

the lives of the /Xam-ka !ei, whose sustaining beliefs were connected to the idea of place in a way that Bleek and Lloyd apparently never quite understood.

Beside the Bitterpits Bleek wrote //Kabbo's name. Time after time the old man asked Bleek if would speak to the Cape Colony's governor, Sir Henry Barkly, about having the people who had used threat and force to take his place from him removed. He wanted to return and continue the life he had lived before the coming of the Boers.

I must remain at my own place, the name of which I have told you. You know it. You know, having put it down. My name is plain beside it.

As much as //Kabbo wanted to go back to /Xam-ka !au so that he might see his people, he none the less gave Lloyd and Bleek to understand quite how difficult life there had become. The Boers had taken the water sources and killed the game. They were exterminating the ostriches for sport without ritual or respect.

In May 1873 Wilhelm Bleek's first *Report* on the Bushman Work was published and presented to Parliament. After gentle pleas for more financial assistance and for the government to consider publishing the contents of the notebooks Bleek gave a brief account of his expenditure and then an index of the material collected so far. The sections were divided into categories:

I. The Mantis
II. Moon and Stars
III. Stars
IV. Fables
V. Legends

with each sub-entry accompanied by a brief description of the material, a page reference and an initial denoting whether the passage was recorded by Bleek or by Lloyd – who refused to be mentioned by name anywhere in the document even though half the entries listed in it were hers. An *L* appears beside the page number of every passage she transcribed to indicate in which notebook it might be found, but there is no indication of what the initial itself stands for. This was at her insistence.

By the time of the *Report*'s publication, Bleek and Lloyd knew very well that the material it catalogued was important for both humanitarian and scientific reasons since even if science chose to ignore it, which was unthinkable, they would have saved something beyond value. //Kabbo, who knew better than anyone at The Hill apart from /A!kungta how his people were threatened, took the work very seriously. As Lloyd filled columns with /Xam he would pause, waiting for her to finish before continuing to speak; he knew perfectly well that he was making a paper memory of the /Xam-ka !ei to be recorded in *!gwe* – letters and books – and it pleased him very much.

The /Xam-ka !ei kept *!gwe* too, //Kabbo told Bleek, letters resembling those *which take a message or an account of what happens in another place*. They were a kind of *beating in the flesh* which told them things. If you did not understand them you might even end up dead, perhaps eaten by a lion; they told people *which way they are not to go, and which arrow they had better not use.*

The Bushmen's letters are in their bodies. They speak, they move, they make their bodies move.

They were a tapping in the body where a nearby ostrich was scratching its neck, a tapping at the place of an old man's wound when the old man approached, the feeling of the thong that kept a child held slung over a woman's shoulders in the shoulders of a man waiting for her at the shelter, a tapping in the ribs for the black hair on the springbok's sides known as *the springbok sensation.*

The springbok, when coming, scratches itself with its horns and with its foot; then the Bushman feels the tapping.

The game would walk early, thinking the hunters asleep in the shade of their huts, but the men would be up, alerted by the sensations in their bodies of the animals' walking. There would be a sensation in the feet as the springbok rustled the bushes, a sensation in the face like the black stripe between the springbok's scalp and nose and a sensation in the hollow of the knee where blood from a slain animal would fall as it was carried home.

'The springbok seem to be coming, for I feel the black hair. Climb the Brinkkop there so you may look all about you. For I feel the springbok sensation.'

The other man agrees with him: 'I am wont to feel thus, I feel a sensation in the calves of my legs when the springbok's blood is going to run down them. For I always feel blood when I am about to kill a springbok. The springbok hair lies behind my back.'

The other agrees with him: 'Yes, my brother.'

To survive as a hunter, whether in Arctic tundra, rain forest or a vast semi-desert like /Xam-ka !au, you need to know an awful lot about the animals you are hunting. /Xam hunters spent years perfecting their knowledge of the idiosyncrasies, habits and propensities of game, a life-long process of observation and discussion with other hunters. If the stories of the Early Race were a useful way of passing this information on from one generation to the next, the 'Bushman's letters' were an extremely effective way of making use of it.

Reading these letters the hunter's knowledge, beyond encyclopedic, could be accessed and understood *somatically* – in the body. Running beside antelope tracks with his bow and arrow ready or following the increasingly erratic spoor of an animal he had shot, say, the hunter might feel the *springbok sensation*, identifying with his quarry on a profound level, his memory effectively a physical experience.

San people who still practise traditional hunting methods sometimes perform a ritual 'impersonation' of the animal they are hunting at times like these. The /Xam-ka !ei probably did the same.

Ritual has been the making of our species. Employed in this way, to ends like these, it is a man-made sense as much as it is a decision-making tool. What we call superstition is what remains when ritual, an ancient inheritance that is not easily lost, is no longer imperative to survival.

/Xam-ka !au was land, ritual, *kukummi* – things told – and the people who performed and told them. In Mowbray //Kabbo was cut off from all four.

Two years and two months after his son-in-law had left with a new pair of trousers and a letter, //Kabbo was still waiting for his wife and his daughter. No one had heard anything from the Northern Cape. In the winter of 1873, a damp, cold time on the Cape, //Kabbo sat down with Wilhelm Bleek and made it clear that this would be the last he would be spending in Mowbray. He had agreed to stay until spring only because Bleek had promised him a new pair of boots and a rifle; now he wanted them.

July 1873:

You know that I sit waiting for the moon to turn back for me, that I may return to my place, that I may listen to all the people's stories when I visit them; that I may listen to the stories they tell. They listen to the Flat Bushman's stories from the other side of the place. Those are the stories they tell. They are listening to them while the sun becomes a little warm. That I may sit in the sun, that I may, sitting, listen to the stories that come there, stories that have come from a distance.

A story is like the wind, it comes from afar, and we feel it.

While he was shivering on the Cape, doing his woman's work, the people he knew were visiting and hearing stories. *I feel that people of another place are here — they do not possess my stories*, he said. *They do not talk my language. They visit their like, while they feel that work's people they are, those who work, keeping houses in order.*

He was not a servant, one of *work's people*. He was a visiting person, a listening person, a smoking person.

As for me I am waiting that the moon may turn back for me, that I may set my feet forward in the path. I am only waiting for the moon that I may tell my master that now I should sit among my fellow men, who walking meet their like. They are listening to them; for, I do think of visits, that I ought to visit. That I ought to talk to my fellow men.

My three names float along to my place; I will go to sit there, that I may listen and turn my ears back, towards my heels, while I feel that a story is the wind.

Stories float along to another place. Then, while they do not see our bodies go along, our names pass through these people. Our names float to a different place.

The mountains lie between the two different roads. A man's name passes behind the mountain's back. The road is around his place, because the road curves. The other people's ears go to meet the returning man's names, the names he brings back. He will examine the place. For the trees of the place seem to be handsome, because they have grown tall while the man of the place, //Kabbo, has not been able to see them, walk among them. He came to live somewhere different, somewhere that was not his place. He is the one who thinks of his place, that he must be the one to return.

He only awaits the return of the moon; that the moon may go round, that he may return home, that he may see the waterpits he used to drink from. He will work, putting the old hut in order, while he feels that he has gathered his children together, that they may work, putting the water in order for him, for he went away, leaving the place, while strangers walked there instead.

Their place it is not; for //Kabbo's father's father's place it was. And then it was //Kabbo's father's place, when //Kabbo's father's father died. And when //Kabbo's father died, it was //Kabbo's elder brother's place. //Kabbo's elder brother died and then it was //Kabbo's place. And then //Kabbo married when grown up, bringing !Kwabba-ang to the place, because he felt that he was alone. Therefore, he grew old with his wife at the place, while he felt that his children were married.

His children's children talked and fed themselves; they talked with understanding.

//Kabbo's sentence had expired on 23 October 1871. It was now August 1873. As the month came to the end, promising spring, //Kabbo declared that he would leave. He had been waiting for the new moon, he told Bleek, and now it had come.

August 1873:

I must sit waiting for the Sundays on which I remain here, when I teach you. I do not wait for any more moons, for this is the moon I told you about. I desired that it should return for me. For I have sat waiting for the boots that I must put on to walk in, strong for the road. For the sun will go along, burning strongly. And then the earth becomes hot, while I am still half-way. I must go together with the warm sun, while the ground is hot. For it is not a little road. It is a great road; it is long. I should reach my place, when the trees are dry, for I shall walk, letting the flowers become dry while I still follow the path.

Then, autumn will quickly be upon us there, when I am sitting at my own place. For I shall not go to other places. I must remain at my own place, the name of which I have told you. You know it. You know, having put it down. My name is plain beside it.

His name was on the map that Bleek had made, the map that showed the world how he had been robbed of his birthright.

It is there that I sit waiting for the gun; and then he will send the gun to me there, in a cart. While he thinks that I have not forgotten; that my body may be quiet, as it was when I was with him; while I feel that I shoot, feeding myself. For it was because of starvation that I was bound – starvation's food – when I turned back, following the sheep.

It is a gun that takes care of an old man; with it, we kill the springbok that go through the cold; we go to eat in the cold. Satisfied with food, we lie down in our huts in the cold.

The gun is strong against the wind. It satisfies a man with food in the very middle of the cold.

Kumm:

/Kaggen and the Ticks

/Kaggen stole fire, tools and clothes from the Ticks for the benefit of the people who came after the Early Race: the /Xam-ka !ei.

This is what he did.

The old man had been walking about in the veld. He had wanted to visit someone and hear *kukummi*, and when he saw the Ticks' shelters he was delighted. With his arrows rattling in his quiver, he set off to see them.

He should have known better. The Ticks' shelters were black. All their possessions were black. They were black, angry people and they hated everyone and everything. When they saw /Kaggen coming they put their heads together and quickly agreed to do what they always did in situations like this: they would hide in the wool of their sheep and leave a little child to look after the pot on the fire. No one with a greedy bone in their body could possibly resist.

Enter /Kaggen, of course, who immediately appraised the situation like this:

houses, black, all empty
pot of food, steaming
no one but a little child to guard the pot.

Excellent, thought /Kaggen. 'Ah!' he said aloud. 'These people must have seen me coming. They've obviously heard about my terrifying reputation as a fighter and run away, leaving only this little child.'

Concealed in the wool, the Ticks could scarcely believe their ears.

'I'm going to put down my quiver, eat some of their meat and then I suppose I'll beat this little child up. He's a Tick. He doesn't look too bright.'

/Kaggen took hold of the pot.

One of the Ticks came down from the sheep where he had been hiding.

Where did you come from? /Kaggen asked.

The Tick said nothing; he just took the pot from /Kaggen's hands and put it back on the fire. Another Tick fell down and took the pot to a safe distance, away from the flying fists and feet that would soon be threatening it. Another Tick came out of the wool. And then another and another, until there were Ticks everywhere. A big, strapping young Tick slipped down beside /Kaggen and stepped on one side of his *kaross*. His brother flanked him and stepped on the other.

All right, thought /Kaggen. Better be off, then.

When he tried to move he discovered he was held fast. Then there was a seething scrum with a bloody /Kaggen at the bottom and the entire extended family of Ticks, young and old, brother and sister, piling in.

/Kaggen slipped out of his *kaross*, crawled out of the scrum and ran away. For once he did not use one of his catchphrases as he fled, but he did call his hartebeest-skin bag and *kaross*, his stick and his quiver when he was at a safe distance. As he flew away, his possessions – his *hartebeest's children* – followed him of their own accord. He landed safely in a *vlei* and swam across it. He climbed up the bank on the other side and then he began his whining limp home.

'Someone beat me up!' he told /Ni when he got home. 'I don't know where they came from! They appeared out of nowhere and they . . . they laid into me!'

/Ni looked at his grandfather.

'You went to the Ticks' place, didn't you? No one goes there. You just walk past. Everyone knows that. They all hide in the wool of their sheep and when someone comes to visit they come down and beat him to a pulp.'

Nobody goes to them, because they drink blood, they are black people, they are bloody-handed. Their houses are always black, because they are angry folk.

'Yes! Yes! That's exactly what happened!' said /Kaggen, shaking. 'And I think I'm dying! I've been beaten so hard I'm going to die! Look at me shiver!'

Very carefully, /Ni replied: 'No, Grandfather, you're shivering because you've just come out of cold water. And you went into the water covered in cuts.'

'Don't lecture me, /Ni! I'm older than you!' he said. 'All I wanted to do was go and hear some stories, I've been beaten up and now I get this when I come home! *I'm* the one who ought to be angry! I'm going to bed now and I don't want to hear any of you tell me they didn't get a decent night's rest, because I'm going to be writhing in pain all night!'

At that he lay down and covered his head.

You always do this, said /Ni.

That night /Kaggen dreamed that all the Ticks' houses rose up and travelled to where he slept. He dreamed that the Ticks' sheep followed the houses. He dreamed that the Ticks' clothes, their pots, their throwing sticks, their knives and all their tools passed silently along after the sheep.

It would be bad for the Ticks when *they* woke up.

For they will have to drink blood, because they no longer have a fire, as they used to have. Real people will henceforth cook, while they walk entirely in

the dark; they will have to stand biting things' bodies, they will have to
drink things' blood and no longer eat cooked meat.

Morning came, and with it the bleating of sheep outside the shelter where /Kaggen and his family slept. /Kaggen woke his grandson.

'Can you hear a kind of bleating noise outside?' he asked. 'Sort of like . . . sheep?'

/Ni said nothing.

'Whoever did this must have been a great magician, don't you think? It's odd, but last night I had a dream that all the Ticks' sheep, their houses and all their possessions rose up and came through the air to us! Isn't that a strange dream?'

Show-off.

/Ni heard the bleating and when he saw the sheep outside he woke his parents !Xo and /Kwammang-a, the Porcupine and the Rainbow, and everybody else in his family. He was delighted that they now had *karosses* to keep them warm, tools with which to butcher animals and fire to cook the flesh. /Kaggen's wife the Hyrax, on the other hand, wanted to know what her husband had been thinking. She asked him why he took the sheep. They had never had any need of sheep before.

It seemed right to me, because those people attacked me; they wanted to kill
me in their anger. Then I felt that I wished those angry people should no
longer warm themselves at a fire, because they fought me at their fire; they
cannot cook. They cannot roast meat for themselves. For they walk about
in their flesh.

In these pots here the Flat Bushman shall some day cook, because they
shall have a fire. We who are here shall then be as the Ticks are. We shall
eat different things, because we too shall lack fire. You, /Ni, Ichneumon,
shall then go to dwell in the hills with your mother. She shall truly become

a Porcupine, she shall live in a hole, while Grandmother Hyrax shall live in a mountain den, for her name really is Hyrax.

I shall have wings, I shall fly when I am green, I shall be a little green thing.

Today the Ticks have no houses. They bite hares' ears to fill themselves with blood. Today they are blood-bellies and men look for them in sheep's wool so they can throw them on the ground and crush them.

!Gi:xa:

'Sorcerer'

Too homesick and lonely to stay, probably sick of being a curiosity, //Kabbo left Mowbray with /A!kungta on 15 October 1873 having promised that he would eventually come back with his wife !Kwabba-ang. Two of Bleek's associates in Victoria West let him know that the men had made it that far, and that both had found their wives. Since //Kabbo's arrest in 1869, however, !Kwabba-ang had grown very frail and //Kabbo decided that he would stay and look after her.

Although they kept abreast of his whereabouts and welfare, more or less, the linguists resigned themselves to losing //Kabbo and began to consider how they might best carry on the Bushman Work without him. We do not know what happened to /A!kungta after he returned to the Northern Cape other than that he was reunited with his wife Ka.

The previous summer, for the first time in years, Jemima and Wilhelm had decided that they would not go to Kalk Bay for their annual fortnight beside the sea, out of the heat. Jemima, who was heavily pregnant and did not feel up to the journey, suggested instead that they take a short holiday in Sea Point, a hamlet of fishing cottages and villas on the road along the shore towards Hout Bay. Wilhelm agreed. The two had planned to go without their daughters or Jemima's sisters, but Wilhelm said that since he felt in especially good health he might as well make the short journey to the library every day. And since it was not *too* far from the library to The Hill by train, he might just drop in on his children.

In that case, Jemima pointed out, they may as well stay at

home in the shadow of Devil's Peak with their family at hand. They did. A month later Jemima gave birth to her fourth daughter, Dorothea.

Bleek's health held up until the winter when he caught two colds in a row, both serious enough to keep him housebound. It took him far longer than usual to recover. Dr Stewart, the family doctor – a specialist in chest conditions – was called in and declared that on no account was Bleek to expose himself to wet weather. From then on, Wilhelm took special care to stay out of the rain.

Despite //Kabbo and /A!kungta's departure, Bleek and Lloyd's Bushman Work continued. Just over two weeks after the two /Xam men set off, two more prisoners were released from the Breakwater to the rather more benign custody of Dr and Mrs Bleek and the Lloyd sisters. They were 4434 David Hoesar, whose /Xam name was Dia!kwain, and his brother-in-law 4435 Klaas Katkop, or ≠Kasing. When they arrived at the end of 1873, both had served three years of their five-year sentences for culpable homicide.

Before their arrests the two had been forced to find work as hands on one of the dusty ranches that now divided much of the Northern Cape where the farmers treated their employees so callously that conditions were difficult to distinguish from slavery. Both had seen close relatives murdered and friends and family flogged to death. They worked for the farmers because the alternative was starvation or summary execution for stock theft; at least on the farms the prospect of random murder was reduced as the owners would not kill their own employees. Not without an excuse, at least.

The Boer had been beating him about herding the sheep, that he had not herded the sheep well.

On the last day of January 1869, a Sunday, the two had
been camped with their wives and other families in a place
known as !Narries, a rise some distance off the track connecting
the infant towns of Brandvlei and Loerisfontein. It is desolate,
hilly country. That day a man called Joseph Kruger rode out
to !Narries from his farm, Gifvlei, to reclaim a sheep that he
believed had been stolen from him. Dia!kwain and ≠Kasing
may well have taken it; we do not know. What exactly passed
at !Narries is not absolutely certain but we can safely assume
that the farmer demanded back his animal, which would
already have been eaten, or that he receive payment, which
no one could have provided. We do know that from horseback
Kruger declared that he would come back with a commando
of men to shoot everyone there in the camp.

While the people are still coming to attack us, at the time when
they intend to reach us, in the morning, the mist – our mist – sits.
They shoot at us in the mist.

Massacre was about to come to Dia!kwain's family and he
would not have it. Dia!kwain had a gun and he used it, hitting
Kruger in his body. ≠Kasing shot next, hitting the man's
saddle.

Kruger fled; his friends found his corpse some kilometres
from where he had been shot and buried him at Gifvlei. When
they reported his death to the police in the young town of
Kenhardt more than a hundred kilometres to the north, the
special magistrate there charged with the responsibility of
ending the menace posed by the /Xam-ka !ei sent some men
to capture the farmer's murderers.

Farmboys fresh in the Northern Cape from the citrus plantations and ranches in the milder south, they were not the best
men for the job; they did not know the terrain and spent

longer looking for fodder for their horses than for dangerous Bushmen. Before too long they stopped off at one of the farms in the area and recruited three Special Constables. Jacob Kotze, Jan Swart and Job Fleuris, all Bastards, as people of mixed European and African descent were then known, were promised a proper wage and a cash reward for the successful capture of the /Xam killers. They rode off into the veld to find Dia!kwain, his brother-in-law ≠Kasing and their known accomplices, Klaas Hoesar (probably Dia!kwain's brother //Xwa:gan-te) and another /Xam-speaking man known as Jantje Japhta, *the terror of the Aachterveld*, according to the magistrate at Kenhardt, the *swiftest runners in the Country*, feared as expert riflemen, incorrigible thieves responsible for countless stock thefts.

The constables caught Dia!kwain, Klaas Hoesar and Jantje Japhta first. Japhta was shot in the leg trying to escape. ≠Kasing managed to evade the men for another two weeks, but the constables knew the region as well as he did and they eventually caught him. When he arrived at the Breakwater Station his left wrist was fractured.

Kotze, Swart and Fleuris received £1 5s. each in addition to their pay in reward for their difficult and potentially life-threatening work.

When Dia!kwain and ≠Kasing were tried for killing Kruger neither denied that they had shot the man. They had been acting in self-defence, they claimed, and had killed to protect their families. The judge, finding that they had been provoked, convicted them of culpable homicide rather than murder and sent them to the Breakwater Station to discover the reformative nature of five years of hard labour.

Used to the frontier justice of their farms, Kruger's friends were infuriated that the /Xam men had escaped the gallows. They would have preferred to have seen the men hanged from a beam, whipped to death or shot. Imagine them cursing British justice, rehearsing their disgust that the life of a godless yellow-skinned Bosjeman thief was now worth more than the life of a Christian man who had toiled for years for little reward under a pitiless sun. ≠Kasing and Dia!kwain were now much safer in prison.

Jemima and Wilhelm Bleek's eldest daughters Edith and Mabel were both terribly excited, if a little scared, when they learned that ≠Kasing was coming. He had, after all, taken the life of another man. By now they were used to the idea of sharing their home with convicts, but a murderer was different from a cattle thief. He arrived on the first day of November 1873; Lloyd sat with him immediately.

≠Kasing was just over five feet tall, a man of about forty if the Descriptions Register at the Breakwater prison is to be believed. With his double tooth and the strength of his gaze the children thought his appearance *fierce*. Unlike Dia!kwain, who had had been punished in prison for *disobedience* and for possessing *dagga*, cannabis, ≠Kasing was a model prisoner who had been moved from the probation to the good conduct class on 29 July 1870.

Dia!kwain was about twenty-five when he was admitted to the Breakwater, making him something less than thirty when he moved to the Bleeks in December, a month after his brother-in-law. That he had been rewarded with six shillings for good schoolwork in June 1872 suggests that his stock had risen with the prison authorities so far that they were able to entertain the idea that a convicted killer could be discharged into the house of a consumptive academic, his frail wife, her sisters and four little girls, the eldest of whom was ten, the youngest of whom, Dorothea, was barely seven months. He was just under five feet three inches tall and was always remembered by the Bleek family as a remarkably gentle man,

although the scar on his face, a sharp semi-circle under his
eye, and the scar on his wrist, suggested otherwise.

So I kicked him and knocked him down, and he got up, he seized
my throat. I was laden with ostrich eggshells of water, having been
to dig up water, and I was carrying a gun as well.

Dia!kwain's mother /Ko:ang, related to //Kabbo through
marriage, was from an area known as the Strandberg, the same
place as /A!kungta. She had been called ≠Kamme-ang by her
parents at birth, and kept this name – her *little name* – until she
earned another from the members of her extended family, as
was the tradition. She was better known as /Ko:ang, meaning
Start Back, because when you told her anything she would
always start back as if she were surprised. /Ko:ang had disappeared years ago, *probably killed by the Boers*, Dia!kwain
thought.

His father ≠Gwai-/ka was better known by his adult name,
Xättin. It meant Clay Hand, a name earned after he put his
foot into a crack in the clay running in front of a springbok
herd during a hunt, falling down and dislocating his thumb.

He had an elder brother, K'obo, and three sisters, one of
whom, !Kweiten ta //ken, was married to ≠Kasing. The
others, Fight Story and Springbok Skin, had lives and children
of their own in the Cape Thirstland.

While ≠Kasing was on the whole a reticent man who spoke
mostly about practical matters, objects and customs, Dia!kwain
was voluble, pleased to discuss ritual and myth. It was sometimes difficult to distinguish between his own history, which
as it turned out was by and large very painful, and the more
fanciful *kukummi* he related. His narrative skills were strong,
his most unlikely stories ballasted by detail that smacked of
remembered experience.

Edith remembered Dia!kwain better than his brother-in-law. He was a *soft-hearted mortal, who would not, unprovoked, have hurt a fly*, she was to recall. While he was staying with the Bleeks, someone gave him a puppy as a pet. The dog had an attack of *distemper*, she remembered, and it upset him very much; when *he spoke of 'my dock's eye'*, tears of sympathy stood in his own.

A few weeks after Dia!kwain's arrival Wilhelm caught a very bad cold and went with Jemima to Kalk Bay sick, remaining ill for much of the summer of 1874. Although his health had generally improved since he had moved to The Hill he was always conscious that he would probably not have time to complete all the work he intended to do and for years now he had been working to ready the Grey Collection for his successor, quietly filling one of the corner cupboards at the library with papers relating to the catalogue and the contents of the collection itself. It was a chore that distracted him from his research but this branch of his work brought in most of The Hill's income and it had to be done.

At every meeting of the Library Committee he asked to be provided with clerical assistance and the money required to print the completed portions of the inventory. The Committee by and large ignored him, for reasons of *jealousy* in the case of the Chief Librarian Thomas Maskew, and *prejudice* in the case of the Committee at large, Jemima believed. Doctor Dale, the chairman of the Library Committee, saw no place for native fairytales in his library at all.

Whatever the explanation, for years of increasingly desperate letter-writing Bleek had only managed to gain the temporary loan of Mr Maskew's clerk for the purpose of making some fair copies of a few rough texts gathered from sub-Saharan Africa and the Pacific. He was writing and publishing papers and corresponding with linguists, missionaries, naturalists and officials from Europe to Australia, but had begun to think that he might not have time to complete all the work he wanted to do, as he wrote to Sir George:

For my children and for the completion of many important works begun, I wish much to [carry] on, but I feel every year more that this may not entirely depend on one's wish; and that the end may be nearer at hand than one has any idea of.

Not that George Grey was particularly voluble these days. He had not written to Bleek for more than a year. *You do not know what a pleasure it would be to me to see your handwriting again, even only in an address on a piece of paper etc.*, Bleek wrote hopefully.

Dia!kwain grew up near the Sak River on the east of /Xam-ka !ei with his extended family, among whom was /Xarrang-/xarrang, known as ≠Naä-ang. She was a difficult old woman with an ostrich's head, almost flat at the back and covered with hair that looked like feathers, and she walked with a sort of hopping scuttle that made Dia!kwain think she wanted to run away from wherever she was: an ostrich's walk.

She kept weather under her *kaross* and she could lift the side of the skin to make the wind blow. When she was angry the wind would rise and blow dust and stones into people's eyes; it would blow away their mats and shake the bushes and the shelters.

/Xarrang/xarrang became angry when she was scolded and you would have to be brave or ignorant to do it. The consensus in the camp and among her dispersed neighbours and relatives was that it was not really worthwhile to take the old woman to task. Whenever she was scolded she would be cross, and then she would cry.

It seemed as if the wind cried with her, when her tears fell. Then the wind did not want them to fall, for it was not willing she should cry. For the wind used to blow whenever she cried, because the wind did not want the tears from her eyes to fall.

!Xugendi, Dia!kwain's grandfather, used to call on her to blow away the mosquitoes that would keep him awake, biting his eyes.

When my grandfather spoke thus, it seemed as if the wind had heard him, for the wind blew the mosquitoes away.

This was after she had died. !Xugendi continued to call on her after her death because the wind blew when it heard her name. The wind had been her ally and Dia!kwain believed it still blew to avenge itself on the people who had scolded her while she lived. People would ask themselves what they had done to offend the old woman when it seemed she was loose with the sides of her *kaross* and the wind was up; sometimes it seemed as though she were being difficult for the sake of it, acting like a child, with her thoughts all over the place, as though death had robbed her of her sense. Still, if you were stalking in the hunting ground it could prove useful to ask her for her help – she might be able to give the wind a nudge for you and keep you downwind.

/Xarrang/xarrang was Dia!kwain's mother-in-law. He married her daughter Mietche.

There were many remarkable people in Dia!kwain's family. His aunt Tano-!khauken used to turn herself into a lioness and travel to see how things were with her people. The old woman would catch the smell of their shelters and roar to let them know it was her; later she would visit in person, as a woman, to discover whether or not anyone had heard her. Dia!kwain's mother /Ko:ang would tell her sister that she was pleased that she had come, and that she should remember as much as she could about the place where they were. Her watching them afforded them a kind of protection. Tano-!khauken replied that she would not forget them.

She lived at a place called /Khau-!kau, but wherever you were she would come and find you if you made free with her name. Parents would be very angry with their children if they heard that they had used her name at night. When people thought she was asleep she was really walking about and seeing things that others could not see. Tano-!khauken *had her nose*: she knew things.

In the same way that //Kabbo was a *mantis's man*, she was a *springbok's woman*, a *!gi:xa* with control over animals. Once, having promised /Ko:ang that she would send the springbok towards her so that she and family might eat meat, Dia!kwain's elder brother K'obo fell sick after eating an animal that their father had shot. It was a short-horned springbok that belonged to Tano-!khauken's son, and it was not the kind of animal that you simply killed and ate.

Tano-!khauken was not angry with Xättin for killing the animal, she told /Ko:ang, but surprised. It was not a food springbok he had killed but a springbok she kept on a thong. She would tell it where she wanted it to go and then release it into a herd. All the other springbok would find themselves following it as it walked towards the bows and arrows of the hunters in her family.

Xättin had brought home the corporeal manifestation of a spirit creature and his wife, immediately recognizing that there was something unusual about it, had begun to make a cap for her sister from the animal's scalp, sewing it so that the ears would stand up whenever she wore it. She knew it was not a real springbok. *That was why she knew that she would soon hear a story about it* and why she had made the special cap for her sister, a cap that was worn only by people who could control the game.

The old woman told /Ko:ang that she had known that Xättin had shot the animal. She did not have to be there to have seen him hunt it, or to know that K'obo had been taken ill once he had eaten it. She had made Xättin sick, but only to teach him a lesson.

She thought she would not really take K'obo away from mother. She would have done so if anyone else had killed the springbok, she would have made his heart ache too, to let him know not to kill such a springbok.

She was glad that /Ko:ang had made the hat for her. It made up for her trouble and it was exactly what she wanted in recompense.

Now she would say no more about it.
Take my old cap, keep it and see whether the springbok do not follow it wherever it goes. You must go and stay at your home, where you usually walk about, you must look whether one springbok will not appear, you will see it where you are walking about; you must keep on looking for others, for you say, I must let the springbok travel, you believe that I really own springbok, that I am a springbok's sorceress.

Tano-!khauken, /Xarrang/xarrang, //Kabbo and the old man who stole the Ticks' things in a dream all had something in common. They were skilled at the practices of the *!gi:xa*, a word Lucy Lloyd translated as 'sorcerer'.

Dia!kwain began to explain to Lloyd and Bleek a little of

what it meant to be a *!gi:xa* in stories and descriptions of the rituals and the daily lives of the /Xam-ka !ei and, importantly, with the aid of copies of the rock art of the Southern San.

On the other side of the subcontinent from /Xam-ka !au was Zululand, the independent state to the north of Natal. Governed by King Mpande, the corpulent half-brother of the famous king Shaka kaSezangakhona, it owed its creation to a dynastic struggle remembered as *the breaking of the rope that held the nation together*, a collision of the violent ambitions of the Boers and Shaka's immediate family.

Its coming into being meant the expulsion of the Hlubi, a people with historical ties to many of the inhabitants of what are today Swaziland and Lesotho. Forced from their land during Mpande's nation building, the Hlubi crossed the Thukela River into Natal and settled in the foothills of the Natal Drakensberg, mountains today known in Zulu as uKhahlamba, or 'barrier of up-pointed spears', where they established themselves with a degree of independence from the British colonial government.

In 1873 their leader, a man called Langalibalele – Scorching Sun, so named because he was born during a particularly severe drought – left his livestock behind to cross the Drakensberg with thousands of his people. The Natalian government wanted to arrest him for his refusal to register his people's rifles, a pretext to disarm an increasingly prosperous and strong community in a colony that was only going to need more land and more labour. Langalibalele fled into the Malutis, the mountains of what is today Lesotho, and the Colony came looking for him.

The task of finding him and his people fell to J. M. Orpen,

the region's chief magistrate, who sent well-provisioned scouts to look for them. Several weeks later all Orpen could be sure of was that they were on the other side of several impassable tributaries of the Senqu, beyond a week's march away, moving through spectacular and elevated country of steep valleys and shallow rivers.

Bridlepaths take counter-intuitive directions in Lesotho, shortcutting over promontories and crossing and re-crossing watercourses; if you ask for directions in this part of southern Africa you are very likely to be pointed the way you have just come. In the last decades of the 1800s the land was all but unknown to the colonists, for whom travel without a guide was supremely difficult, and if Orpen were to navigate the country's gorges, plateaus and passes to find Langalibalele he would have to find someone who knew them. This was how he came to hear about Qing, or !King as Bleek later spelled the man's name.

Qing was one of the last surviving San people of the region, then employed as a hunter by the son of a local Basotho chief. He was young, an expert horseman apparently given to disappearing into stony *kloofs* when distracted by the prospect of game. The San people of what is today Lesotho had no one like Wilhelm Bleek or Lucy Lloyd to record their beliefs and customs and no one like //Kabbo or Dia!kwain to speak on their behalf at any length. Everything we know about the oral traditions of the first people of this part of southern Africa comes from the notes that J. M. Orpen made while sitting down talking to Qing, smoking over the camp-fires they lit in the course of their journey.

Orpen had been asked by an amateur geologist and anthropologist called George Stow, an eccentric, difficult man unfashionably fascinated by the Bushmen, to make copies of any rock paintings he should find. Greatly assisted by Qing,

Orpen found several. He also recorded Qing's explanations of the paintings they copied, others they saw on the way, and the myths and beliefs of the San people of the Malutis. Qing pointed out images of men with the heads of reebok, for example, and explained that they depicted *men who had died and now lived in rivers, and were spoilt at the same time as the elands and by the dancers of which you have seen paintings.*

These somewhat cryptic words were published the next year in a Cape Town journal called the *Cape Monthly Magazine* alongside copies of the drawings and an essay by Wilhelm Bleek under the title 'A Glimpse of the Mythology of the Maluti Bushmen'.

Now the world's greatest expert on Bushman mythology (or rather the world's greatest *acknowledged* expert on the Bushmen, considering what Lucy Lloyd then knew), Bleek had been invited by the editors of the *Cape Monthly* to write a paper giving his thoughts on Orpen's article, which he submitted just as it was going to press, having shown the copied paintings to Dia!kwain and ≠Kasing for their own comments and explanations.

The general consensus in southern Africa was that Bushman art comprised crude depictions of the everyday lives of a people with no sense of the spiritual, a belief that persisted well into the second half of the twentieth century. Bleek disagreed. In his paper he wrote that the paintings were *a truly artistic conception of the ideas which most deeply moved the Bushman mind and filled it with religious feelings*; he believed that the paintings *illustrated* the mythology of the San people, and he believed it absolutely.

Quite how far the paintings actually do illustrate San mythology has proved to be contentious, but that they are the material expression of a particular aesthetic and spiritual conception of the world is today beyond question.

Orpen's mission was quickly over. Langalibalele was arrested and sent to Robben Island as a political prisoner. His tribe was 'disbanded', meaning that hundreds of the men were killed and the women and children were relocated to the British colonies, where they became servants.

No one knows what happened to Qing, a man who deserves to be remembered.

Bleek called for records of South Africa's paintings to be made, preferably in the form of photographs, so that the general public could be in no doubt of the beauty and accomplishment of the art, and he exhorted Orpen to continue in his work, hoping others would follow his example.

Following the publication of Orpen's copies in the *Cape Monthly Magazine* farmers and travellers across South Africa sent information about rock paintings and sketches of their own to Mowbray. Among the packages that arrived were forty-two hardbacked facsimiles made by George Stow, the difficult, eccentric amateur geologist and anthropologist who had first asked Orpen to make copies on his behalf. Bleek had heard of Stow's collection and was delighted to see some of it. He thought the pictures so magnificent that their publication could only serve to *effect a radical change in the ideas generally entertained with regard to the Bushman and their mental condition.*

They are of the greatest possible interest, he wrote, *and evince an infinitely higher taste, and a far greater artistic faculty than our liveliest imagination could have anticipated.* Wilhelm Bleek and Lucy Lloyd used the pictures to prompt information from the /Xam men staying with them, and Dia!kwain, whose narrations were particularly detailed and imaginative, was especially pleased to oblige.

One of Stow's copies shows a line of six figures standing with their arms held out before them, bent at the elbow. The figure on the far right, a man, holds a long stick upright. Below the two figures on the left of the line is a single steenbok, one of the world's smallest antelopes, which seems to be running to the left, out of the picture.

Dia!kwain believed the people in the copy were dancing because they were stamping their legs. The man *in the front* was showing the people how to dance, which was why he was the one holding the dancing stick. He was dancing before the others

for the people know that he is the one who always dances first, because he is a great sorcerer. That is why he dances first, for he wants the people who are learning to dance as he does. For he is dancing, teaching sorcery to the people.

His dancing made his nose bleed, and he would make his students smell the blood. The blood from a sorcerer's nose was always cold, no matter how hot the day, and it cooled whoever it touched. It was potent in its scent and powerful in itself.

The /Xam word Dia!kwain used for 'sorcerer', of course, was *!gi:xa*. *!Gi:xa* is a compound word made up from *!gi*, meaning power, magic or potency, and *xa*, which indicates possession. Sometimes the word was used for something considered simply 'magical' or 'supernatural' – a lion with its tail in its mouth speaking with a man's voice, for example, was not a human 'sorcerer' but was still a *!gi:xa* – but when Dia!kwain called the man in the picture dancing with the stick a *!gi:xa* he meant *someone who possesses power*.

A *!gi:xa* was a perfectly normal person but at times his or her experiences were very strange indeed.

A man who is a *!gi:xa* will not lay down his *kaross*, even if it is hot, because he knows that the place will not seem hot to him, for his inside is cold. Therefore if he puts down his *kaross*, he would shiver, he would be cold. For the doings of sorcery are not easy.

The plural of *!gi:xa* is *!gi:ten* and among the /Xam-ka !ei there were *!gi:ten* of the game, who would predict or influence the movements of the herds, *!gi:ten* of the rain and *!gi:ten* who healed the sick. Every /Xam band had members who could perform one or other of these roles, men and women who worked to the benefit of their families and their friends.

There was another kind of *!gi:xa*, however, whose actions were wholly negative. They would make you ill by summoning toxic creatures – lions, owls and moths – to plant inside you where they would sit invisibly, eating your flesh and poisoning you. These maleficent *!gi:ten*, who liked to work their magic from a great distance, or even from beyond the grave, would also poison people with /*ko-lti: sickness sticks, harm's things*. Dia!kwain said that the sticks were more or less the size of a pencil and that they were alive.

They call them bits of wood, for the things are like sticks.
They were very pretty when I used to see them.

Pretty they may have been, but their purpose was unkind, and the task of the healer was to take these sticks from the sick person's body by *snoring* them out with his or her nose and then sneezing them away.

A living *!gi:xa* could also go to the place where the wicked *!gi:ten* lived, a frightening and painful journey to the world of the dead, where he or she would actually fight evil-doers to prevent them working themselves or their invisible animal proxies into the sick. The motives of these invisible people, who sometimes came to the world of the living in the form of lions, were bad. They ate the flesh of the dead and they always wanted company or slaves. They had to kill you to have you, and so resistance was the best course.

If you had been a notable *!gi:xa* in life it was likely that you would continue to be so in death, either for the benefit or to the detriment of those you left behind. A living *!gi:xa* of the rain might invoke a deceased rain-maker years after his passing by calling on him personally, although the skills of the dead were pretty much available to all. Anyone could ask. If mosquitoes were troubling you in the night you could always call on poor /Xarrang/xarrang to blow them away, but you would have to remember her with respect at other times unless you wanted the wind to blow your reed mat from your shelter.

Hearing Dia!kwain talk of *!gi:ten* it was often difficult to tell if he was talking about the living or the dead. This was because a dead *!gi:xa* was no less powerful than a live one, and the effect of a *!gi:xa*'s actions was more important than whether he or she was alive or not. The dead were very present, the /Xam believed, and all *!gi:ten*, breathing or buried, had an important influence on the everyday lives of the /Xam-ka !ei.

Upon death, the heart of a *!gi:xa* who made people sick would appear in the night sky and fall into a waterpit with a noise like a quiver full of rattling arrows: a shooting star. If a nursing mother saw a shooting star she would express the milk from her breast so that her baby could not drink it. If she did not it would be as if a breath had been over the baby's heart and a fire had burned a mark over it; the sparks trailing a shooting star were the star's lice and they would sit over the child's heart, killing it.

For they have fire, and the fire become hot when the star falls; the star's light is fire. That is what goes to breathe over the baby's heart.

Only the invisible *!gi:ten*, the distant and the dead, were to be *really* feared. Some even took slaves whom they would force to collect locusts and the flesh of the newly buried. The other kind of *!gi:ten* – the living, visible kind – were nothing to be afraid of, and not only because their skills were useful. They were your aunts and uncles, your brothers and sisters, your parents.

Family, however, can be annoying. As a *!gi:xa* of the game, Dia!kwain's uncle /Uhere had a measure of control over ostriches. For a hunter to get on his bad side meant a difficult search for a more tractable source of protein. If /Uhere were angry with you then ostriches would act as if they had seen you, no matter how well-concealed you might be, and would run from you the moment you saw them. You would be puzzling over the birds' behaviour and wondering how you could have been detected, but it would have been /Uhere's doing. Eventually someone would have to take him aside and ask him what he was about.

'You don't seem to understand that some of us have children to feed,' he would have to be told. 'You may be angry, but you're behaving like a child and it's not helping any of us.'

In the end /Uhere would relent and promise that the hunter would catch a bird the next day, even it were just a *!kauï-kwa*, the lean runty ostrich whose egg had incubated on the outside of the clutch, in the cool.

!Gi:ten were people with a particularly large quantity of *!gi*, potency, or capable of obtaining it from the animals

or powerful places about them somehow, but that did not necessarily confer any particular degree of *status*. Like the more traditional San people still surviving, the /Xam-ka !ei were particularly democratic. There was no word in their language for 'chief' and leadership duties for any particular task were more or less spontaneously delegated according to who was most skilled at the matter in hand, be it hunting, butchering, curing skins or curing the sick.

If the /Xam-ka !ei were anything like the surviving San people who preserve their traditional practices, something like half of the men and a quarter of the women would have been skilled at the work of the *!gi:xa*.

Sometimes a man is a sorcerer and the woman is not a sorceress, her husband is the sorcerer. Another man's wife is a sorceress, the man is not a sorcerer. Another is a sorcerer, the man himself, his wife is also a sorceress. They are both sorcerers, the woman is one, the man is one. This is the custom among the /Xam-ka !ei.

For many *!gi:ten*, their abilities were closely bound with their skill at entering and controlling a state of trance. It was certainly not the only means by which cures were effected, the rains were worked or the movements of game predicted or influenced, but its importance to the /Xam-ka !ei is obvious from its appearance in so much of their myth and folklore and from the richness of the metaphorical terms used to explain and describe it.

Trance was activated in the dance described by Dia!kwain, a ritual performed to conjure *!gi*, energy. Some would dance and others would clap. The dancers made a train and moved in a circle, either around the clappers or inside a wider circle formed by onlookers and musicians; the 'dance step' was an active shuffle, highly rhythmic, performed with the aim of facilitating the deepest concentration. It seems that sometimes there would have been more than a dozen *!gi:ten* dancing, at other times only one, depending on the nature of the task at hand or the occasion.

People would assemble to dance after a successful hunt, for example, or as part of the wider rituals that marked such rites of passage as a woman's first menstruation or a young man's first eland kill. They would gather to dance for marriages, at certain seasonal times, or to cure sick individuals, the 'patient' sometimes lying down in the middle of the circle. Rattles made from the ears of springbok were worn wrapped round the dancers' legs and a hunting bow with a calabash attached as a resonator was sometimes struck with a stick: the rhythms were complex, the syncopation fierce.

Songs particularly rich in *!gi* would be sung and the dancers would follow each other one way and then the other until they had produced a circular furrow in the ground with their footsteps and the *!gi* produced in their bellies was beginning to 'boil'. Once it was boiling it would climb the *!gi:xa*'s spine, powerfully constricting the muscles in the stomach and causing the dancer to bend forwards in pain, before appearing on the dancer's skin as perspiration. Sweat imbued with *!gi* could be powerful stuff: /Kaggen rubbed his sweat onto the Blue Crane at the waterpool for a reason. Eventually the *!gi* would arrive in the dancer's head with the powerful 'explosion' that caused him or her to bleed from the nose. Dancers could collapse and might have to be supported by others; they could execute backflips; they could stand on their feet shouting or run out into the veld to fight the spirit creatures that only they could see. The dance could last for hours.

In the first decades of the 1800s, a French explorer called Arbousset witnessed it in the mountains where Qing lived:

The movement consists of irregular jumps; it is as if one saw a herd of calves leaping, to use a native comparison. They gambol together till all are fatigued and covered with perspiration. The thousand cries which they make, are so violent that it is not unusual to see some one sink to the ground exhausted and covered with blood, which pours from the nostrils; it is on this account that this dance is called mokoma, *or the dance of blood.*

Trance frequently brought with it nasal haemorrhage. Blood would stream from the trancer's nose, sometimes to be spread across the face. This blood was more 'potent' still than perspiration.

The dance was not a 'mystery' or a secret event witnessed only by the initiated but a part of the shared cultural life of the band. Children would have run around the furrows, imitating the dancers in fun. The use of trance as a means of healing, prediction, rain-making, fighting off malevolent *!gi:ten*, influencing the movement of game, or for other social and spiritual necessities we do not yet understand, was simply part of life.

None the less, *!gi* was fierce and powerful, difficult to manage without pain; a trancer could knock you over by pointing his finger at you. The word */a*, remember, meant 'fight', or 'curse', or 'harm', but it also meant 'a concentration of power'.

There is a word used by the Tungus people of central Asia that is useful in helping us to understand what the /Xam people meant when they described people like //Kabbo and Dia!kwain's aunt Tano-!khauken as *!gi:xa* or *!gi:ten*: *shaman*. Hunting and gathering cultures throughout the world are shamanic and all their shamans have surprisingly similar abilities. They travel great distances, see through the eyes of distant creatures and even take the form of specific animals, the better to run or fly about the places in which they live. /Xam shamans were no different.

When Dia!kwain was about eleven, invisible, distant !*gi:ten* tried to kill him by shooting something into his liver. They wanted to take him from his parents and have him as their slave, bringing them food and dipping up their water, and they were thwarted only when he was 'snored' back into health by a woman from the Hartbees River called !Kwarra-ang.

Still alive in 1874 and living on land that had been taken from the /Xam by the Boers, she was a curer whose husband ≠Gerri:sse had been shot dead by a farmer while out collecting poison for his arrows, preparing for a springbok hunt. The farmer's name was Hans Basson, Dia!kwain remembered; he had shot ≠Gerri:sse and his young son together.

People said that !Kwarra-ang's snoring was not what it used to be. In the past, they said, she used to snore people with great skill and could bring the sick back from the brink of death. Now they said that she took for ever to smell out the sickness and once she had found its cause she could not be trusted to effect a complete cure. Dia!kwain had cause to disagree with them.

When she healed him !Kwarra-ang put her nose to his body to smell out the sickness and the invisible wound that was causing it.

We do not see the wound, for the person's skin is over it. But his nose enters the man's flesh underneath. His nose smells underneath the skin, and he works upon the man's flesh.

Soon she found what had been shot into his belly and took it from his liver; she left the shelter to dispose of it and then came back to close the wound under his skin.

Her nose sews up the wound.

Now her nose was bleeding and she rubbed Dia!kwain with the blood so that the scent would prevent anything from getting back into him.

She who is a *!gi:xa*, her blood scent should be upon me.

With nasal blood on him, he resembled a *!gi:xa* and was protected.

!Kwarra-ang still had the power to cure, whatever anyone might say, but Dia!kwain remembered that she was not happy. She knew that people said her nose was weak, that she did not snore anyone nicely any more and that she practically ate people when she put her face to their bodies. Her 'patients' took advantage of her poor reputation now and never wanted to reward her for her work – when they even remembered where she lived, that is. No one visited her now that her nose was not what it had once been. People only came to see her when they were ill, and once she had cured them they did not want to pay her for what she had done.

It was no wonder she was bitter; the work was not at all easy.

'The next time someone comes to me in pain I should tell them to snore themselves,' she told Dia!kwain. 'Or I should wait until the very last minute before I heal them, until they're on the verge of death, and then there'll be no arguing about who owes what.'

She had to be careful. A reward was a serious business and she had lost friends.

'If those people came back again, no matter how much pain they're in, I'd tell them: no, sorry, nothing I can do,' Dia!kwain remembered her saying. !Kwarra-ang thought that these ingrates were lucky it was her. Another *!gi:xa* would cut the sick person's arteries with her snoring, killing them to punish them for their lack of gratitude.

What she really wanted for her efforts was a real knife, a metal one.

For then my heart is happy, for I feel that they have cooled my heart, and my heart is not angry. For when they have made my heart happy, then I am happy. For, I am sure if the harmful things come to me, that had been killing them, I should be able to keep them away from them, they would not know them.

I should see them; they would not see them.

Kumm:

The man who shot the Rain

The people say that the Rain's bull goes out from his pit, and the pit becomes dry, while it feels that the Rain has gone out – the Rain's bull. Therefore the pit dries up, on account of it.

The Rain, !Khwa, lived where there was water. That was his body and his home. If the waterpit were dry then !Khwa was walking about, either on the land or in the sky. His breath was mist, and his scent was the glorious smell of rain on the dry ground.

A man (I do not know his name, but he was one of the First at Sitting People) once hunted the Rain, as the Rain was grazing there. The Rain was like an eland.

The man tracked the eland cautiously; he put down his bag and readied his bow and his poisoned arrow. Lying down, concealed, he shot the animal, which sprang to one side and ran away from him. He picked up his bag, walked to his arrow, put it into his bag, and went home where he lay down and slept, thinking to follow the animal's tracks and bring the meat home the next day.

Early next morning he told the people that he had shot the Rain. And they followed up the Rain; they went to track its footprints.

As they were following the eland's tracks a mist came up, and they walked through it, right up to where the antelope lay.

They followed the footprints right up to the Rain. They caught sight of the Rain lying down, and they went up to it. They cut up the Rain. They kept cutting off meat. They kept putting it to roast, but the meat kept vanishing, being burnt up in the fire.

It may as well have been evaporating.

This is what they did: they went to take out the meat.

When they went through the ashes to see if they could find the meat, they couldn't. It had completely disappeared.

The fire burnt out; the fire died down.
   Then an old man said: 'I thought I would go when this eland's meat was finished, but although I roasted it I have not eaten it. So now I will go while its meat sits there.'
   And another answered, 'We will all do so, because we did not know what sort of eland it was. Let us go, because it is an eland whose meat we do not eat.'

   As they all got up to go the Rain shut them into the shelter. The Rain's navel came: a cyclone of fierce wind, hail and raindrops.

The Rain's navel shut them into the hut, and they sat waiting for the Rain's navel.

   !Khwa, the Rain, turned the men into frogs. They hopped from the hut into the veld.
   The man who'd shot the eland hopped away too. He hopped off to the *vlei*.

The Bushmen do not kill frogs, while they feel that the rain does not fall if we kill frogs. And the place becomes dry. Therefore the Bushmen become lean, on account of it, when the rain does not fall; and the springbok are not there, on account of it, the locusts are not there. And the locusts disappear. The springbok also vanish.

!Khwa:

The Rain

George Stow – amateur geologist, anthropologist and the first genuine rock art researcher – copied a rock painting *under the great precipice of Klein Aasvogelkop*, a sugarloaf hill rising out of the plain south of the Caledon River west of a town called Rouxville, and sent it to Wilhelm Bleek in 1874.

The creature in the copy is painted in a pink colour with red details on a yellow-orange wash used by Stow to represent the colour of the rock surface. Although it does not exactly resemble any creature of the natural world there is something of the hippopotamus or cow about it. It is painted facing to the right, head down and mouth open, with thirteen evenly spaced white 'hairs' or 'teeth' emerging from its top jaw and a 'beard' of what could be hair, or water, or blood, coming from its neck. It has two curved yellow lines nested on its broad back with two red shapes hanging from the lower of the two. Its wide tail, half as long as the body to which it is attached, is a fountain painted in shades – in this copy – of yellow and red and pink.

It has anything up to eight limbs, depending on whether you interpret its appendages as udders or legs. It is certainly difficult to identify the elongated bell hanging from its belly, dotted with red spots and finished with what could be nine triangular nipples or even claws.

The painting was explained:

She rain with the rainbow over her.

A half-circle of two colours, open at the bottom, encloses this *she rain* with a thick band of yellow above, where /Kaggen sat, and a thinner line of red below that was /Kwammang-a's colour in the rainbow. The light-coloured, soaking, 'she rain' brought fertility; the darker 'he rain' violence, hail and lightning, to be warded off by the lighting of fires and placated by the burning of horns.

At the end of the summer of 1874, a week before Dorothea Bleek's first birthday, Dia!kwain and ≠Kasing set off to visit /Xam-ka !au.

It had been nearly five years since the two had seen their wives and the places they knew and they were terribly homesick. Although they promised that they would come back to Mowbray with their wives as soon as they could, Lloyd and Bleek must have felt anxious to see them go; three years before /Hang≠kass'o had promised the same and had simply disappeared. Unlike /Hang≠kass'o, however, the two men had been settled at The Hill for nearly five months now. Wilhelm and Lucy, still impatient to record testimony from women, were willing to risk never seeing the men again.

Bleek's friend Dr Meyer wrote to him to let him know that it had taken the two men twelve days to get to Calvinia, 430 kilometres to the north.

Nearly two weeks after they had left, the superintendent of the Cape Town Botanical Gardens, Mr McGibbon, a tall and somewhat grim man who would poke children with his stick when he caught them stealing flowers, made a pile of weeds pulled from the flowerbeds and set it alight.

The library is at the bottom of the gardens, separated from the lawns and the trees by iron railings and a statue of Sir

George Grey. There was nothing to prevent the smoke from McGibbon's bonfire filling the room where Bleek was working. Soon he began to cough. After a while he began to bring up blood, and thought it would be better if he took the train home.

He struggled up the path to the front door of The Hill and the moment Jemima saw him it was quite obvious to her that there was something seriously wrong. Immediately she sent for Dr Stewart, who came and did what he could. Before he went, he took Jemima to one side to tell her that he *did not like the look of things*; from now on her husband would have to more careful than he had ever been.

Wilhelm was impatient to get back to work and as soon as the haemorrhage healed he went back to Cape Town on the 9.30 a.m. train. For some reason Jemima felt uneasy that morning, and followed him to the library to discover him coughing up blood in a room full of smoke from another pile of McGibbon's burning weeds.

She took him home again at once. Although the fresh haemorrhage healed after a few days, Bleek had the feeling that death had come closer to him than it had been for years. He told Jemima how much *he wished the doctor would tell him the truth about himself*; she remembered him saying that he wanted to know whether he had *weeks, or months, and saying, that could he but know how he* really *was, he could then tell what things to try quickly to finish off, and what to lay quietly on one side.*

She went to see Dr Stewart alone in order to speak to him frankly, and to discover the truth for herself. Stewart told her that he had considered Bleek's health to be precarious ever since he had become his doctor. He believed that her husband could live for years if he took care, but that it would take only a serious cold in the chest to finish him. As careful as Wilhelm Bleek was, a bad chest cold was hardly unavoidable.

Putting it as gently as she could, Jemima told her husband *the sense* of what the doctor had told her. She had decided that although she was going to bring him bad news his situation was better than he had feared, and that he needed to know the facts if he were to decide which part of his work he wanted completed.

When Wilhelm was strong enough to leave the house, he and Jemima began to take the air again; there were many good walks through the meadows about Mowbray. As they went, they talked about the future. They would not be sending their daughters to Germany for their education now, something Wilhelm would have found terribly difficult had his health been perfect. It was not simply that he wanted to spend the months or years he had left to him watching the girls grow up but that they were constitutionally better suited, he believed, to life in the southern hemisphere.

On his death they should carry on without him, Jemima managing the house and Lucy continuing the /Xam work. Both should do everything they could to ensure the continuation of the government grants without which they could not afford to feed and clothe their /Xam-speaking residents.

Jemima wrote that her husband insisted that although *he told me all this, as his opinion of what might be best and wisest for me to do, if left alone, yet that I must by no means consider myself bound, or even hampered in thought, by any of his expressed wishes.* It was impossible to foresee what the exact circumstances would be, after all. *Only don't lose your head and you will come all right*, he repeated.

Autumn approached as they waited for Dia!kwain and his brother-in-law ≠Kasing to come back from the dry north.

A storm in the Northern Cape is a memorable thing. Twigs and dust blow about your knees, preceding the *rush of the storm* itself which arrives, as Dia!kwain described it, like the wind from a cannonball. Red and yellow lightning flashes pave the way for a cloudburst of terrifying strength; the rain and wind could flatten your shelter and wash your things away.

There was one word in the /Xam language for 'rain' and 'water': !Khwa. !Khwa was responsible for storms and for the welcome succour of rain, neither a god nor a blind force of nature but something occupying a liminal space between living myth and metaphor.

He was clouds, rain and standing water but also the being that brought them, so raindrops themselves were *!khwa //ki* – literally, 'the Water's liquid' or 'the Rain's liquid'. His influence was felt tangibly since a full cistern or *vlei* kept you alive and good rain provided grazing for the herds, while flash floods, cyclones and torrential rain were frightening at best and potentially very dangerous.

Animal metaphors were used to describe the rain and the clouds. /Xam people would speak of the 'Rain's body': cloud that walked on the columns of falling rain known as the 'Rain's legs'. Mist was the 'Rain's breath', associated with the she-rain *!khwa /aiti*, drizzle, and the 'Rain's hair' was either the wispy strands of rain falling from distant clouds or the 'lining' of clouds, silver or dark. The rain's tracks could be read like any animal tracks, with the forceful 'male' precipitation leaving deeper prints in the dust, different from the gentle 'female' drizzle's shallow spoor.

The 'Rain's ribs' seem to have been long strands of dark, heavy clouds. You could drink the 'Rain's tail' but the 'Rain's navel' was frightening weather – hail, wind and fierce rain – strong enough to keep you trapped in your shelter. The appearance of !Khwa's navel, probably a cyclone, was a frightening prelude to the transformations suffered by those who had done him wrong. While both /Kaggen and !Khwa were capable of inflicting transformation, of the two !Khwa was quicker to anger and far more dangerous. First his whirlwind came to scoop the disrespectful, the ignorant and the foolish into the air and then a terrifying journey to the waterpits and springs, where the transgressors would be turned into frogs or flowers, followed.

This is what the old people say, the rain wants to kill us when it is angry with us. The rain attacks the hut angrily, and the hail beats down on us breaking down the huts, and the cold wind gets in to the people in consequence.

It drives out the people; and the man, because of whom the rain is angry with the people, is the one whom the wind lifts up, and blows into the sky and drops down into a pond. Then he stays in the pond and becomes a frog.

Drought would come if the /Xam killed frogs because, along with the cobra, the puff-adder and the water tortoise, they were things *the Rain puts aside as the Rain's meat*, and had to be treated respectfully. *Therefore Bushmen fear them not a little. These things are what the rain throws at us, because he feels he is a strong thing.*

!Khwa could be spoken to, soothed or annoyed: if you heard thunder on a clear, sunny day, a woman had just thrown a stone into standing water. Worse would happen if a woman dipped up water in the rain without first sprinkling on it *buchu*, the aromatic herb that made the rain placid.

For !Khwa loves *buchu* very much, for *buchu* is aromatic. It glides along quickly, shutting its eyes, gliding along when it smells things of unequalled scent.

The !Khwa described in the stories set in the time of the Early Race sometimes went looking for food in the form of a large animal like an eland, the *waterbull*. His horns were *black below, and white at the upper end, as if scraped*; he would leave the waterpit empty as he went into the world, his breath filling the flats and hills with mist. You could smell him coming.

The people say that there is no scent as sweet, hence the people say that it is fragrant.

Although the Rain's ribs, the Rain's hair, the Rain's navel and the massive 'legs' of raindrops supporting clouds as they 'walked' across the veld were metaphors, there were times when !Khwa's animal manifestations were absolutely real. If the Rain were only an animal for the purposes of describing the weather in the everyday world, a sleep or a circular dance away for the *!gi:ten* of the rain was !Khwa-ka xoro, the rain animal. The *rain's men* of the /Xam-ka !ei knew how to find the rain animal as he grazed, or to coax him from the water where he lived, and most often they did it in a state of trance.

What they did with the rainbull once they had caught it affected the lives of all, but the animal would always resist them for all it was worth – and no wonder. The *rain's men* were shamanic butchers.

How to kill the rain.

!Khwa-ka !gi:ten, the shamans of the rain, would lie in wait for !Khwa-ka xoro, the rain animal, to come out to graze, leaving the waterpit dry. The men would approach downwind, silently, so that the creature would not be aware of their coming, an old and experienced *rain's man* taking the lead with his apprentices following. It was the apprentices' job to hold the thong once the old man had put the looped end over the creature's black and white horns and drawn it tight about its neck; the animal would always attempt to escape back to the waterpit and it was their task to stop it. If it resisted them successfully then there could be no more attempts that day and the *!gi:ten* would have to go back to the camp to apologize. They would go sheepishly, arguing over whose fault it was that the creature had escaped.

Everyone waiting at the camp would be angry since there would be no rain, the leaves would not sprout and the springbok would not come to eat the new shoots. The rain was as important for the hunt as it was for the gathering of *veldkos*.

Those trying to capture the rain animal took the aromatic leaves of the *buchu* bush with them since the smell was the only thing that would pacify the creature once the shamans had their hands on it. Without the smell of *buchu* the animal could even break the thong around its neck, which would rip its way home through the sky with a noise like a huge *!kummi* – a bullroarer.

Once they had caught it the rain-makers would walk the animal towards the dry places, where they would kill it, breaking its ribs and scattering its blood and flesh on the places that needed rain. This happened in the world of trance, the spirit-filled, Bushmanland-shaped template over the 'real world': there, where the people sat, thirsty, the north wind would pick up, blowing the rainclouds before it and bringing rain.

Then the wild onion leaves sprout for the people, and they dig and feed themselves with them. The people who are at home see the rainclouds and say to each other 'The *!gi:ten* really seem to have their hands upon the rain animal, for you see that the rainclouds come gliding along. For the rainclouds are fine, and it looks as if they are truly going to make rain fall for us.'

Slaughter in a state of trance was not the only method there was of making it rain.

Before he left Mowbray to see his wife, //Kabbo spoke about a *!gi:xa* of the rain called /Kaunu, a *rain's man* who used to live in the hills to the south of the Bitterpits. The man was known by the names !Khwa-ka /kaunu, Rain's New Grass, given him because of his skill, and /Kaunu !kwa, New Grass Leg, given him after he once cut his leg on the new season's sharp grass. He went grey young. Many people were scared of him because of his owl's eyes – big, predator's eyes, even larger than those of an ostrich.

/Kaunu had been //Kabbo's father's 'person', meaning that they were close, and after the death of //Kabbo's father he became //Kabbo's person too. He taught them both about the rain.

You would go to see Rain's New Grass when the ground was so parched that the withered bushes were sunbleached and everything was desiccated white. *Please let it be wet*, you might ask him, *that the bushes may grow beautiful. For a place is beautiful when it is sprouting, when the mountain tops are green.*

This kind of talk made /Kaunu angry, on the whole, and provoked him to foul language. You would have to be persistent and try to explain how the Rain's legs walked past you, how you had been delegated to come and speak to him by the others and how you never complained when the rain *did* come, like *they* did, but merely covered yourself with your *kaross* to keep dry and lit a fire to keep warm.

If he finally assented he would work at night, when everyone slept, striking his bowstring with a stick. Some might hear him playing in the night, turn over and drift off back to sleep. By the time everyone was awake there would be a *cloak of rain* hiding the sun and soon water would be falling so abundantly that people had to dig channels to drain it from their shelters. With the wind from the north it would blow all day and night, only letting up the following dawn.

One night, years before //Kabbo came to Mowbray, an argument broke out amongst the women in /Kaunu's band and the *rain's man* left his shelter to find his wife and soothe her. That night was mortally tense. On his way back to his shelter his grandson !Kauken-ka-/a, who was angry with him, shot him with an arrow and killed him.

//Kabbo remembered what the grey-haired man with the predator's eyes had taught him.

During the night of 10 October 1871, three months after his son-in-law /Hang≠kass'o had left Mowbray with a letter, some money and an old pair of Wilhelm Bleek's trousers, it rained in the night. Two days later Lucy Lloyd made some notes in tiny letters on the first page of her twelfth notebook.

Jantje Tooren [//Kabbo] told me on the 11th that he had asked for rain on the previous night, when lying down (in his bed) to make the garden wet, as his arm and chest were painful, and that it had come in the night. He told this with an appearance of satisfaction, and so I today asked him about it, and got the history, which appears to be that of a dream. He says he saw the rain coming, and also saw and spoke to his wife, his son, and his daughter in his dream.

//Kabbo – Dream – told Lucy Lloyd:

I dreamt that I told the rain to fall for me, for my arm ached, my chest ached. Therefore I dreamt that I spoke. The rain assented to me, the rain would fall for me, that I might gently sit, for my chest ached.

He had been digging and the ground was hard for want of rain. His muscles were sore.

The rain water should first wet the garden for me; that I might sit in peace, while the rain was wetting the garden-earth. And I first sat, the rain wet the garden bushes, as I sat quietly, for I used to dream when I was at my home, I dreamt; the rain assented to me when I was at my place. The rain fell for me, for the rain felt I was thirsty; that was why I dreamt of the rain, that rain should fall for me, that I might drink, for I was dying of thirst. Then the rain fell, I drank, because the rain used to assent to me.

Lucy Lloyd believed that in the middle of relating his dream he had drifted off into a sort of nostalgic reverie about life in /Xam-ka !au. She wrote: *The whole is, I believe, not a dream. I think he has branched off into ordinary Bushman life, in the course of it.*

For //Kabbo, this was not quite true. Lloyd's confusion came about because, telling her of his dream, he had put himself in Cape Town and in /Xam-ka !au in the same breath. It was, it seemed, inexplicable.

//Kabbo continued:

I said to my wife, that rain should fall for us, that we might drink. I spoke to my wife about it. 'O wife, I have been dreaming of rain, that rain should fall for us, that we might drink.' Thus I spoke. My wife agreed with me. I also spoke to my son: 'O my son! I have been dreaming that rain should fall for us that we may drink; for we are thirsty.' I said to him: 'We shall drink tomorrow; I see clouds.'

I said to him: 'Do you not see the cloud? We shall drink tomorrow.'

I spoke, my daughter's child was silent. 'The rain will come to us, we shall drink.'

The child was silent. The rain fell, the rain moistened the ground, the water ran off, the water's child. We drank it, we fill the springbok skin, we put away water, we put them away.

He then went on to describe a hunt for food, in which he seemed to be participating, and then a conversation to which he could not have been party:

I think that /Hang≠kass'o has seen Suobba-//kein, I think that Suobba-//kein has called my name, for I sneeze. I think that my wife calls my name, for I sneeze, I think that my son calls my name, I think that my daughter calls my name. I think so, for I sneeze.

I think that /Hang≠kass'o says to my daughter 'These are Father's trousers; his master gave them to him, telling him to give them to me.' That is what I think. Her mother asks: 'Are those father's trousers there?' Her daughter's husband says to her: 'Your husband's trousers are there, which he gave me.' I thus think, for I sneeze.

My wife asks him: 'Are these Father-in-law's trousers there?' She says to her son-in-law: 'Husband seems to have wanted me to talk to him. I will go to him, for he is definitely staying at his master's.'

This is what I think. She has said to me that her son should definitely be with me. 'We will go to him.'

That is what I think, for I sneezed. She told all the people that she would go to me, for I was at my master's. My master had taken /A!kungta. While /A!kungta was working there, my master went and said to me I should come to him. He said so, I agreed that I should do so. I came to be with /A!kungta . . . My master also said that I should tell him [/Hang ≠kass'o] to come to our house, when he had got our women. Our wives should come with him, he should bring them.

Bleek, //Kabbo told his family, would buy a knife and new tobacco bag for /Hang≠kass'o when he came back, and spoke of the journey they could expect on the way home:

This is what I said: 'Our Master says this: this is his letter, and with it you will get food as you go along . . . This letter is to make all white men take care of you. It's from our master. Our master has made it for you. I said: 'You must take this letter to Beaufort West: our Master says so. Beaufort's magistrate shall see it.' I said so, /Hang≠kass'o assented. 'This letter is the one to take to Victoria West.' I said so. 'The Magistrate of Victoria West shall see it.'

Lucy Lloyd was recording the words of a shaman – a *!gi:xa* – as he described how he had made it rain and then engaged himself in more mundane chores, dipping up water and hunting porcupines, in a place hundreds of kilometres away. Lloyd would have been less confused had she known something about the other shamanic cultures of the world, defined in part by journeys of the spirit made by people expert in the use of the imagination.

//Kabbo believed that he had made a journey to /Xam-ka !au during a 'dream', and as far as he was concerned his visit to his family was as real, in its way, as the rain that had assented to his request to fall.

Sometimes !Khwa came unbidden and angry, without request or warning.

If you wanted rain, a gentle she rain was preferred, the kind that would strike up in a mist and sow herself on the dry ground without too much wind and violence – certainly without the lightning or the painful hail that came with the dark, angry male rain whose clouds blotted out the sun and shook the people's shelters with his wind.

At its fiercest, the male rain was capable of destroying an entire town. //Kabbo's daughter saw it happen.

Victoria West, the Karoo town where the men of //Kabbo's family were held on their way to the Breakwater, was founded in the bottom of a valley. On the night of 27 February 1871 a rampaging male rain filled the valley floor, which, it turns out, was an ancient watercourse with life left in it. The stiff rain that fell in the town itself was quite violent upstream and after dusk it battered its way down the high street as a flash flood nearly two metres high that destroyed the town's raw brick cottages and carried bales of wool, sheep, horses and goats in its wake. The citizens found the bodies of their dead miles downstream the next day; the only building undamaged was the town hall, which they used as a mortuary.

Sara saw it while her father and /Hang≠kass'o, her husband, were in prison at the Breakwater. /Hang≠kass'o later told Lucy Lloyd:

I was listening to Sara; she was the one who said that there were drums attached to the rain's body. The drums fell down in the midst of Victoria West, the brick houses.

(because brick houses are in the middle of Victoria West. A ravine it is; because a rain which came angrily to the people by night it is. Therefore, the /Xam-ka !ei do not a little fear the Darkness's rain. They make a great fire, which is not small, while they desire that the rainclouds may divide; when they behold that this rain, it does not a little lighten; it does not a little thunder. For, the darkness's rain's doings are not nice.)

I was listening to Sara, to that which she spoke. Sara said that the rain was not strong.

(therefore she did not think that the houses would break in pieces; she also did not think that the people would be killed).

*The water filled the houses; the houses they altogether carried away. Another
house broke in the upper part; it came crashing down upon the skulls of
people. The people were yonder being altogether carried away by the water;
they and the houses' things; while the drums fell down among the houses.
The water altogether yonder carried away the sacks of wool. The pigs were
yonder carried away with the sheep. The house-things which had been stored
up, the houses which the water broke to pieces, they all, altogether, went
with the people. The people screamed as they watched.*

Sara said that the thing sounded like a bell which people are striking.

(sorcery's bell it was, a rain which kills people, its bell).

*It sounded !kam, !kam, !kam, !kam, !kam, !kam, !kam, while she listened;
while the water felt that all the people were being carried away, carried away
along in the middle of the river-bed; while the people felt that the rain-liquid
was that which took them away. The rain-liquid was that which carried
taking away all the things, carried taking away the people, and the dogs,
and the pigs, and the sacks of sheep's wool.*

Three months after they had left for the Northern Cape,
Dia!kwain and his brother-in-law ≠Kasing came back to The
Hill with !Kweiten ta //ken and her sons, who were six and
two. It was winter, the second week of June 1874. For some
reason ≠Kasing and !Kweiten ta //ken had decided that they
should leave their two daughters in Wellington, a fruit farmer's
market town not far to the north of Stellenbosch, and it was
not until October that the family was reunited.

Dia!kwain must have been pleased to have had his sister
and his nephews and nieces with him but he did not come back
to Mowbray with his wife. While he had been imprisoned at
the Breakwater she had been taken by another man, a Bastard

Bushman, and had gone with him *far away*, somewhere near the town of Klaarvole, he thought. He had also discovered that his uncle had been killed in the company of some other /Xam men, their arms tied, driven off a precipice.

His incarceration had saved his life but destroyed his family.

Lucy Lloyd and Wilhelm Bleek were delighted to see Dia!kwain and ≠Kasing again, but the presence in the house of Dia!kwain's sister must have been especially pleasing. Finally they had the opportunity to record /Xam culture through the eyes of a woman.

The first part of her name, !Kweiten, was a word with at least two meanings. The word was used of a kind of water flower and for what Lucy Lloyd translated as 'thunderbolt'. Both were things to do with !Khwa.

When the Rain was angry with a young woman he would exercise his powers of transformation through lightning or the whirlwind.

!Khwa lightens, killing them; they become stars.

If they were not transformed into stars these women could expect to become the beautiful *!kweiten* flowers that stood in water and would mysteriously vanish right before your eyes were you to try and gather them.

Therefore mother and the others told us that we ought not to go to the flowers we see standing in the water, even if we see their beauty. For they are girls whom the rain has taken away, they resemble flowers; for they are the Water's wives, and we look at them, leaving them alone. For we should also be like them in what they do.

A thunderbolt, the other meaning of *!kweiten*, was one of the shiny, black and pointy stones that came from the sky when there was lightning.

They disturb the ground where they fall.

They could very well have been the black dolerite boulders of the *brinkkops* of /Xam-ka !au, which would help to explain how these hills were connected with the rain and why rain-makers were referred to as *brinkkops' men*.

Although !Kweiten ta //ken was not a rain-maker herself she knew enough about the Rain to describe its children, as Lucy Lloyd noted:

!Kweiten ta //ken has not seen these things herself but she heard that they were beautiful, and striped like a /habba, i.e. zebra. The Water was large as a bull, and the Water's children were the size of calves, being the children of great things.

Towards the end of that spring, ≠Kasing and !Kweiten ta //ken's two other children arrived from Wellington, reaching Mowbray on 25 October and forming a miniature /Xam band there. The two made domed shelters in the garden from the branches of the trees surrounding the lawn and lived there with their children, a few paces from the back door of The Hill.

While there could be something almost severe in the gaze of her husband, who clearly did not enjoy having his photograph taken, !Kweiten ta //ken had a far milder air about her, something she shared with her brother – although both she and Dia!kwain were clearly capable of standing up for themselves if they were ever provoked. Photographs taken of the two capture the same expression. She had her brother's cheekbones and forehead, although she was broader, rounder in the shoulders. Short by European standards, her feet were so small that she could wear Edith's outgrown boots: Edith, who was now eleven, thought her *pretty, hot-tempered* and *lively*.

Her children were lively too, although very well behaved. They obeyed their parents perfectly, and Edith never remembered seeing them squabbling or fighting; instead they played quietly in the fields and meadows about the The Hill.

Edith did recall that the whole family very much liked to listen to music. On Sundays they were invited into the house to hear Jemima play the piano and all of them, even the smallest of the boys, would sit perfectly still as they listened. One of their particular favourites was the Dead March from Handel's *Saul*.

!Kweiten was not to provide Lucy Lloyd and Wilhelm Bleek with quite the quantity of testimony that they had expected but she did have a few beautifully detailed stories. Women played important roles in the few *kukummi* she offered, many of which dealt with the beliefs and rituals associated with women's rites of passage. !Khwa was especially interested in the propriety of women at these times, as the *kumm* of the Girl and the Frogs, one of the few stories she told to Lloyd at the height of the summer of 1874, shows.

Neither a girl nor a woman, a *maiden* lay apart from the camp in the isolation of the shelter built to see her through safely from her life as a child to her life as an adult. Between adulthood and childhood you did not belong with adults or with children. You were taken out of the daily life of the camp and the elder men or women would finally explain to you what the passage really meant. It was a time of crisis requiring the observance of ritual, special food and celebrations. The maiden was not suffering all of this in the right spirit.

She had been a difficult child, this not-quite-a-woman, and in her special shelter it did not seem likely that she would be growing out of it soon. When her *mothers* – her birth mother and the elder women of the camp now helping with the appropriate rites – brought her the ritually prepared food her condition required, she refused to touch it. Maybe she was annoyed that she could not eat what she wanted, since certain foods were not permitted her, her mothers thought. Maybe she was simply awkward and did not appreciate the vital importance of the safe journey from childhood to maturity. No one in the camp dared to voice the thought, but we can: maybe she was just bad.

No one had seen a thing pass her lips for days and yet she did not seem to be hungry at all. By rights she should have been starving. It was a mystery.

Out foraging for *Bushman rice* – ant chrysalids – one day, the women made up their minds to get to the bottom of it all. After some discussion they told the girl's little sister to hide in the maiden's shelter and keep watch so that the next day, when everyone else was out of the camp hunting or foraging, she could find out what was what.

The little girl did as she was told and crept in, hiding herself as carefully as she could. She did not have to wait too long before she saw her sister put her head out of the door and look about to make sure that there was no one watching. When she was certain that the camp was deserted, she stole away.

The little girl stayed hidden. After a while her sister came back, carrying something with her: an animal the size of a calf, striped like a /habba, a zebra, and quite beautiful.

The Water was large as a bull, and the Water's children were the size of calves, being the children of great things.

She skinned it, boiled it in a pot, and then ate it.

Although the younger girl did not know what the thing was, she saw enough of it to be able to describe it to her mother later. The older woman recognized it immediately. *It is a Water-child.* Of all the things in the world a young woman could choose to eat at such an important time, this was the worst by far. She was breaking the rules of isolation and putting herself and the young men of the camp at terrible risk simply by leaving her shelter like that, which was bad enough, but creeping to the waterpit to kill and eat one of the Water's magnificent offspring? This meant terrible, terrible trouble.

Nevertheless, the girl's mother did nothing. She did not tell anyone what she had heard. Perhaps she was frightened of the consequences for her daughter. Perhaps she hoped that the Water would not find out.

And her mother did not speak about it; she again went out to seek for Bushman rice.

It was a mistake to have done nothing.

And when she was seeking about for food, the clouds came up. And she spoke, she said: 'Something is not right at home; for a whirlwind is bringing things to the spring.'

It was !Khwa's whirlwind and it hoisted the woman's daughter, not quite a girl, not quite a woman, into the sky. It carried her to the water and dropped her in, where she became a frog. All the elder women were next – the whirlwind picked them up from where they walked in the veld and dropped them into the spring, where they all became frogs. Next were the young woman's mother and father, picked up from where they were walking on the hunting ground and carried to the spring.

Then the people one after another go out and fly up into the sky, the cold wind blows them up into it. Then they keep coming out of it, floating down and falling into the pond, where they become frogs.

!Khwa's whirlwind took all their possessions, too:

Meanwhile the karosses become springbok which lie down and roll, thereby shaking out the water from their skins, while the sticks and branches of the hut become bushes. The skins of which people have made the quivers turn into springbok, as the quivers stand about there, they get ears.

The arrows of the girl's father turned into the reeds from which they were made and stood on their ends at the water's edge; their sleeping mats turned back into grass.

Meanwhile the rain turns altogether in a pond, because its body goes into it.

Like //Kabbo, Dia!kwain had seen rain-making from close quarters.

Once, when he was still a boy playing about the camp with his little sister !Kweiten, his elder brother K'obo came with his wife Du-//hu to spend a few days away from home. When K'obo and Du-//hu decided that it was time to go back to their children they found that it was far too hot to leave; the earth had been soaking up the sun for days and they decided that it would be better if they waited for it to cool before they set off home. A few days later, however, the earth was no cooler. It was still not safe to begin the journey they had to make – but they really could not stay.

Du-//hu spoke to Xättin, Dia!kwain's father, telling him that she wished that she and her husband might *return home, that rain might fall for them, for the sun was burning not a little, that the ground be made cool for them, the hill which they had to pass.*

She wanted to see if the Rain's hair could not be made to pass over the hills so that the ground might cool under the clouds' shadow. Xättin's response was that rain really did not look likely to him. Did it look likely to her?

This was not what she had expected to hear. It did not seem especially friendly, since she knew that Xättin was a man who knew a thing or two about the rain having been taught by !Nuin /kuïten, a renowned *rain's man* who had been dead for many years. Was Xättin teasing? Was he angry with her?

Once she had asked for his help a second time Xättin stood up and walked out into the heat of the day and told Dia!kwain to come with him; they were going to climb the nearby *brinkkop* and sit on top looking for springbok. They walked from the camp towards the bare hill. As they climbed,

Father said that he knew that my brother's people were waiting where they were. They wanted to return home. He also wanted them to return to their home. Then we climbed up the hill, when the sun stood above it.

They were not climbing the hill to spot springbok at all. They were there to help K'obo and Du-//hu on their way home to their children.

When they had climbed to the top of the *brinkkop*, Xättin spoke to !Nuin /kuïten, the dead man who had taught him years before. He told him that the young people wanted to see their children but they were sitting in the camp below waiting for the earth to cool. He asked him if he would take the heat out of the ground for them.

'You who seem to be !Nuin /kuïten, you used to say to me that once you had died you would hear me if I called upon you. You would let rain fall for me'

he said.

And when Father spoke thus, the rainclouds came gliding up, the rain did not pass over, for the rainclouds covered the sky.

Dia!kwain was beside himself. *Tata-we*, hey, father, *look*: he said. Rainclouds are covering the sky!

Angrily, Xättin told his son to stop talking: you were silent when the rainclouds approached. As he spoke a wind blew, following the clouds, and on it was the soft, round smell of new rain on dry earth. The Rain's breath.

The people say that there is no scent as sweet, hence the people say that it is fragrant.

Despite his bad back, which made the descent difficult and always gave him cause to grumble, Xättin was pleased with himself as he climbed down the *brinkkop* and made his way back to the camp, where his son and daughter-in-law were sat before the shelters. He greeted them and told them that !Nuin /kuïten had heard him; the old man had let the wind blow for them and now it was cooling the air and the ground. Xättin suggested that they go inside to see what would follow the wind.

They went inside the hut and waited until the rain broke.

Then Father said 'Du-//hu, I think you told me that you were returning home. I heard that you were seated on the ground.'

The spring of 1874 was wet. Soon after ≠Kasing and !Kweiten ta //ken's children arrived at The Hill from Wellington, Bleek made his way to the library on a rainy day, quite against Dr Stewart's orders. He went to take the keys from the chief librarian, Thomas Maskew, to save him the trouble of making the building secure in the evening and opening it up in the morning. Maskew's eldest son was mortally ill, and although Bleek was not particularly fond of the chief librarian, he felt for him. He and Jemima had lost two children of their own.

Jemima blamed the rain for the cold he brought home with him. Wilhelm was coughing for weeks.

Summer brought more trouble still. The landlord of The Hill, struck by the 'mania' for selling property then sweeping through Cape Town, gave the Bleeks and the Lloyd sisters notice to leave their home of five years. With their situation uncertain, and money tighter than ever in the Bleek household, ≠Kasing, !Kweiten ta //ken and the children all left for /Xam-ka !au in the first two weeks of 1875, exactly seven months after they had all come down together from the Northern Cape. !Kweiten had contributed less than 200 pages of material during her stay, but since his return ≠Kasing had contributed nothing at all.

He had given important information on specific details of life in /Xam-ka !au, identifying medicinal plants *found in the hut of a Bushman sorcerer*, for example, but unlike Dia!kwain it seemed that he did not feel especially comfortable in the transcription sessions. It seems that he was not a practised narrator, at any rate, and Lloyd and Bleek were either unwilling or unable to stop him from going home. He and his wife were very keen to go back to the Northern Cape, despite the real dangers that their home now held and the privations that they would inevitably suffer there.

Dia!kwain stayed, as homesick as he clearly was. His wife had left him, his parents were dead and he was not certain where his children were. Mowbray seemed more attractive than the constant threat and hunger that now defined life in /Xam-ka !au. He was treated with respect at The Hill and he and the Lloyd/Bleek family were genuinely fond of each other.

If he stayed he would not be wanting for conversation with /Xam-speakers, either; as his sister and her husband prepared to leave, Lucy and Wilhelm heard excellent news from //Kabbo. The old man had sent word through one of Bleek's associates, a landowner in the Northern Cape called Devenish, that he intended to come back to the Cape Peninsula and continue the work he had left off the year before. Lloyd and Bleek were delighted; they considered //Kabbo a 'mine' of information, and if he brought his wife with him then they would have the testimony of someone who would surely remember the myths, rites and beliefs pertaining to women.

Dia!kwain stayed in Mowbray as the Bleeks and the Lloyd sisters discussed whether or not they should buy their house from their landlord. It would certainly make things easier, Jemima argued, if they had somewhere of their own. Still harbouring dreams of travel, Wilhelm argued that he did not want to be tied to anywhere permanently, but eventually conceded that if they *were* going to buy somewhere then it must not have a thatched roof, since the fire risk to the texts and manuscripts in his library was too great.

Finally the state of Wilhelm Bleek's health decided them.

The Hill was a damp, airless place and hardly ideal for an occupant with consumption. Instead of buying it, they would rent somewhere else.

Their landlord was not the only man on the Peninsula selling his property, however. When Charlton House came up for sale, a big house in Mowbray on the other side of the road from Cape Town to Rondebosch, about ten minutes' walk away, it looked as if they might have found a splendid compromise. In fact, considering their unique circumstances, it was almost perfect. In February 1875, at the height of summer, they bought it and moved in.

With a conservatory running along the side of the house and a bright drawing room quickly identified by Bleek as the perfect place in which to take breakfast, Charlton House was larger and squarer than The Hill. Its corners were firmer and its roof, happily, was tiled. It was a little grander than their old place but every bit as welcoming, a whitewashed building with shuttered windows and an elegant *stoep* approached via a tree-lined drive that ended in a loop around a single tree. Behind the house was a lawn bounded by eucalyptus trees where children could play and people living in shelters could have some privacy.

For a next-door neighbour they had the eminent astronomer Sir Thomas Maclear, an old man regarded as something of an institution in Cape Town having recently retired as Astronomer Royal after more than forty years of service. Jemima came to develop a great deal of affection for Maclear, first known to Bleek as the senior of the Grey Collection's trustees, who had already helped Wilhelm and Lucy in their researches by providing the Latin names of heavenly bodies identified by their /Xam 'informants' at the observatory down the incline. Thanks to him we know that the dastardly lions Belt and Mat were the pointers to the Southern Cross, Castor and Pollux were the Eland's Wives and Orion's Belt was the Three Female Tortoises Hung on a Stick.

There are pages and pages of myth, ritual and belief concerning the stars in the notebooks, although they amount to only a fraction of the material contained in the 7,200 half-pages and eighty-four books Lloyd and Bleek had filled when they moved house. From the translated texts there were some 11,000 words to be indexed for the Bushman–English dictionary that Wilhelm was preparing, ready to be cut out on individual scraps of paper and reassembled alphabetically for the printers in Cape Town.

Maclear may have been happy to have the Bleeks and the Lloyd sisters as his neighbours but he was not so pleased to have Dia!kwain so close. *Disgusting trespass in the Paddock . . . The person, a Bushman of Dr Bleek's . . . I always dreaded the proximity of Dr Bleek's Bushmen*, he recorded in his diary less than two months after they moved to Charlton House. There were certainly others who considered the transplant of 'wild' human beings into Mowbray, a square of rural England grafted on to the Cape Peninsula, as somewhere between curious and dangerous.

The move was made without too much damage to Wilhelm Bleek's fragile health – although he still wore himself out in an effort to save his wife and her sisters from 'fatigue' – but barely a month after they were settled, he learned that his mother had died in Bonn at the age of seventy-two. Jemima thought it fortunate in the circumstances that her husband, who was heartbroken, had a new home to distract him. The two put their minds to Charlton House and its gardens.

Despite the series of colds he had suffered, the stress of moving house and the news of his mother's death, Wilhelm's health actually began to improve as the autumn of 1875 set in. Jemima fell pregnant in April and Wilhelm returned to his *Comparative Grammar of South African Languages*, readying the second part for publication. The first had won him plaudits across the whole of Europe and had made him famous in academic circles. When he put it aside to concentrate on the language of the /Xam it had been considered an eccentric decision in the extreme: what could anyone possibly learn from a people whose system of numbering ended at three?

Academia's incomprehension did not bother Bleek in the slightest, since he believed that the work recording the /Xam language and its cultural expressions was the most valuable thing he could hope to achieve in his life. He was convinced that the material would answer questions about the origins of the speech and history of the human race: science would thank him in the future. None the less, twenty-five years after he had begun his research into southern African languages, his *Comparative Grammar* still ran to only one of the three parts he had intended, and with Lucy Lloyd concentrating on the /Xam project he wanted to get something actually completed before his death. His sore lungs were a persistent reminder that his time was short.

Everyone believed that the move had done Wilhelm good, despite all the bad news and anxiety he had been forced to endure, and his constitution seemed more robust than it had for some time. It did not seem that the winter would be especially troubling for him that year. Following Dr Stewart's advice to go to work in the library at eleven o'clock rather than at half-past nine so as to avoid the *raw morning air*, and coming home on the three o'clock rather than the four o'clock train to get out of the winter damp and cold before evening, it seemed as if he had found a way to protect his fragile health and still work productively.

Dead people who come out of the ground are those of whom my parents used to say, that they rode the rain, because the thongs with which they held it were like the horse's reins, they bound the rain. Thus they rode the rain, because they owned it. Therefore people say, when there is a big rain, that the sorcerer has gone to loosen the thong.

Then the rain falls and increases, where first a little rain leg has passed by. The rain liquid it is which comes from the clouds. It is that that the people call the Rain's leg, when it does not rain everywhere.

Kumm:

*The two brothers of the Early Race
who hunted lions*

In the time of the Early Race there lived two brothers who hunted lions. Hunting lions for food was hardly safe, that's true, but the people of the Early Race were foolish, remember, and didn't understand things well.

These brothers hunted with throwing sticks, knobkerries, made from the thigh bones of animals. The elder brother made his from the bones of elephants and giraffes, large enough to break the skull of even the biggest lion, and the younger brother made his from ostrich bones. A lion would charge and the brothers would throw their knobkerries at its head with all their strength; any lion would fall after a blow from a giraffe's bone but sometimes the two would carry on beating the animal they had hit until they saw blood coming from its ear just to make sure it was dead. Lions are clever creatures and sometimes they would be faking. It was a good idea to be sure.

One day they left the camp to hunt and came across a lion before they'd even found any tracks. He saw the two brothers at the same moment they saw him and in a heartbeat he charged them. The elder brother threw his elephant-bone knobkerrie and hit the lion in the face, knocking him down, and the younger brother threw his ostrich bone to finish the animal off. The two butchered it right there in the veld and carried the meat home to the younger brother's wife and children.

Again, the brothers went hunting. Soon they found the tracks of two lions. They were the spoor of a lion and a lioness, and they were fresh. They began to creep along them, right up to the lions themselves. The animals saw them and charged them.

And the elder brother knocked down a lion while the younger brother knocked down a lioness. And they cut up the lions. They carried them to the hut where they unpacked the meat, sliced it, and hung it on the bushes to dry. And then they went out to hunt again.

Again they found the tracks of a lion, and they followed the tracks until they found the lion that laid them. The lion charged them.

And the elder brother threw, hitting the lion, while his younger brother also knocked down that lion. And they cut up that lion.

They took the meat home, they unloaded it, they sliced it, and they put it to dry.

And they did it again, when day broke, they went hunting again.

They found the tracks of a pair of lions and followed them until they came across the animals that made them, both asleep. The lions woke up and charged them. One tried to seize the elder brother but he hit it in the face with his elephant-bone knobkerrie, beating it through. The brothers killed both of the lions, butchered them there in the veld and took the meat home to slice and dry in the sun.

Then the elder brother stayed at home while his younger brother went hunting alone. His younger brother went hunting, he did not say he had yet seen a lion.

Careful.

He hunted, he hunted, he hunted.

He went a long way through the dusty scrub and the reflective grass of /Xam-ka !au before he found any spoor in the red soil.

He hunted, he hunted, he hunted.
    And he found lions, and the place was not near. And he went and saw lions. And the lions charged him. And he did this because when he wanted to do as he always did, he threw, hitting the bone on the lion's head.

    Back at the camp the elder brother felt a wind. This was his brother's lion-killing wind, he thought, the one that always blew when they had killed lions together. Everybody is born with a wind.
    He sang:

> *O my little brother*
> *My little brother's wind feels like this*
> *When he seems to have killed a lion.*

    But the younger brother's children thought differently. They said that their father's wind was like this because a lion had killed *him* – this wasn't a hunter's wind blowing because he had made a kill but the wind that struck itself up to blow away a dead man's footprints.
    Their uncle wouldn't hear them.
    Many nights passed and the younger brother didn't come home, and still the elder brother sang that it was his brother's lion-killing wind that blew. The children told him again: *Father's wind feels like this when a lion seems to have killed him.*

And their uncle said: *Oh dear, leave off! Why do you speak like this? Your father does not come back because there are two lions. That is why he will not come. He does so because he seems still to be slicing lion's meat, because he wants it to dry. He will come.*

Many nights passed, and the man continued to sing. The children's mother said to the children: *We will go away, for a lion must have killed Father. You see that Father does not come, and a lion must have killed him. Therefore let us go, Uncle will quietly stay there, we will go, he can stay there quietly at the hut.*

And they left. The mother left her brother-in-law and the children left their uncle alone at the door to his shelter; night fell and he sang.

> *O my little brother*
> *My little brother's wind feels like this*
> *When my little brother has killed a lion.*

And he saw stars. Curious stars, floating low, where stars didn't go. *Brother, brother, can these be stars?* he said. And he sang:

> *My younger brother's wind feels like this*
> *When he has killed a lion.*

He said: *Brother, brother, what can that be? Stars must be shining above me.* He sang again and then he said: *Brother, brother, what is it that stars are shining above me?* while the lions' eyes shone as they approached him, because there were two lions, walking a dead man's tracks back to his camp, as they had been since the younger brother's ostrich bone had left his hand only to break on a carnivore's hard skull.

And the lions heard him singing there. And as he was singing and looking out there, he saw the lion's eyes shining, approaching him. Then he said they were stars. The lions seized him, while he thought they were stars.

He cried, *Ai, ai, ai, auuuuu.* One of the lions dragged him out of the hut and bit him to death.

And the lion carried him off, the lion took him away; the lions took him away; the lions went and ate him up. When the lions seemed to have finished him, the lions went.

!Khwe a tsu !kung-so:

The North Wind

Everybody is born with a wind.

The northeast wind, *!kauöken*, was the mountain wind. The northwest wind, *!khweten /ne ta //k'hwi //xuï*, lay in the quagga's knuckle. *!Kauä*, the east wind, was cold and stiff. The southeast wind lay on the east wind's horn. The west wind blew the rainclouds away; the south wind blew from 'above' and raised dust.

!Khwe a tsu !kung-so, the north wind, was the most pleasant wind of all; it blew from *underneath*, from the Kalahari over the Orange River, pushing rainclouds before it and blowing dust into the sky. *!Khwe a tsu !kung-so* was Dia!kwain's wind. He said that there was no wind as nice. It was warm as it blew the cold east wind away when he had killed an ostrich, letting him lay down his *kaross* of hartebeest skin. The north wind was Dia!kwain's father's wind too. It always blew when Xättin hunted springbok.

The wind blowing at your birth had a certain temperature, or direction, and it was your wind for life. When a hunter made a kill on the hunting ground the *!gi* – the energy or 'potency' – in the animal he killed interacted with his wind and made it blow.

When a man kills something, he is cold, his wind is cold. When he kills anything, he is cold, for the thing's wind is not a little cold. So people say: 'Our brother there, his wind feels like this when he makes a kill, his wind is so cold.'

There was another time your wind blew, too. The elder brother, desperate in his heartbreak, misread this other wind for his little brother's lion-killing wind.

The wind blows when we die; for, we who are people, we have wind; our clouds come out when we die. So when we die the wind blows dust, because it intends to blow away our tracks, with which we had walked about, while we still had nothing the matter with us. Our spoor which the wind intends to blow away, they would still be plainly visible. For it would seem as if we still lived.

It is no surprise that on the death of a /Xam person the wind arrived to remove their footprints.

/Xam trackers were skilled enough to recognize the prints of an animal shot amongst its herd and then follow it out of the mass to where it lay dying. As with all hunter cultures, the skill of tracking was of fundamental importance to the /Xam-ka !ei, a people for whom tracks were not merely arrows pointing to a source of protein but part of a great and complex web of *signs* that wrote themselves across the landscape and into the lives and bodies of those capable of understanding them. These signs were auspices, 'omens' in the flights of moths and beetles, the behaviour of springbok and kudu, shooting stars, sensations in the body, the noises and smells of the veld. Significance could be found anywhere and all these signs were useful, in their own ways, as clues offered by an unforgiving, difficult place to be acted on to the benefit of the survival prospects of those skilled at interpretation.

You made signs, too. Everywhere you went you wrote yourself into the landscape with tracks that were unique to you.

The same beliefs that found ritual expression in the proscription of the hunter crossing the spoor of the poisoned eland and saw engraved and painted prints of lion and eland, and ten-toed rain creatures marching into rivers and springs on stone surfaces across southern Africa, saw human tracks as *evidence*, material and spiritual. Only living creatures leave tracks and you were not truly dead until the ephemeral marks you left in the course of your progress through your days had gone.

It was the last task of your wind to take them.

Kumm:

The origin of death

The Moon is bad tempered, and sinister, and means you ill. If you look at the Moon when you've struck an animal with a poisoned arrow he'll send dew like liquid honey to cool the animal's wound and the poison will be no stronger than water.

The Moon's water is that which cures it. And the animal lives, on account of it.

And should you look the moon in the face between killing and butchering the animal you've shot, he'll eat the fat and your kill will be lean.

The Moon travels all night. He doesn't stop, and if you look at him when you're hunting then the game won't stop either. Putting your hands on an animal that night will be as difficult as putting your hands on the Moon himself, who will guide the game you're stalking to a place where there's nothing for you to drink, and there you'll die of thirst.

And never laugh at him.

You seem to think that the Moon has forgotten. Yet it knows; it understands when people are talking at their houses.

Even though far off, it will become angry and will enter the sky because it wishes darkness to lie upon the people, so that people would not be able to see the ground as the ground would be dark. As its anger becomes cool, it gently goes out, when the people are asleep. And when they awake, they see it, standing brightly and making the earth light.

The people say to each other: 'You are the ones that laughed at the old

man, and when you do, that is what the old man will do – he becomes
angry when he hears people laughing at him. For people will laugh, they
look at him and they say that his stomach has become black. This is why
he goes into the sky angrily, for he wants us to lie in darkness.'

For darkness resembles fear, when trees do not stand in brightness so that
people become afraid of the trees. The trees with darkness in them.

Why is the Moon's stomach black? Because that's where
he carries the dead. The Sun chases the Moon with a knife,
cutting away at him until there's nothing but his spinal cord
left, and he passes over the night sky with */nu !ke* – the spirits
of the dead – sitting in the gap. It isn't a lucky time to be
under the Moon, then, with a crescentful of corpses passing
overhead.

Mother spoke, she said: 'The Moon is carrying people who are dead. You can
see for yourself how it lies, and it lies hollow, because it is killing itself by
carrying people who are dead. This is why it is hollow. It is not a //kaura, for
it is a bad Moon, threatening. You can expect to hear something when the
Moon lies like this. Someone has died.'

The Moon has always had to do with death. He created death,
and so we can blame him that we die – although the Moon
himself would blame the Hare.

This is what the Hare did in the time of the First at Sitting
People and how we all came to die.

The Hare wept and wept and wept because his mother was
dead. He was such a foolish man that he did not know that
everyone who died came back again, as surely as the Moon
disappeared every month and came back a sliver. He wept and

wept until the Moon eventually told him to stop, but he still wouldn't listen.

'My mother's dead!' he cried. 'She's dead and she's not coming back!'

Inconsolable.

The Moon explained that he didn't need to weep because his mother was not *altogether* dead. She meant to come back from her death; everybody did. It was called *sleep*. The Hare, however, replied that *he was not willing to be silent; for he knew that his mother would not again return alive. She was altogether dead.*

'Listen to me,' said the Moon. 'She's going to come back.'

But the Hare wouldn't listen, no matter how many times the Moon told him. He just continued to weep, refusing to hear sense, until finally the Moon struck his mouth, splitting it.

He spoke. The mother-hare lay dead. The Moon said: 'Yes little Hare. Cry strongly, mother will not return for mother is truly dead. Mother dies, mother shall die away entirely. You, my children, do miss mother; do not miss me.'

This is how the Moon spoke: 'I die, I again become the new Moon. Hare dies, man dies entirely. His children miss him. I die, I return alive. The Sun pierces me. I return, alive. Do not miss me, my children. The Sun stabs me with his knife. I die, I speak as I am dying, because, while I die, I am yet alive. The Sun cuts one part of me with his knife. Then I speak quickly: "O Sun! Leave the spinal cord for the children." And so the Sun leaves it. He spares the spinal cord because I spoke.

'Then I limp back feebly. Then it is the other half of my chest. Then my other side lives; I die away while my one side lives. My other side decays. With the side that is whole I walk. Then I return home to the children and then they see it, as it comes up. The see that it is the Moon's side, the other side. Then my stomach stands on it because it really becomes another Moon now.

'That Moon is whole, because I am a new Moon.

'Then I stand opposite the Sunset sky, when I am a crescent Moon. When I am merely the Moon's side. And I really do live, for I feel that I really will return alive. I will become a new Moon. Then I lighten the earth a little and I lighten the bushes a little. I feel that I am shining brightly upon the bushes, because I am the one who is used to acting in this fashion. This is how I speak. The Sun will then agree with me and I am then likely to return again, alive. I have always done so.'

This is what the Moon says: 'When a man dies, he is really dead.'

He speaks thus: 'Thus Hare should cry really very much, for mother has really gone. As for me, I shall die, but I shall return again, living, so that I might stand again opposite the evening sun.'

He says: 'When I die, really I grow, opposite dawn. When man does, he really goes!'

Thus speaks the Moon. He speaks because the Mantis made him speak.

The Moon cursed all the people because of the Hare, the foolish man who wouldn't listen.

'I had intended that you who are men should resemble me and do the things I do; that I do not altogether dying go away. You who are men are those who did this deed. I had thought to give you joy. The Hare, when I intended to tell him about it – while I felt that I knew that the Hare's mother had not really died, for she slept – the Hare was the one who said to me that his mother did not sleep; for his mother had altogether died.'

If the Hare had assented to the Moon then we who are people should have resembled the Moon. The Hare's doings were those on account of which the Moon cursed us, and we die altogether.

We got off lightly compared with the Hare. He became a timid thing, afraid to go about other people, wild, with his lip split for ever. Years later the /Xam-ka !ei would hunt him and eat him, leaving his thighs which were still human flesh like theirs. Their dogs would chase him. He would spring away and double back, and when the dogs caught him they would tear him to pieces and he would die – really die, altogether dead, for good. He would lie in bare places, not in bushes or under trees, and he'd be infested with lice. No matter how much he shook his head as he ran, he'd never shake the lice loose.

Having said this, the Moon remained silent; he never spoke about it again.

/Nu !ke:

The Dead

George Stow sent Wilhelm Bleek a copy of a rock painting made in a cave on the steep side of the right bank of the Lower Black Kei River, an hour's walk from a farm called Upper Longreach. He copied eleven of the figures in a shelter full of hippo, dancers and eland.

The man in the top right-hand corner of the copy sits with his knees raised. The two spindly figures below him are bent double at the waist and the others are either in the same position, bent double at their waists, or standing on all fours with parti-coloured backs and bodies, spotted or striped. One of them seems to have feathers. Dia!kwain said of this picture: *People killed by lightning. Spotted skins are cheetah skins, the others springbok.*

In this sentence both 'killed' and 'lightning' are metaphors: they are shamans, *!gi:ten*, 'dying' in the dance that propelled a person to the world of the spirit.

As a young man Dia!kwain once went a whole month without killing a springbok with his first shot. His aim had been off so consistently that it had become uncanny. He could not explain it.

At the end of the month he hit a springbok, breaking its leg. As he made towards the animal to finish it he saw it get up and lick the break as though it were grazing. It raised its head to look at him, calling aloud, looked away, and then

licked itself again. It hobbled from him as he approached and
it was still alive when he came to it. He killed it and carried
the meat home to Mietche, his first wife.

When he got home and told her how the animal had
behaved, she asked him why he hadn't left it alone. What was
he supposed to have done? he asked. It was obviously going
to die once he'd shot it, and they had to eat. Of course he
couldn't have left it. She reminded him that it had been weeks
since he'd killed a springbok outright; the animals weren't
letting themselves be killed.

The springbok were offering presentiments of death, she
said, and the two of them could expect to hear news of it
soon. Dia!kwain said nothing.

He went out into the veld to hunt again and spent the night
in the open, waking in the *morning's mouth* to see a herd of
gemsbok not far off. He began to stalk them. Although they
could not have seen him they seemed to be aware of him and
kept looking in his direction as he crept closer. When they
ran off towards the dry watercourse behind the hill known as
the Spitzkop, Dia!kwain made for the other side, thinking to
head them off. He came down to the watercourse and stole
along it as quietly as he could but the gemsbok seemed to
know he was coming and turned into the wind, away from
him. Then he just sat down in the riverbed to watch them,
curious as to what they would do.

They ran away. They had not seen him – they simply ran.
Dia!kwain decided to let them go.

Su !kuiten:ta, Snore White Lying, an old man whose
mother had been a healer, had been watching him from the
top of the Spitzkop. His mother had been a very fair-skinned
woman who healed people by lying down beside them when
she snored them, a method that eventually earned her the

mistrust of her neighbours. Her son had inherited the name
that described her complexion and her curing technique.

Dia!kwain saw him sitting on the hilltop and went to speak
to him. They discussed the gemsbok, and the behaviour of
the springbok that would not let themselves be killed, and then
they started for home together, the younger man eventually
leaving the older behind.

When he arrived back at his shelter Mietche was gasping,
taking breath *with a puff-adder's ribs*, with difficulty and in pain.

*She was breathing as if she were seeking her heart, panting, for she felt as if
she could not perceive her heart when she breathed.*

He asked Mietche what was making her take breath with
such pain and she replied that it felt as if something were
sticking in the hollow on the back of her neck. Something
had hurt her, she knew, but she did not know precisely what.
Her arms had become so weak that she had not had the
strength to hold their youngest child to her breast. Truë, their
eldest daughter, had been holding the baby there. Soon Su
!kuiten:ta arrived and reminded Dia!kwain of the springbok;
the younger man asked him what he should do, as there wasn't
even cow's milk to hand for the baby. Su !kuiten:ta replied
that all they could do was to wait and see.

Mietche died at dusk.

After the funeral the next afternoon, as he walked across
the vast salt pan known as the Deception Pan with his mother
and his sisters !Kweiten ta //ken, /A:kumm and Whai:ttu,
Whai:ttu saw a girl sitting in the open a little way off. She was
right in the middle of the salt pan, looking in the direction of
the funeral ground. She didn't move.

'Look!' Whai:ttu said. 'Is that a little girl sitting over there?'

!Kweiten thought there was, adding that it seemed as if the little girl was wearing the cap that Mietche used to wear while she was alive.

No one recognized the little girl and no one greeted her, which would have been unthinkable at any other time. Instead they carried on towards Whai:ttu's place, leaving the little girl under the sun, looking in the direction of the grave.

As they walked, Dia!kwain's mother /Ko:ang reminded them that this was what the *angry people* did when they had just taken someone away. The people she was referring to were the sour *!gi:ten*, jealous of the living, who would shoot sickness sticks into people or sit in them in the shape of a moth or an owl and eat them from the inside. She reminded her son and her daughters that once the angry people had taken someone they would show you who they had, just to be sure that you had seen. There really was someone sitting there, wearing Mietche's cap.

Ghosts did not necessarily appear as the image of their living body and interpretation was called for.

And we went to their home. And we talked there for a little while.

As the sun began to set Dia!kwain thought about going home and decided that he would go the way he had come, across the salt pan, to see if the girl was still there. He looked carefully as he went but when he came to the place where he thought that she had been sitting, there was no one. He had thought that they might have been mistaken that afternoon, that it could have been a bush, but the space where she had sat was empty. There was nothing there at all.

I saw that I did not perceive it, at the place where it had sat. And I agreed that it must have been a different kind of thing.

*For my mothers used to tell me that when the !gi:ten take us away, at
the moment when they intend to take us quite away, that is when our friend
is right before us, while he wants us to see him, because he feels that he still
thinks of us. So his outer skin still looks at us, because he feels that he does
not want to go away and leave us. The part of him with which he still
thinks of us: that is what comes before us.*

A herd of springbok was lying on Dia!kwain's wife's grave
the next morning, and Dia!kwain remembered that they had
never stopped there before.

*And Snore White Lying said, now I could see why the springbok which I
had shot had been behaving so strangely.*
    However, we should not go on talking about it, but should be silent.

Everyone and everything that dies – Boers, Bushmen, black
people, *ostriches, gemsbok, the things that the Bushmen have shot,
as also the Bushmen that other men have shot* – go to a great hole
as wide as the distance between the Breakwater and Table
Mountain. Once you were dead and buried you walked the
path of the !Khwe //na s'o !kwe, the people of the Early
Race, to this great hole where you would live and walk
around, while your heart went into the sky and became a star.
    !Gi:ten went through the waterpit, metaphorically and liter-
ally passing through !Khwa into the realm of the dead; there
they would fight maleficent spirits and effect healing. Otherwise they could snore them out of the sick person in the world
of the living and fight them there:

*He kills the other who has bewitched us. He makes the other go from the
place out of which he snores him . . . When he has beaten him to make him*

soft, he scoops him up with the earth on which he has pounded him soft, he beats him away.

The waterpit was both the body and the home of !Khwa, a place of transformation and creation, as /Kaggen's sister the Blue Crane and the first eland would attest. It was a place to dip up water and a meniscus pierced to reach the dead, a place of great spiritual and material importance.

Although living shamans knew ways to enter the world of the dead it took great tolerance to pain and disorientation, since the process of producing and controlling the *!gi* you needed for the journey was not a simple matter at all. It took skill and practice and it was no shame if you discovered you were not up to the task and ended your shamanic training before you were 'qualified'. Everybody understood how difficult and frightening it could be.

You had to die to visit the dead; this was not an easy thing.

Dr Stewart had work to do in the middle of June 1875.

Some old friends of the Lloyd sisters from Natal days were in Cape Town that winter and in some kind of *great trouble*. Wilhelm Bleek did everything he could to help them, not just because they were old friends of his wife but *on the common ground of humanity*. His efforts caused him to be detained in Cape Town an hour later than was usual for two days running, and he complained that the short walk home from the train station was particularly damp and cold. Within a couple of days he was housebound with another cold, serious enough for Jemima to call the doctor to Charlton House. A few days later, on 24 June, the patient was up and about and thought himself well enough to return to the library.

Inevitably he was coughing up blood the next morning. Although Bleek's life was not threatened he was sufficiently unwell to make Dr Stewart anxious and it was not until July that he declared him fit to go back to work. There was no reason that Wilhelm should not return to the library, Stewart said, but from now on he should go outside only when the weather was *congenial*.

On 17 July, Wilhelm returned to work at the library and continued to travel into Cape Town whenever the winter weather allowed it. On very rainy days he simply stayed at home. He was generally well, but *tho' he had so far recovered, there were many little things about his health and ways which kept me very anxious and made me look with painful longing for our trying winter weather to be over, and the dry summer warmth to come and do him good*, Jemima later wrote.

There was a word for people who had passed on but still retained a particular kind of influence on the affairs of the living: /nu !ke. It translates to 'spirit people', although this does not quite capture the sense in the /Xam. The word /nu had associations with age, spirit and death. Dia!kwain said that his mother.

used to tell me that the /nu !ke were those who had been game sorcerers. When they died their thoughts, with which they had been !gi:xa and worked magic, continued, although they died and we did not see them; still their magic doings went about here.

Their magic doings are like a person who always lives, they do not altogether die; thus he still lives in his !gi.

/Ko:ang, Start Back, would beat the ground with a stone

when she wanted to call the attention of the /*nu* !*ke*. She could not see them, of course, but she knew that they were listening. When her husband could not find anything to kill, she would call upon *her sorcerers who had owned game* and speak to them: Xättin had climbed the *brinkkop* with his son to call upon his old teacher !Nuin /kuïten to the same end.

As Start Back beat the ground with a stone she would say 'My /*nu* !*ke*, have you forgotten about me? When you had bodies you used to talk to me, as if you loved me. *But it seems as if you had in dying taken your thoughts away from me.* While you still thought of me you would send my husband some creature for him to kill, something old and lean. I didn't mind, because it came from you; I knew that.'

That is what Mother kept telling us, the /nu !ke would first give us an old thing, we must eat it first. Later they would give us something good.

About 100 kilometres from //Kabbo's Bitterpits are a few high hills where there are thousands of engravings of eland, giraffe, ostrich, inexplicable pictograms and the tracks of a family of seven-toed creatures so perfectly executed that it has been seriously suggested that they are fossil prints disproving evolution. They are not, of course; there are engravings like these loping into watercourses and pools in many places in southern Africa.

These engravings are found on the slopes of a high, broad hill that affords a spectacular view of the flat red and brown earth, low scrub and quivertrees all around. It is very tempting to walk on them in order to see them all – which you must not do, no matter how enthusiastic your guide might be for you to follow them. Your shoes take off some of the dark desert patina with every step you make, destroying the things you have come to see. Engravings are made by an artist cutting or chipping through this patina to reveal the lighter rock below it and they are more fragile than they look.

Chipping, cutting and the soles of walking shoes are not the only way that the patina is removed, however. On the north and east of the hill, where it is easiest to find shade in the late afternoon, the brown rock is punctuated by white patches where seeds have been ground over many thousands of years. In some places, flat-bottomed grindstones have been left sitting on their 'pestles' more than a century after the last women to use them went to find water or work.

A short, steep walk from here on one of the hill's crests there are stretches of smooth, level rock where rainwater collects in natural depressions and hollows. About the water pools between the boulders and ledges on the hill's crest are other white patches, made not by grinding but by pounding. The purpose here was not kitchen work but ritual, as Dia!kwain's mother /Ko:ang would have recognized.

This is where her */nu !ke*, her old, long-gone spirit people, would have been called from the ground by the pounding of stones.

All people become spirit people when they die. My grandfather used to say, spirit people. He said, You have uttered for us the old people's names, as if the old people were not dead people, and they come to harm us on account of it, because they do not possess their thinking strings[1] with which they understood.

Therefore they are wanting to come and harm us, if we utter their name

---

[1] *//Khu//khuken*: the /Xam-ka !ei believed that the seat of thought was in the neck, evidenced by the pulsing of the arteries. These were the *thinking strings*.

by night. And, we dream about them, if we utter their names by night.[1]
They (that is, the children) do not utter their names by night, for, when the
sun is high, then, they utter their names.

As July 1875 gave way to August, Dia!kwain was unusually
preoccupied with death. It had been a difficult winter for him.
He was terribly homesick – //Kabbo had still not arrived, as
he had said he would – and had developed a worryingly
persistent cough that only worsened as the winter wore on.

Although he was not a particularly morbid man by any
means, every *kumm* of any length recorded that winter had
something to do with mortality. As spring grew nearer Lucy
recorded that a dead person's gall sat green in the sky when
someone died and that when the Moon came *lying down*,
standing hollow in the sky, it was carrying dead people and
killing itself as it came. It could be a dangerous time.

You may expect to hear something when the moon lies in this manner.
Someone has died.

<hr />

[1] *Moon it is, when the place is light.*

Kumm:

*The dream which Dia!kwain had before he heard
of the death of his father*

30 July 1875:

When I was with a Boer I dreamt that my father and I were cutting up a sheep. The Boer came up to us as we were cutting it up and said that he would beat us to death. The dream told me that I asked the Boer not to kill us at once but to let us pay for it by working for him instead. For I did not want him to kill my father, I wanted to work off what my father owed for the sheep. I would work out both what I owed and what my father owed. And the dream said to me that I saw my father lying dead under the warm sun.

2 August 1875:

And I wept when I thought I saw that my father had died. And I asked the Boer, did he think it was such a big thing that we had killed, that he acted like this? He should have let us work it out and not have acted as he did.

And when day broke I arose and told my wife that a dream had told me we were cutting up a Boer's sheep. I saw Father standing there dead. I told her that she seemed to think we should not hear news of that which the dream told me. And the wind was in the north.

The north wind was his father's wind.

And I asked her did she not see that the sky looked as if it were going to rain? It was just as the dream had told me; dust was covering the sky. Therefore I should go and talk with the Boer, I should see what was happening that had made me dream of Father, that the Boer had killed us. The dream had told it to me, just as if a person had spoken.

Therefore we will go and listen at the huts, and see whether we do not hear news.

And Father's eye was blinking before I had gone, it ached as if rain were really going to fall. It was raining heavily, as I had told my wife. I said to my wife: 'You did not see how when I told you I was dreaming of Father, someone's eye was blinking there. The blinking eye of a someone who seems to be dying is there. That is why you see rainwater coming down like this. For you seem to think my dream was not clear. I shall see a thing which my dream told me about. I shall see it. Then you will see, although you did not agree with me when I told you the dream, and what the dream did to me.'

We returned home to where we lived with the Boer and we stayed there two nights. Then the next night Mother came to us there. And I asked her what was happening to the rainclouds, that they were coming up in front there just as if it were going to rain. For Father had said they acted like that when rain was going to fall. Therefore I wondered what was going to happen when the rainclouds did like this.

The wind blew, as if it were begging from me, just as the wind had done in my dream, when I dreamt about Father, that the Boer was killing us, because we had cut up his sheep; the Boer killed us, when the sheep bleated. The dream had told me this.

And Mother said to me, I seemed to have disbelieved the dream and to have thought I should see Father again, though the dream had told me I would not. Yet now I saw her, and she had come to tell us that Father had died, leaving us. That was why we saw that the clouds (Rain's hair) did not leave the sky, but stayed in the sky. And Mother asked me, did I not see that the dream I had dreamt had spoken the truth? Now we saw what had made me dream it.

So the dream I had told her about had not deceived me.

Then I asked Mother, what had happened to Father? And she said that it was his back, which he had always complained about to us, which he had died of. And Mother said, I seemed to think the springbok had not known when Father's heart fell, the springbok had not acted as if they saw us at the hut. The springbok had passed the hut as if they were not afraid. Mother did not know where the springbok came from.

'There were plenty, and they came and played as they approached the hut where Father lay dead. The springbok appeared to be moving away, and the wind really blew following them. They were running before that wind. It was really Father's wind and you yourself feel how it is blowing. You know it used to always to blow like that whenever Father was shooting game.'

Then I told Mother that I had felt the wind was blowing that way. I had known what was happening when I felt the wind, when the rain was falling on the ground. Then I was sure I should see something happen; I should feel the wind, I should see something.

I spoke to my wife and told her about it. I asked her whether she did not believe that I was feeling my inside aching. As the wind blew past I felt my inside biting. She seemed not to believe that I felt like that when one of my people was dying.

My inside always ached when it was one of my people.

/Xam-ka-!ke-ta !gwe:

'The Bushman's Letters'

As Dia!kwain described the dream that had told him of his father's death, Bleek worked on the *Bushman Dictionary* and the second part of his *Comparative Grammar of South African Languages*. That August the two men talked about George Stow's copies of rock art and Bleek even asked the /Xam man if he would make some drawings of his own. Dia!kwain smiled, seemingly *pleased*, but did nothing.

As Wilhelm walked to the back door on the way to the train station the next morning he found a little painting pinned to the wall in the back porch. It was of a family of four ostriches: a male, two females and a chick. Dia!kwain later drew a picture of the rain animal !Khwa-ka xoro in blue pencil, giving him tiny antlers like antennae and sticks for legs, and then three more in black.

5 August 1875:

The hair of our head will resemble clouds, when we die, when we in this manner make clouds. These things are those which resemble clouds, and we think that they are dead. We, who do not know, we are those who think in this manner, that (they) are clouds

We, who know, when we see that they are like this, we know that they are a person's clouds; (that they) are the hair of his head. We, who know, we are those who think thus, while we feel that we seeing recognize the clouds, how the clouds do in this manner form themselves.

On 12 August Mr Trimen, the caretaker of the South African Museum, came to Mowbray to see the copies of rock paintings that George Stow had sent. On the thirteenth, the chief clerk under the Secretary for Native Affairs, Mr Bright, came to see them too. On the fifteenth, Bleek was bright and well and spent the day in the company of a Polish botanist whom he had invited to Charlton House. He had a splendid day.

That night he did not sleep well but he was up early, *bright and happy and unusually busy* the next morning, writing the *Second Report* for Parliament on the progress of the Bushman Work, helping Jemima with the household's quarterly accounts and indexing the words of his *Bushman Dictionary* ready for Lucy to start pasting onto paper in final readiness for delivery to the printer. Wilhelm always breakfasted alone in the drawing room because it caught the morning sun, but he joined his wife, then pregnant, and her sisters for lunch and supper, and had the energy to play with his daughters in the evening.

Just before dinner, and then again just after he had eaten, Wilhelm complained that he was tired. He went to bed before his wife. She followed him at a quarter to eleven and the two of them chatted as she prepared the *little comforts* he might need in the night. At eleven she put out her candle, said goodnight, and lay down beside him.

But then, before either of us had fallen asleep, a want of power in moving his right arm attracted my attention, and I spoke to him, but received no answer. Striking a light I saw he was awake and looking at me, and that he tried to speak but could not. When he saw (or felt) that the effort was in vain, a sort of wondering half puzzled look came into his eyes and then a very sweet smile.

Jemima tried to get him to drink some wine and he did, but he did not speak. She wanted to go upstairs to fetch her sisters but was frightened to leave him alone. Very soon he began to be distressed: a violent sickness came over him and he began to breathe painfully, *with a puff-adder's ribs, as though he could not perceive his heart when he breathed.*

He did not speak but he was conscious enough to communicate to his wife that she should not distress herself; she thought that he was trying to calm her down for the sake of their unborn child. In one of the lulls in his sickness Jemima ran upstairs to fetch her sisters: Lucy, Frances and one of her half-sisters were then all living upstairs. One of them went to fetch Dr Stewart and the other, probably Lucy, stayed with Wilhelm, who soon found it so difficult to take a breath that eventually he was barely capable of any kind of communication at all.

Dr Stewart arrived at ten minutes past midnight. *He is very ill*, he said, and *There is nothing we can do*, a few moments after that. *Suffusion of the lungs was taking place owing to some internal haemorrhage caused by some weak place in his left lung having suddenly given way*, the doctor told Jemima. Wilhelm lay very still. The only movements he made were with his hand.

You must not think he is suffering, said the doctor. Bleek was already unconscious then, and dead by 2.15 a.m. He was forty-eight.

When you died and your heart fell down from your neck into your chest, a star fell too, to let everybody learn what it knew. People would see it and would prepare themselves to hear the news. The hammerkop knew what the falling star meant, and the bird would fly overhead, crying. People would say: 'Didn't you hear the hammerkop when the star fell? It came to tell us that someone close to us – *our person* – is dead.'

People would talk to each other, agreeing that the hammerkop was not something that came to deceive. It would not visit without the purpose lent it by what it knew. The hammerkop knew so much because it lived in a pool of water *in which we see all things; the things which are in the sky we see in the water while we stand by the water's edge. We see all things. The stars look like fires which burn.*

That was why when the women heard a hammerkop they would say to it: 'Go and plunge into the Orange River, where the stars stand in the water, because I know what you've come to tell me.' *That is the place where its stories should go in.*

Jemima wrote to Wilhelm's old patron Sir George Grey in Auckland, telling him of her husband's last hours.

So far as the awful suddenness with which this long impending blow fell would allow one to think or feel any thing, save pain, I think my chief thought (. . . dread at my poor little ones' waking hour and what must then come upon them too) was thankfulness that my darling had had so short a time to suffer.

But Oh dear Sir George, perhaps you can fancy what our empty home and life is now he has gone.

At more or less nine in the morning on Wednesday 18 August, a hearse and a single carriage left Charlton House for the Anglican cemetery in the village of Wynberg where Wilhelm was buried in the same grave as his son Ernst and his daughter Hermine. It was a private ceremony attended only

by Jemima Bleek, Lucy and Frances Lloyd, *and three gentlemen,*
one of whom was the Rev. Henry Tyndall.

A person who rains, who dies, the rain falls, taking away his footsteps, so
that his footsteps may no longer be there. The rain presently falling takes
away his footsteps when we have just put him in. When we have just put
him into the grave, and we are filling in the earth, the rain falls, before we
have covered it. Then the rain falls, falls, falls, and we cover it with bushes;
afterwards we cover it, laying the bushes upon the earth, when we intend to
heap on stones, to heap, laying stones upon the bushes; in order that the
bushes may also not be bare. Therefore, we heap on stones, shutting in the
bushes.

Bleek's obituary in the *Cape Argus* the next day said that had
the funeral not been private the ceremony would have been
attended by hundreds of people and that this *typical representa-*
tive of the German student and scholar would be missed *by the*
numerous friends in South Africa to whom his name was a household
word, but by whom his familiar visage shall be beheld no more.

Heartening, perhaps, but hardly compensation for the loss
that Jemima, her sisters and Dia!kwain had suffered. Although
not entirely unexpected, Wilhelm's death meant even more
insecurity for everyone at Charlton House. The Bushman
Work was threatened since the annual grants provided by the
colonial government to defray the costs – without which
the research was all but impossible – had been paid to an
internationally respected man of science with a doctorate and
not to a former schoolteacher with a gift for languages who

had gone out of her way to obscure her role in the project. Bleek had had to badger the government constantly to guarantee even that. With the loss of the £250 a year he had earned as custodian of the Grey Collection at the South African Public Library it did not look likely that the family would be able to afford to accommodate any /Xam speakers.

Dia!kwain had quite personal concerns of his own as well. He had lost one of the few people in his life with whom he could converse from day to day in his own language and it had been seven months since he had had the opportunity to speak to anyone with /Xam as their native tongue.

Since his sister !Kweiten ta //ken had left for /Xam-ka !au in January, no one had heard anything of either her or her husband ≠Kasing. He had been staying for the arrival of //Kabbo for more than seven months, alone and homesick, worried about the well-being of his sister and her children; in the past seven years they had spent a matter of months together.

Three days after Wilhelm's death he dictated a letter in /Xam to Lucy Lloyd, who translated it into English before sending it on to her associate Dr Meyer in Calvinia for him to forward.

Charlton House
Mowbray
Nr Cape Town
20th August 1875

From 'David Hoesar' (or Dia!kwain) to his sister 'Rachel' (or !Kweiten-ta-kein) wife of 'Klaas Katkop' and her family

I have been wanting to say, why can it be that Rachel and her family do not send me a letter? That I might hear whether they went to the place which they intended to return; as, in case that they had returned, they would have sent me a letter. Therefore I am thinking that I want to hear whether they have returned; for if they had returned, they would have told me, that I might know that they had got home. They must please speak to me.

Will Dr Meyer, when he has become well again, be so kind as to dispatch a letter to Middlepost, to Gert van Wyk; at whose place my sister 'Griet Lynx' (or Springbok-skin) used to live, that one of them may let me know whether they are still well there. They must let me know why it is that they do not seem as if they remembered me, that they do not speak to me, and why Rachel has not told me that she has returned home well – for, a silence reigns, if she has returned. Therefore, I know not why she has not told me that I might know that she has returned. Therefore, I desire that Dr Meyer, when he has become well again, will, at his good pleasure, allow Rachel and her family to know; that they may acquaint me, that I may know what has happened to them.

For, I had thought to return; my master, he was the one who told me that I should first wait a little, as he did not yet desire that I should return (home), going away from him; for, I had thought of returning. He, in August's Moon – that was the one in which he died, leaving us. Therefore, I know not what I shall still do about it; for, my mistress still weeps; – this is why it I still sit melancholy on account of it. ★

They must let me hear what they say. For, I still behold my mistress; therefore, I want them to let me know. For, I do not yet wish to leave my mistress, while she still weeps. For, a Husband (man) to give his consent to my going is not with my mistress.

So, these things they are those on account of which I first yet a little behold what she will do.

★*(ie on account of what has occurred.)*

Dead people, *!ke e /kuka*, were *old people*. Not because of their advanced age but because they had gone to the past.

!Ke e /kuka could come back as animals to see how their families were getting on. Soon after her father's funeral, Dorothea was woken up by a noise from her window, an owl calling with a noise something like breathing. She was frightened, alone in her room, and told her Aunt Lucy. Dia!kwain was delighted when he heard and told Lucy that this was no surprise.

It was Wilhelm Bleek come back to see *how his little children were getting on*, as of course he would. He loved his children.

A year before his death, Wilhelm had added a codicil to his will expressing his wish that Jemima should collect his manuscripts and philological papers and see to their publication. With Lucy in mind, the codicil finished:

I hereby gratefully acknowledge the great help she has been to me in my literary labours. But particularly I request her to continue and work well out our joint Bushman studies, in which her quicker ear and great industry has been of so important service to science. I appeal to all friends of science to assist her in such ways as they can in her work of collecting, working out, and publishing the records of this dying out race, the accurate knowledge of whose language and ways seems destined to solve some exceedingly important ethnological questions. So far to-day; other alternations may be noticed another day.

Signed
W. H. I. Bleek

With the reading of her brother-in-law's will, the course of Lucy Lloyd's remaining years was decided once and for all. The following decade, in particular, would be difficult and terribly frustrating for her.

Anything that hindered the *collecting, working out and publishing* with which she had been tasked, work she would do anything to accomplish, now stood in the way of solemn obligations to science and to the memory of her brother-in-law – but to fulfil these obligations she would have to contend with the hypocrisy and vanity of a respected member of the establishment.

Dr Langham Dale, the chairman of the Committee of the South African Public Library, was to self-regard what /Kaggen was to bad manners. Bleek had detested him and Lloyd would soon discover why.

Three days after Wilhelm Bleek's funeral the astronomer Sir Thomas Maclear called on Jemima and Lucy to offer his condolences as a neighbour, and to discuss the collection's security as senior trustee of the Grey Collection. He had been thinking about the immediate future, he said, and thought it urgent that they find a temporary custodian. Bleek's former position could be filled only by a qualified philologist, possibly from overseas. As it might be several months before a permanent replacement was appointed it was his hope that Lucy Lloyd would stand in.

Mrs Bleek is a very nice clever woman. I wonder how Bleek managed to capture her, he wrote later that day to Charles Fairbridge, a member of both the trustees of the Grey Collection and the Library Committee. Not that Wilhelm Bleek did not deserve her; rather she was *very nervous. I am under the impression that Bleek's sister in law Miss Lucy Lloyd, who was his secretary, would be the best temporary custodian of the Grey Collection,*

Maclear added. *She enjoys the repute of being a good linguist, particularly German of course.*

Maclear had his work cut out to convince the Committee of her merits since Lloyd did not have a university degree, she had little Greek or Latin and she was altogether too female. On the other hand, no one better understood Bleek's working methods or could navigate through the scrawl on his manuscripts; she would be perfect to ready things for Bleek's successor – or to mind the shop while they decided whether to appoint one or not. Dr Dale, the chairman, did not think that Bleek's work on languages and folklore from around the world had any place in his library at all.

Fairbridge apart, the Committee did not recognize the importance of Bleek's work. One member, a cabinet minister with a say in the colony's budget, had recently objected to the annual grant of £150 paid to Bleek by the government for his /Xam research, insisting that *the money would be far better spent in keeping the sons of three Kafirs at school* instead.

For his part Fairbridge had already suggested a permanent replacement for Bleek, an expert on the Nama dialect of the Khoe languages called Theophilus Hahn who ran a trading post in a sandblasted backwater north of the Orange River. He was known both to Bleek, having exchanged correspondence with him on the subject of Khoe languages, and to Fairbridge and Maclear, having visited the library some months previously when he had impressed them both with a memorable display of Nama click sounds. Aside from the man's facility with explosive consonants, however, Maclear told Fairbridge he *was ignorant of his attainments.*

They were few. Hahn had published next to nothing. He wrote a lot of letters, he was a linguist and he lived in southern Africa. He had little else going for him apart from his skill at generating controversy.

A few days after Maclear's visit to Charlton House, a joint meeting of the Committee of the South African Public Library and the Trustees of the Grey Collection was called. Immediately afterwards Dr Dale went to Mowbray with an offer for Lucy Lloyd: if she were willing she could complete the inventory of the Grey Collection begun by her brother-in-law and prepare the ground for Bleek's successor. She would be paid a half salary of £125 a year and Maskew, the chief librarian, would act as custodian.

Three committee members had been nominated to help her to index the Greek and Latin texts and Dr Dale gave his word that he would ensure that a government-funded Chair for Languages would be instituted, giving the Cape Colony a full-time professional tasked with research into southern African philology. The combined salaries of the curator of Grey's Collection and the Chair for Languages should be enough to tempt a properly qualified philologist from Europe to continue the work her brother-in-law had begun.

Deciding that the library work would occupy her only for a matter of months, Lloyd wrote to Dr Dale after his visit to explain that although a *specific branch of work entrusted to her fulfilment by the late Librarian of the Grey Collection* rendered her time *of double value* she would undertake to see printed the detailed inventories that Bleek had been unable to complete *through the want of assistance afforded to him in his labours* – a pointed dig at the Library Committee, who had never given him the support he had needed.

However, she specified certain conditions. She wanted to be trusted with the keys to the library (allowing her to set her own hours, the easier to continue her work with Dia!kwain) and the aid of a committee member, Professor Cameron, for her smooth settling in. She also required that *the duties of the correspondence of the Grey Library be entrusted to my execution.*

The Committee agreed to all her conditions, but for her the last was the most important. Like Dr Dale, a man quite proud of his belief in the superiority of European culture, Maskew, now acting custodian, was blind to the importance of Bleek's work. He saw no urgency in the task of collecting oral material from the world's indigenous peoples and Lloyd knew he would not write a single letter to that end if the correspondence were to be put in his charge.

In the archives of the South African Public Library there are letters in Lucy Lloyd's handwriting addressed from the South African Public Library and received from Madagascar, sub-Saharan Africa and the colonies of the Pacific. There are transcriptions of myths, descriptions of rituals and traditions and printed missionary texts collected by priests, officials and explorers; we can thank Lucy Lloyd for the preservation of Christian prayers from Umtata, testimony from Sembuland that she apparently translated herself, *A Collection of words used by the Natives about Lucla, that is at the head of the 'Great Bight' between South and West Australia* and Tasmanian *Legends of the Deluge*.

She did not have Bleek's analytical skills but she could save material for a successor who did – material such as the story of Madagascar's Lost Sons of God, Rakoriako and Ravao, boys sought by

the stones that were below the ground, or the trees that pervaded the earth, or the people who dwelt upon the earth, and the water and the beasts. Likewise the living creatures and the things without life, each and all things . . .

The story explains why dogs bark, why whales move ceaselessly and how we came to inherit the arrangement of roots and stones we have.

Dr Dale had wanted an end to this sort of thing in his library. He had not reckoned for Lloyd's capability or her dedication. Expecting a secretary he got a scientist; he took it quite personally.

Lloyd's /Xam texts already well outnumbered Bleek's in 1875, and the work of *collecting* material continued at Charlton House when Lloyd sat down with Dia!kwain and an open notebook three weeks after Bleek's death. Within days of that she put her mind to the *working out and publishing* of the material she already had.

Although Wilhelm Bleek had not made an entry into a notebook since the landlord of The Hill had given him notice to move house, he had been methodically consolidating the /Xam research and it was now up to Lucy to finish the manuscripts he had begun. The first of these tasks was the completion of the *Second Report Concerning Bushman Researches*, all but ready for publication on its author's death.

Like the first *Report* of 1873, the *Second Report* was an inventory of the transcriptions recorded in the notebooks categorized under 'Mythology', 'Fables', 'Legends' and 'Poetry', with sections headed 'The Mantis', 'Sun and Moon', 'Stars', 'Animal Fables', 'Legends', 'Poetry', and 'History (Natural and Personal)', all containing detailed descriptions of the indexed passages:

112. *Death. – The place to which the Bushmen go after death. The various ways of dying and being killed. A man is accidentally wounded by another, when they were both hunting springbok. Dialogue, in which the wounded man begs them to speak gently, not angrily, to the one who shot him. Unfortunate shots are believed to be due to such causes as the children at home*

playing on a man's bed, etc., and are ascribed to the remissness of wives. The dying man's last speech to his wife, in which he gives her advice, etc. The widow's lament, in which she says that she should like to cry herself to death; and does not want to eat food. Her mother-in-law comforts her. After the burial of the deceased, his widow returns home to her father, where her brothers receive her very well. She relates her sorrow to her family, and expresses her intention not to marry again, for fear of meeting with a husband who had not the good qualities of the deceased. A general conversation ensues, ending in an almost interminable description of springbok hunting, etc. . . .

Bleek had thanked her in the acknowledgements:

The valuable assistance which I have derived from the collections made for me (indicated by the letter L), as well as from the practical knowledge of the language acquired by the collector, may in some degree be understood by those who notice how great a share of the texts noted in my analysis bear that initial.

Again, the letter *L* was the only evidence of Lucy Lloyd's contribution.

On 16 December 1875, four months after her father's funeral, the last of Wilhelm and Jemima Bleek's daughters was born. Jemima called her Wilhelmine Henriette Anna after her father.

Christmas came, the family's first without Wilhelm, but the summer weather did nothing to improve the condition of Dia!kwain's chest. Nor was there any sign of //Kabbo or his wife //Kwabba–ang; Dia!kwain had been waiting for months, alone in Mowbray with only Lucy Lloyd to speak to in his own language, as cut off from his place and people as ever.

In February Lucy Lloyd received a letter from the Northern

Cape with the news that //Kabbo had died, and within days, missing the few relations he had left and the fugitive *kukummi* still available to him, Dia!kwain announced his intention to leave Charlton House.

Dr Stewart was called to examine the /Xam man's chest and found his lungs *seriously affected*, but no one could convince him to stay. A gentle man, popular with the children, he had become a valuable support to Jemima in her bereavement. Everyone was sad to see him go; although he promised that he would be back he was sick enough for Lloyd to worry that she would never see him again.

Dia!kwain did not die from lung disease.

He went first to Calvinia, a little town at the foot of the Hantam Mountains on the edge of the Karoo, where Lloyd helped him to find work with a farmer called Meyer. Today Calvinia is an eccentric, pretty place with some well-preserved Cape Dutch buildings but in 1876 it was little more than a collection of dusty roads, stockades and trading posts serving the fledgling sheep farms spread out across the flats. Meyer's farm was a wagon ride from here.

After a few months he left his wages with Meyer for safe-keeping and set off towards his old home near !Narries to see !Kweiten ta //ken and ≠Kasing. He intended to stay for three weeks and then come back to Charlton House via Meyer's farm, he told Meyer, but he vanished without ever fetching his money.

Lloyd heard nothing more of Dia!kwain for almost ten years, when two of his relatives, /Xam men known as Jan Plat and Friedrich Horlnoop, came to Charlton House. Jan Plat, being married to one of the daughters of Dia!kwain's sister Whai:ttu – Springbok Skin – was the closer relation.

When Lloyd asked him if he knew what had happened to Dia!kwain, he told her that they had left Calvinia together.

*We went out from Calvinia, we came to Zwartwater, we came to Louriet,
we travelling went to Rondeklip, we went out from 'Rondeklip', we went
to 'Forzefontein' . . . we went to 'Kopjes Kraal', we went to 'Hoek von
Schuurberg'. We went to 'Melk Kraal'.*

Eventually, Plat said, Dia!kwain found work *keeping sheep* for
a farmer called *NL* at a place called Klaver Vlei.

Jan Plat heard afterwards that [Dia!kwain] *accompanied NL to Kenhardt,
and has heard, too that* [he] *went to the Free State with NL, which does
not seem improbable to me, as* [he] *had told me that he thought that one or
two sons of his had gone there; and, as far as I remember it was one of his
thoughts to hear about his sons, if he could, when he left us.*

Dia!kwain never left the Northern Cape, he never found his
sons and he probably never found work with a farmer called NL.

When he returned to !Narries some time around the turn
of 1876 and 1877, friends of a dead farmer called Joseph Kruger
of Gifvlei learned that the Bosjeman who had killed him at
the end of the 1860s had finally come back from prison in
Cape Town. To see justice done they tracked him down and
murdered him.

We do not know where he is buried.

*Finished, our thoughts, ascending, leave us, while our bodies are those which
lie in the earth. Therefore, our thoughts leave us.*

Your *thinking strings* sat in your throat pulsing your thoughts
and as long as they *stood up* you were alive. When you died,

your heart fell from your throat into the middle of your body. This marked one kind of death.

The other kind of death was marked by the nosebleeds in the paintings of the circular dance that /Kaggen gave to the people who danced it. For the /Xam-ka !ei, death was a metaphor for unconsciousness and trance.

In trance, of course, you could visit the dead. Having walked the path of the Early Race to the *great hole* as wide as the distance from the Breakwater to Table Mountain, the dead had gone to join the First at Sitting People there in the past. The *!gi:xa* who would visit the dead was travelling to the past too, because the past, according to the /Xam-ka !ei, was a place.

After Dia!kwain's departure in March 1876 there were no /Xam-speaking people permanently resident at Charlton House. Lucy Lloyd continued her work at the library. As the Committee had done nothing to find a permanent replacement for Bleek in the seven months since his death, she had been forced to take matters into her own hands and had written to potential candidates in Europe.

At the end of that winter, her associate Mr Devenish in the Northern Cape wrote with some of the first good news she had received for many months: five years after he had left, //Kabbo's son-in-law Klein Jantje − /Hang≠kass'o − intended to return to Mowbray. Happily he was to bring with him //Kabbo's wife !Kwabba-ang and his own wife Suobba-//kein, //Kabbo's daughter, as he had promised all those years ago. Lloyd had only two hundred pages of text taken from /Xam women and now she would be able to take the testimony of the wife of the old man she still considered her best informant. Doubtless she would be as knowledgeable and wise as her late husband.

She prepared to receive them in the last months of 1876 but when January 1877 came there was still no sign of them. Lloyd was disappointed but not surprised; it was not the first time that /Hang≠kass'o had not made good on a promise.

He arrived at Charlton House in January 1878, quite alone, without warning and sadder than he had been when Lucy Lloyd last saw him as he set off for the north in a pair of Bleek's old trousers. His journey had somehow taken him a year and he had come without his wife, his mother-in-law or either of his children.

//Kabbo's Oude Lies had died suddenly in January 1877, he explained, and he and his own wife, mourning, had decided to delay their journey. In the comparative cool of April they left their son with friends and set off with their baby towards Cape Town by way of Beaufort West, the town where he and //Kabbo had been imprisoned for a short time on his first journey to the Breakwater.

Somewhere between Vanwyksvlei and Beaufort West, /Hang≠kass'o and Suobba-//kein lost their baby. We do not know what caused its death, but we do know what happened to the baby's mother. When the couple arrived at Beaufort West she was beaten by a policeman so badly that she died from her injuries. //Kabbo's wife, his daughter and his youngest grandchild were now dead; /Hang≠kass'o went on alone.

He was about thirty now, a measured, grave man of five feet. At Charlton House he found himself with no one to speak to in his own language apart from Lucy Lloyd. The only immediate family he had left apart from his brother-in-law //Goo-ka-!kui was his son !Hu!hun, with friends in one of the dusty young towns of the Cape interior. His family had been all but destroyed and it was important that he be with his son, but when Lucy tried to arrange for the little boy to

come to Cape Town she discovered that he had been inden-
tured on a farm and that the farmer who now employed him
– *owned* might be a more accurate word – would not let him
go. With the assistance of the Civil Commissioners of Victoria
West Lucy Lloyd tried to gain his release but it was no good.
The farmer would not listen.

It took a single generation to seal the extinction of the
/Xam language. //Kabbo had been a *!gi:xa* of the rain who
remembered a time when it had been possible to survive
without recourse to stock theft or labour as a shepherd.
!Hu!hun, his grandson, was growing up speaking Afrikaans
and would never see the rituals his father had performed or
hear the stories that explained them.

He could have learned an enormous amount from his father.
It is strange that /Hang≠kass'o made no contribution to the
notebooks during his first stay as he was a superb narrator
whose knowledge of ritual practices and myth easily matched
that of Dia!kwain and even approached that of his father-in-
law. Perhaps Lucy Lloyd was surprised to discover quite how
much he knew and quite how prepared he was to share it.

Much of the beauty of //Kabbo's testimony had been in its
fascinating digressions; dictating a *kumm* over a few days he
would never stick to the narrative, or indeed the 'rules' of
narration, preferring to explore details and offer extended
explanations on the material he was dictating. /Hang≠kass'o,
on the other hand, stuck to the point. He made use of story-
telling formulae like repetition and chorus-chanting that
served to make his narration easier to follow, reserving his
explanations and addenda for the notebook pages facing the
transcriptions, lines filled when Lloyd later read him back
what she had recorded.

This was just as true of material that would not have been
subject to the 'laws' of public speaking. He was precise and

thorough as he gave descriptions of the daily practices of
the /Xam-ka !ei like the making of clay pots and musical
instruments or the significance of the markings on arrows. He
described how pigments used in rituals and in rock paintings
were gathered and applied to hunters so that their foreheads
would *resemble the hunting leopard*; his accounts of rain-making
elegantly restated the extent to which the spiritual was incorporated into the most everyday parts of /Xam culture.

Wilhelm Bleek would have been pleased with the information /Hang≠kass'o offered when he was shown the copies
of rock paintings made by George Stow.

A poised, graceful man, he was *gentle and kindly*, and despite
his gravity he delighted in the Bleeks' children. He would
play catch with Wilhelmine, a little over two years old on his
arrival, and made small presents for all the girls on their
birthdays: miniature bows and arrows, dolls' furniture or San
musical instruments. He raised a deaf kitten and called it Kauki
tui, *the one that does not hear*.

When /Hang≠kass'o told Lucy Lloyd about the death of
his mother-in-law, *pale with awe at the remembrance*, he described
ghostly fires burning on the other side of a river, Edith Bleek
recollected. Apparently he found it difficult to make out quite
who was there on the other bank and what they were doing,
but there was a pot on a fire and he did not want to imagine
what was inside it.

/Hang≠kass'o was keen to share the stories of the /Xam
people with the Bleek children, and they loved to hear them.
He would throw himself into each story with vigour, giving
a short précis in English before speaking in /Xam with gestures
and sound effects appropriate to the death of a greedy lion on
a hot stone or a sad frog hopping away from his humanity into
the rain.

Kumm:

The sending of the crows

Dia!kwain; 10 March 1874:

The men went to hunt, and slept in the hunting ground. They slept a second night in the hunting ground. On the morning after the third night, one of the women said: 'What can be the matter, that the men sleep another night in the hunting ground? For they had intended, they said, that they would sleep two nights in the hunting ground. We should see if we can send the !gauru — *the white crow* — *that it may look.'*

Another woman said: 'The !gauru *always flies heavily. Instead you ought to send the* /xuru — *the black crow* — *that it might go, that it may see where the people are. For the men intended, they said, that they would not remain long. The* /xuru *might see them.'*

And they cut up a sheep, and took the fat from around the sheep's stomach and they put it around the /xuru's *throat for food. They said: '/Xuru-we! Oh,* /xuru, *fly! That you may see what the men have been doing, for they had intended, they said, that they should not remain away so long.'*

And so the /xuru *flew away. And so it flew, but it did not perceive the men. And so it turned back. And so it arrived back at the houses.*

And the women questioned it to find out whether or not it had seen the men. And it answered that it had not been able to see the men. Because the men seemed to have gone to a place that he did not know. He did not know where they had gone.

And the women said: 'Someone take the sheep's fat from the /xuru's *throat and put it on the throat of the* !kagen — *the pied crow* — *so that he may be the one to fly instead; for he always flies far. For the* /xuru *always does this. He does nothing. He neither flies far, nor looks about well.'*

And then the !kagen flew away, with the sheep's fat around his neck. And from the air he took the path the men had hunted. And he went seeking, and he perceived the people's vultures, vultures which were eating the men; and so he went up to them. The men lay dead.

And he saw that a Boer commando must have been those who killed the people.

And so he flew to the camp. He went to tell the people that a Boer commando had killed the men. And that was why the men did not return. Because they had been killed by a Boer commando.

And one of the women said: 'Did you hear when I said that the men had intended that they would not be long?'

And another woman said: 'Leave the sheep's fat on the !kagen's neck, for it was he who came to tell us nicely about it, that our menfolk are all murdered.'

He had told truly, and they saw that he was good.

Today the /xuru, the black crow, has only a little white on the back of his neck, because the women took the sheep's fat from him to give to the !kagen, the pied crow. They let the !kagen keep it, which is why he has still has a white chest to this day.

Kukummi:

Things Told

Some forty kilometres down a pitted gravel road off a perfectly straight highway to the Namibian border you will see a post-box and an orange gate marking the entrance to a sheep farm of about 20,000 hectares. At the bottom of a shallow depression ten kilometres or so on the other side of this orange gate there is a farmhouse with a dusty lawn shaded by trees; along the edge of the yard runs a long pipe balanced on top of uneven concrete blocks, leaking water from a famously dependable spring near by. Without this spring to water the lawn, the trees and the sheep, no farm would have been founded here.

On the other side of the fence separating the yard from the open veld is a steep-sided rise with a particularly exploded aspect covered in now-familiar boulders of black-patinated dolerite. The view from the top is of very distant hills and bright, arid valleys and plains. It must have been an excellent place for spotting animals.

It still is. About the brow of the hill are engravings of ostrich, eland and an animal something like a gemsbok filled in with scratches and scored with ritual 'cuts', more than a metre from nose to tail. The fold of fat between the animal's forelegs is disproportionately large and its hindquarters and belly have been scored with vertical lines. At least six figures dance around it, two of whom are partly animal, having what appear to be tails, wings and the heads of antelope or birds. They have their arms raised, while another figure seems to be lying on his back with his arms or wings behind him. Another leans back from his hips, his legs curved and elongated. All of these postures and features are associated with depictions of *!gi:ten* in trance.

Attached to the animal itself are three 'cords' of the kind that the rain-makers would use when they led !Khwa-ka xoro, the rain animal, to the dry places.

According to Dia!kwain his father Xättin, a rain-maker taught by a celebrated *rain's man* called !Nuin /kuïten, made engravings of *gemsbok, quagga, ostriches, etc., at a place called !kann, where these animals used to drink before the coming of the Boers.*

The spring here, the only one for forty kilometres that continues to flow even in times of drought, is known as Kans se Vloer. Local tradition has it that the word Kans comes from a Bushman word meaning 'spring'; like dozens of other places in the region the name is derived from an old /Xam name now pronounced without the 'difficult' clicks and as the farm (whose partly Afrikaans name means 'fresh spring') almost certainly takes its name from the word *!kann*, this must be the very place that Dia!kwain had in mind.

In May 1875 Dia!kwain drew a picture of a rain animal for Wilhelm Bleek and pinned it to the wall in the back porch. The creature in it had a body like a cloud, a thin tasselled tail, a gentle hump like that of an eland or a cow and a head with little horns.

It belongs here, on top of this hill, where his father almost certainly engraved very similar creatures. This is a place which could be described as '*powerful*'.

Someone has taken an iron stylus and cut across the extinct antelope and trance animals.

A. J. LeHanie 17/4/1938

WH Louw 1939

PS 50–15
En roep my aan in die dag van benoudheid: ek sal jou uit help,
en jy moet my eer.

'And in the day of trouble great, see that thou shalt call upon
me; I will deliver thee, and thou my name shalt glorify.'

/Xabbi-ang sang to soothe her weeping son.

> *For*
> *That's why I intend to go,*
> *Passing through*
> *!guru-/na's pass.*

> *For*
> *That's why I intend to go,*
> *Passing through*
> */xe-!khwai's pass*

she sang.

Tssatssi had come back from the hunting ground with a
leveret – a young hare – for /Hang≠kass'o, his grandson, who
fell in love with it on the spot.

I played with it; I set it down, it ran; I also ran after it.

Once he had caught it he put it down again and chased
after it.

And I again caught hold of it; and again, I caught hold of it; and I came to set it down.

'You shouldn't be *playing* with it,' /Xabbi-ang said. 'You ought to kill it and lay it out to roast.'

I was not willing to kill the leveret, because I felt that nothing acted as prettily as it did, when it was gently running, gently running along.

/Hang≠kass'o showed Lucy Lloyd how its ears moved when it was running.

Nothing acted as prettily as it did.

/Xabbi-ang told her son to go and dip up some water. /Hang≠kass'o could always be trusted to come back from the waterpit without playing or getting distracted, so naturally he was always the first child they asked. He tied up his pet, took a vessel – a waterskin made from the stomach of a springbok, or an ostrich shell – and left for the water.

When he returned with the water he discovered that his leveret was roasting, and that was when he began to weep.

They must have been deceiving me; they told me to fetch water, while they must have intended that they would kill my leveret, which I had meant to leave, so that it might live on in peace.

He asked his mother and Tssatssi if someone would catch another hare for him and they both refused. You do not play with your food. His mother consoled him by singing to him the song sung by the lizard !Khau as he went on his way to live at the shallow pools among the red sand hills:

For
That's why I intend to go,
Passing through
!guru-/na's pass.

For
That's why I intend to go,
Passing through
/xe-!khwai's pass.

At Charlton House /Hang≠kass'o explained to Lucy who the lizard !Khau was, where the passes were and why the lizard intended to travel through them.

!Khau was a man. He was a lizard. He was one of the Early Race and his descendants, lizards of the genus *Agama*, can be found basking in dry places all over southern Africa. He was going to live at a pool called !Kaugen-/ka/ka and as he was on his way, travelling between some steep hills, they squeezed together and chopped him in half. His front half fell over and lay still, becoming !Guru-/na, the western hill, and his rear half fell over and lay still, becoming /Xe-!khwai, the eastern hill.

Guru-/na and /Xa-!khwai, along with a third smaller hill called /Xe-!khwai ta !kau ka ti-opwa, the lizard's 'head', make up one of the most salient geographical features in the splendidly flat landscape of silver grass and thorny bushes extending north of the town of Vanwyksvlei. /Hang≠kass'o drew a map of the Lizard Mountain for Lucy Lloyd and a hundred years later Janette Deacon, an eminent archaeologist who has studied the geography of /Xam-ka !au for years, mapping the places where Bleek and Lloyd's /Xam informants lived, discovered where it is.

Comparing aerial photographs with /Hang≠kass'o's map she found a perfect match in a hill known as the Strandberg. It is hardly a 'mountain', being a long, broad, steep-sided hump similar in shape to the engraved volcanic cap near the Bitterpits, but it is impossible to miss in this part of the Northern Cape since there is no other geographical feature like it for a day's walk in any direction.

Like the engraved hill at a place Dia!kwain knew as !Kann, the Lizard Mountain is a powerful place where ritual was once enacted; it was a place known to the *brinkkops' men*, the *!gi:ten* of the rain.

Lizards were creatures associated with !Khwa, the Rain, and their movements had a measure of influence on the fall of his liquid. *It lies up on the thorntree*, /Hang≠kass'o told Lloyd of the agama lizard; *it keeps its head towards the place where the north wind blows and bewitches the rain clouds*. Only when the agama lizard had come down from the thorntree would rain come. Shooting arrows into the tree seems to have been a rain-making ritual. It was hoped that the noise of the fletch fizzing past would disturb the lizard sitting there and induce it to come down so that the rain might follow.

As Dia!kwain said, the north wind – *!Khwe a tsu !kung-so* – was the most pleasant wind of all. It was warm and it brought rain. Everybody knew that, not just the *brinkkops' men* like Xättin who climbed the brown hills to call on their dead teachers. It is significant that among the engravings covering the dolerite boulders on the Strandberg there are engravings of rain animals to be found on the north hill, the Lizard's 'head', somewhere the *!gi:ten* of the rain would climb to call on the dead *rain's men*.

In a place as difficult as /Xam-ka !au a deeply intimate

knowledge of landscape was a necessity. Survival depended on knowing the water sources, the migration paths and how, where and when to find food and medicinal plants. The tessellation of the material and the spiritual in the lives of the /Xam-ka !ei meant that most would know which *brinkkops* were good places for spotting game and which were the effective places to perform particular rituals.

The geographically specific *kukummi* of the /Xam-ka !ei belonged to a people who saw the landscape about them in the way they did not only because they had to be alive to its seasonal feeding places, alterations and topography in order to survive but because of a world-view, apparently shared to some degree by hunting and gathering peoples everywhere, that put a singular importance on the idea of place.

When the Boers arrived in the region it had already been inhabited for at least twice as long as the European continent. Those generations of habitation had left the land all but unaltered; there had been no tilling or ploughing and the only buildings were temporary windbreaks of thornbushes and shelters of grass and twigs. The only permanent alterations to the landscape itself were water cisterns, pitfalls for trapping game, engravings, and – rarely – simple finger paintings. There was no 'good' land or 'bad' land here, and you were not its 'master'.

Living in this place you were on such intimate terms with the creatures with which you shared it that you had both familiar and respectful names for many of them and you were constantly on your guard for significance in their movements. Ritual, animals and weather operated on each other subtly and continuously and there were specific places in the landscape where these operations could be influenced, like the Lizard Mountain. This place used to be an agama lizard, the *noisy rejoicer* whose movements foretell the rain.

When the /Xam-ka !ei lost their land to the sheep farmers it was a spiritual catastrophe. The disintegration of their culture and the loss of their land were inextricably linked since the landscape dictated the culture it supported; where an agriculturalist people can rebuild a temple or a shrine should they be forced from their place, the /Xam-ka !ei could not rebuild *vleis*, a rock formation like a standing man or the view of a vast and literally timeless landscape seen from the top of a pile of black igneous boulders. Their ritual and their beliefs worked *there*, directly permitting a lifestyle practised since the first people to make it that far from wherever our species was born crossed the Orange River and invented the stories they needed to survive.

First the /Xam people lost their geographical 'texts', then their culture and finally their language. Bleek and Lloyd preserved a valuable fraction of their literature. Perhaps if either of the two researchers had been able to visit the landscape itself they would have preserved more of the topographical features of the thought-world of the /Xam people as well.

Dr Langham Dale of the Committee of the South African Public Library did not like Lucy Lloyd any more than she liked him, but he was in a difficult position.

He could not dismiss her without having found a permanent successor to her brother-in-law because that would provoke an outcry, but he could not easily make the appointment because that would mean that the library would be stuck for good with a dedicated specialist in the fairy stories of the world's illiterate and ungratefully conquered brown folks. This would clearly be a waste of government money and shelf space, he believed, since a library was a place where people of

European descent went to study the achievements of their peers and ancestors.

The only thing he could do was wait. Eventually, he hoped, Thomas Maskew's temporary custodianship would become permanent, allowing the library to absorb the Grey Collection's European treasures into its main collection. Then there would be no need for a dedicated custodian at all.

It is probably worth pointing out here that as the Cape Colony's Secretary General for Education, Dr Langham Dale was responsible for the institution of segregated education for the people of South Africa. *I do not consider it my business to enforce education on all the aborigines, it would ruin South Africa*, he once said. *If I could produce 60,000 educated Tembus or Fingoes tomorrow, what could you do with them?*

His education policies became one of the defining components of apartheid. It is no exaggeration to say that as far as he was concerned African culture was quite valueless, while anything that challenged his authority as chairman of the Library Committee was an attack on his self-esteem.

Lucy Lloyd, a woman whose passion for the preservation of material from the colonized world found a balance in her detestation of hypocrisy and vanity, did not find it difficult to dislike Dale.

A full year after Bleek's death she was still writing letters from the South African Public Library rather than devoting her time to the Bushman Work in Mowbray, as she had been requested to do in her brother-in-law's will. Dale had done nothing to make an appointment or to see the government institute a Chair for Languages, as he had promised in a fit of sympathy while the Bleek family was still in mourning.

Without the Chair, and the salary that came with it, there was no way the promised *good man* from Europe could be tempted to the Cape. Lloyd, who believed Dale's behaviour an affront to science, had even found a potential successor, an eminent German philologist called Dr Jolly, but it made no difference – Dale and the Committee of the South African Public Library, an *ignorant and obstructive vestry*, would do nothing.

Jemima wrote a pleading letter to Sir George Grey in Auckland in which she included extracts of letters from Max Müller, the world's most famous philologist, and Dr Jolly himself:

The extracts of letters enclosed will shew you that an apparently very suitable candidate is already found; it is therefore only the means which are wanting. I say, mainly, because I fancy that for some reasons of his own Dr Dale may be personally averse to the appointment of another scientific man of Continental training to the Grey Library.

Grey did not take the trouble to reply.

Jemima was quite right about Dale's aversion to Dr Jolly. On the urging of Max Müller, Jolly had already gone so far as to write to Dale to nominate himself for the vacant position, explaining that he understood the opportunities for scientific research that would be afforded him and that he hoped to be able to combine his personal fascinations and researches with the opportunities presented him in Africa, a letter that was surely worthy of a meeting of the Committee.

Dr Dale did not even inform Sir Thomas Maclear, who was still the senior of the Grey Library Trustees, or Mr Fairbridge, who was a member of both the Committee and the Trustees. In fact, not only did Dale fail to consult any of the Trustees or members of the Committee, he decided to decline Dr Jolly's offer altogether and wrote to him to tell him so.

When Lloyd and Bleek discovered what Dale had done they were furious. At a chance meeting with Jemima Bleek, he claimed that he had acted without consultation because a mail steamer was leaving for Europe within days and he had not had the time – but everyone knew when the mail steamers put into Table Bay since there were announcements made in every newspaper, and if you were regularly writing letters to Europe you made it your business to know when each one left. He was lying.

The sisters began a letter-writing campaign designed to alert public figures in Europe and South Africa to Dale's calculated inaction. In the Cape Colony they wrote to, among others, the Prime Minister John Molteno, to the editor of the *Cape Argus*, and to Sir Henry Barkly, the colony's governor. In Europe they wrote to politicians, statesmen and influential scientists like the prodigious philologist William Dwight Whitney and Wilhelm Bleek's cousin, the naturalist Ernst Haekel.

Even without Sir George Grey's assistance Jemima Bleek and Lucy Lloyd succeeded in generating a low swell of minor scandal that prompted Dale to instigate some rearguard face-saving measures. In October he wrote a letter to the *Cape Monthly Magazine* with the stated aim of *throwing some light* on the issue of the appointment of Wilhelm Bleek's successor. A masterpiece of strategic admissions, veiled slights and blatant revisionism, the letter finally concluded that the Colony had no business paying for the continuation of one man's private research.

Immediately the *Cape Argus* and the *Cape Town Daily News* both published columns deploring the situation and pointing out that since Bleek had offered the results of his work to both the international scientific community and the public, it could hardly be called *private*. His work should be a source of pride to the Colony. It was of such importance that it should be resumed by someone capable and qualified as soon as possible.

The next *Cape Monthly Magazine* published a rejoinder from Lucy Lloyd first urging the Committee to make the appointment and then reminding them that she had never been charged with the full completion of the printed catalogue. Although fourteen months had passed since Bleek's death,

the proposed steps have not been taken, and the Bushman work (entrusted to me by Dr Bleek himself, and sufficient to occupy every year of my remaining life) suffers greatly through the prolongation of my library work.

Despite her frustrations with the Library Committee Lucy Lloyd continued to sit with /Hang≠kass'o. He provided her with narratives, like Dia!kwain's, in which 'real' events seem to have been refracted through a sort of prism of myth and /Xam-ka !au was remembered 'out of time'.

Bleek was correct when he wrote that a language was an image of the way its speakers saw the world. /Hang≠kass'o's story of the young man who warned his family of the approach of a Koranna commando come to murder everyone in his village tells us, like Dia!kwain's story of the sending of the crows, that 'the past' means different things to different people.

The parents sent a youth of the Early Race to the water, when the Korannas had descended to the water, /Hang≠kass'o said. (The Koranna, or !Ora, are Khoe people originally from east of the Northern Cape. Their language is today all but extinct.)

He went for water. He went to the foot of the water's little hill. He came to the top of it. And, when he came up to the top, he spotted the Korannas down at the water, while the Korannas also spotted him.

He knew who they were – they were a commando come
to kill him and his family, and if he were to protect himself
he had to keep his wits about him. Rather than running away
he made himself as small as a child and began to sway from
side to side as though he were wanting wits and would never
grow up. In the time of the Early Race, remember, a person's
appearance was not fixed as it is today.

Seeing this little boy come down the hill one of the Koranna
men said: *Shame! Oh! How is it that the people send him to the*
water, while a grown person does not scoop up water?

When the young man came to the bottom of the rise and
reached the waterpit he greeted everyone happily and stupidly.
His disguise was so good that the men actually felt sorry for
him, especially when, filling his ostrich shell, he dipped up as
much mud as he did water. One of the men even took the
boy's shell and filled it properly for him.

Another of the men was not so moved that he had forgotten
why they had come to that part of the country. *We ought to*
knock him down because he will go and tell his people, he said. He
had murder on his mind and saw no reason not to start with
the boy.

'What's the point?' asked the man who had filled the young
man's ostrich shell. 'He's stupid. Look at him! He hasn't got
the sense to tell anyone!'

'It's *you* that's stupid,' the other man replied. 'We should
kill him and then follow his footprints back to his camp.
Think.'

'For the last time, he has no *sense*! Why won't you listen?
It's like he's been taking snuff!' said the first man.

When you take snuff it dries up your brains, of course.

He and the other men filled the young man's ostrich shells.
They even stopped the mouths with grass, put the shells in his
bag and helped him to pick them up. Then they all took hold

of him and carried him to the top of the hill, laughing at him for his stupidity. They sent him on his way and then went back down to the waterpit to prepare themselves for slaughter.

When the youth was out of sight at the bottom of the hill he became a real young man again and quickly went home, singing all the way, to where he lived with his mother. There he told everyone what he had seen.

'There are Koranna men at the water, and they've come to harm us. They've bound on war's things, *harm's things*, black like woodpigeons' tails, and they've come to kill us. We must act now if we want to escape!'

Quickly, the people set a tree stump alight before every house in the camp. When the fires were burning, the women climbed the hill to safety.

Soon they would be gone. And they climbed the mountain, while the fires' stumps smoked at the houses.

Then the men left too. As the Koranna men approached the camp, they saw the fires burning and they crept quietly, readying themselves to kill. They surrounded the shelters only to discover them empty. One of the men said *I want you to see.* He was furious. *For when I said 'Let us kill the child,' you said that the child did not understand, that he was a simpleton: but he told his people.*

/Hang≠kass'o's story was set simultaneously in the time of the First at Sitting People, when it was possible to disguise yourself by altering your shape at will, and the world brought about by the arrival of farmers of European descent.

The Koranna commando does not belong in the mythical

past. They were Khoekhoen, related genetically and linguistic-ally to the /Xam-ka !ei and to southern Africa's other Khoe and San peoples, herders by tradition and culture. Although /Xam people had been interacting with herders for 500 years at the very least, the Koranna were a people whose displace-ment by European farmers to the east was very recent indeed. Koranna 'war parties', commandos, had been visiting them-selves on the /Xam-ka !ei for no more than a generation but in the oral tradition of the /Xam-ka !ei their violence was already located in the mythic past.

This mythic past was not necessarily an *ancient* past, as Dia!kwain's story of the sending of the crows confirms. The /Xam people conflated time and place and landscape defined their culture; genocide and dispossession were leaking into myth because they were killing the past.

In January 1877, a year and a half after her 'temporary' appoint-ment, Lucy Lloyd was still working at the library. Public opinion still prevented Dale from dismissing her, despite the increasingly public trouble he was causing her, and the impor-tance of her brother-in-law's legacy at the library still made her resignation out of the question. She absolutely would not go until the arrival of a *good man* from Europe to continue the work but it was clearer than ever that Dale did not want to make the appointment: although Governor Barkly had now agreed to provide an increased salary from municipal funds, Dale still sat on his hands.

The following September, provoked by Lucy and Jemima's ongoing agitation and the ever-more open criticism of his inaction, Dale wrote another letter to the *Cape Monthly Magazine* presenting his new argument: the irrelevance of the

Trustees of the Grey Collection, sympathetic to Lloyd, and his omnipotent authority as the chairman of the Library Committee, who were not.

His letter did little to help his cause. A columnist in the same edition of the journal wrote:

Will Dr Dale pardon us for saying that we are quite unable to imagine any good purpose for which his letter to the editor of the Magazine can have been written? that it appears to us to be egotistical and – dare we add? – silly?

For a response Lucy Lloyd submitted a selection of Zulu folklore with an afterword appealing to South Africans to recognize the importance of the material she was attempting to preserve. She hoped that once people had read the texts they would be inspired to

lend a helping hand in the work of collecting and recording what is so swiftly passing from beyond our ken, and in gathering what may still be gathered of the ideas, thoughts, and beliefs of the aboriginal races among whom we live . . . For, while we doubt, and hesitate, and think this lightly of the opportunity still within our grasp, such products of the mental life of the aborigines as might even yet be rescued from destruction, are passing away from us for ever.

The contribution was signed, in typically self-effacing fashion, *L.*

A note from the editors followed:

Our contributor, 'L', will be pleased to learn that a qualified candidate for the work of prosecuting research in the interesting field of South African Philology, has come forward in the person of Dr Theoph. Hahn.

She was anything but pleased. This was a disaster.

Dr Johannes Hahn PhD, generally known by his middle name Theophilus, was born at the Ebeneezer mission station on the mouth of the Olifants River in Namaqualand on southern Africa's Atlantic coast. Fifteen years Bleek's junior, he grew up speaking German and Nama, one of the languages of the Khoekhoen. Like Bleek, he received his philological training in a German university under the tutelage of a world-renowned linguist; like Bleek, he evinced a remarkable facility with languages at a young age.

In every other way, J. Theophilus Hahn was Wilhelm Bleek's polar opposite. He was combative, notoriously short-tempered, physically robust and possessed of a natural gift for rubbing people up the wrong way.

Indeed, he was capable of rubbing entire *peoples* up the wrong way.

At the time of Bleek's death in 1875 Hahn was living in a place called Rehoboth, some eighty kilometres south of Windhoek in what is today Namibia. Rehoboth, the *de facto* capital of the Afrikaans-speaking Baster people, was home to about 800 men and women and some 20,000 sheep and there Dr Hahn, a sort of philologist-shopkeeper-cartographer, ran a trading store. How he ended up living a wagon ride from Cape Town canvassing to be Bleek's successor at the library is instructive.

Objecting to the taxes he was required to pay for the right to trade on Baster land, Hahn applied to the governing Baster Council to have his contributions reduced by half. The Council sat to hear him plead his case but he failed to persuade anyone despite his furiously reminding them that he was white and they were not. He left in a rage.

Immediately Hahn wrote to one Hendrik van Zyl – big-game hunter, scandal-generating philanderer and charismatic Boer leader – to invite him and the people he led to settle in Rehoboth, suggesting that with something like fifty men they would be able to oust the Basters and take the entire region for themselves. The Baster Council discovered what he was proposing and they were furious.

I write to ask you who gave you the right to dig wells here and build houses and make dams? From today you are forbidden to turn another spadeful of earth and to place one stone upon another. I tell you further that, from today, you must look for some other place to live in other than Rehoboth

wrote the Baster leader Hermanus van Wyk.

The famous Baster leader Jan Jonker Afrikaner felt similarly after Hahn hired some of his people as servants and then flogged them at the drop of a hat. When he complained, Hahn told him that he had no business *to write letters to a white man* and threatened to punish him with mercenaries.

When the leader of the Herero people, Maherero, was told of Hahn's invitation to the trekking Boers, the philologist had succeeded in annoying the three most important leaders in the corner of southern Africa in which he lived. They united to be rid of him and applied to the Cape government for protection. A special commissioner called William Coates Palgrave was sent to investigate and Hahn drove his wagon south from Rehoboth to the elegant wine-making town of Stellenbosch on the Cape of Good Hope. He could not stay north of the Orange River any longer because everyone there hated him.

Things were different on the Cape, where he had the ear of certain members of the Committee, and it soon became apparent that if Lucy were to succeed in preventing the fruit of two decades of research being turned over to a man whom she considered racist and tactless, and whose achievements in the field of philology were negligible, her actions would probably have to be radical.

In the meantime, /Hang≠kass'o, the only /Xam speaker permanently resident at Charlton House, was lonely. Lucy Lloyd could not simply invite his immediate family down from the Cape Thirstland because he had none left. When J. M. Orpen, the magistrate who had collected Qing's testimony over a decade previously, wrote to her to tell her about *a small Bushman family from the Diamond Fields* she arranged to have them brought to Mowbray to keep him company.

They arrived in January 1879 in poor health after the difficult journey from the diamond boom town of Kimberly – but disappointingly for both /Hang≠kass'o and Lucy Lloyd they were not /Xam-speaking San people but a Koranna-speaking Khoe family. They and /Hang≠kass'o were unable to communicate in anything but Afrikaans.

Orpen was not a linguist. He could not distinguish between the languages of the San and Khoe people, and as the family had apparently declared themselves 'Bushmen-Hottentots' he had mistaken them for /Xam people. The cultural differences between Hottentots and Bushmen were lost on most people of European descent as it was generally believed that Bushmen were merely Hottentots who had lost their cattle. Like the /Xam-ka !ei, the Koranna spoke with clicks and were generally fair-skinned.

Lloyd made the best of the situation by taking the opportunity to record a little Koranna literature and vocabulary from the father of the family, Piet Lynx. Mrs Lynx's health was very bad and Lucy Lloyd let them stay for a whole year, supporting them all the while. During the Lynxes' stay, David Livingstone's sister-in-law Elizabeth Lees Price came to visit

Charlton House after an invitation from Jemima, who had been introduced to her at a social engagement in Cape Town. That the Lloyd sisters impressed Elizabeth very much is apparent from her diary:

Mrs Bleek immediately invited us all out together to her country house at Mowbray . . . These ladies are great students of Bushman and other African languages and habits . . . All the sisters (four) dressed in the same neat way, and the house was very very plain and simply furnished, with very little indeed in the way of ornament, a little too plain and bare I thought, but it was such a relief to feel in the company of people, refined, intellectual and cultivated, yet simple and homely as the humblest of cottagers.

As the Lynxes moved into the garden behind Charlton House, the first edition of the South African Folk-lore Society's *Journal* went to press in Cape Town. It was edited by an unnamed *working Committee of the South African Folk-lore Society* and prefaced by a short essay written by the Society's secretary, who had refused to have her name printed anywhere in it. The first paragraph began:

The journal of the South African Folk-lore Society begins its existence under serious disadvantages. Not the least among these is the continued absence of a trained philologist acquainted with the whole known field of South African languages, to whom doubtful and difficult points could safely be submitted.

Lucy Lloyd, then.

Published with the aim of preserving African literature *rapidly passing away, under the influence of European ideas and the spread of European civilisation*, the *Journal* included 'The Story of the Long Snake', a Xhosa tale contributed by George

McCall Theal, 'The Lion and the Ostrich', a Tswana fable contributed by the Rev. Wookey, and a Tswana nursery tale contributed by a Miss Meeuwsen from the Transvaal.

Drawing on the pick of the creation myths, proverbs, riddles, ritual practices and nursery tales accumulating in Sir George Grey's library, it was a rebuke to the government and the Committee of the South African Public Library, as was every edition that followed.

Shortly after the publication of the first *Journal*, Lucy Lloyd had the opportunity to record a San language other than /Xam. Both she and Wilhelm Bleek had been very keen to see how the language of the /Xam-ka !ei compared with the San languages spoken to the north of the Orange River and in 1879 Lloyd had the opportunity to do the work that Wilhelm Bleek had not been able to achieve.

With the help of William Coates Palgrave, the man sent up from the Cape to investigate Dr Hahn, two young teenagers from the very dry north of what is today Namibia arrived at Charlton House on the first day of September. !Nanni and Tamme had no European names, since there were no farms in their country, and we know little of how they came to be separated from their parents. Both were very thin. Through these boys Lucy Lloyd became the very first person to record the language of the !Xun.

She was surprised at quite how different the /Xam and !Xun languages were. /Hang≠kass'o could not make himself understood to the boys, nor they to him, but apparently he was very pleased to meet the !Xun children none the less. His son !Hu!hun must have been about the same age as !Nanni.

!Nanni and Tamme, who came from places some eighty

kilometres apart and spoke slightly different dialects, seem to have settled in quickly. Like the /Xam men and women before them they were given tasks to perform around the house and in the garden when they were strong enough (!Nanni quickly put on weight while Tamme remained *slight and small*) and were probably paid for their labour. They were given a room of their own in the house and played in the garden, where they built shelters from the eucalyptus trees, one for themselves and another for Jemima's daughters. Edith was then sixteen, Mabel nearly ten.

Seven months after their arrival they were joined by two more !Xun boys, /Uma and Da. /Uma seems to have been about seven when he came, Da about five or six. They arrived wrapped in blankets, Edith Bleek remembered, like *little dolls*. /Uma regained his strength quickly while Da, the youngest, remained slight. He had not passed the rites of passage that would enable him to eat particular foods and so when they were given an ox's head to cook they would not let him eat any of it: he was *too young, not having the cut from the forehead to the bridge of the nose that the elder boys had.*

All the boys were expert in the manufacture of bows and arrows, traded with the children from the village or used to shoot doves, which they cooked. Practically every boy in Mowbray wanted !Xun hunting equipment and if they could not get some by trading tobacco then they would steal into the garden to raid the shelters. There were fist fights.

The elder !Xun boys teased Da to the point that he once fired a shot at /Uma. He had run from the older boy and shut himself in his room; /Uma looked through the keyhole and Da fired a tiny arrow headed with a pin through it, hitting him in the eyelid. It was fortunate, Edith thought, that he was not blinded.

A decade after Wilhelm Bleek and Lucy Lloyd had first moved San people into Mowbray many still considered them a curiosity at best. On one occasion !Xun bows and arrows were very nearly used on strangers. The elder boys, !Nanni and /Uma, had been on their way home from an errand when they were ambushed and beaten with belts by a gang of teenagers. When the boys were noticed leaving Charlton House, furious and armed, they were asked where they were going. Apparently they were quite open about what they intended.

It took a long explanation to show them that this would not do, and that only the law might punish the offenders. Their consent to forgo immediate vengeance was most reluctantly given, and a sharp watch had to be kept all the evening to prevent them slipping away with their weapons. Next day they were taken to point out the ringleaders, who were arrested and punished.

Only !Nanni and /Uma provided much folk-lore, Tamme and Da being very young, but all the boys played a part in capturing a vivid child's-eye view of life in the Namib desert with the coloured pencils and watercolours that Lucy Lloyd gave them.

On pristine white card, writing paper and blotting paper, numbered in black ink and annotated with !Xun and English translations, they depicted insects, birds, carrion creatures and antelope; trees, bushes, tubers and flowers; scenes from the lives of !Xun people of the end of the nineteenth century; unguessable illustrations from !Xun myth.

Sha: *A plant with edible roots, eaten by monkeys and the Bushmen of !Nanni's country. The latter roast it in the fire in fine weather and eat it raw in wet weather.*

1. !Kania: *A fruit-bearing plant, the fruit something resembling an apricot, but much larger. Eaten raw, and said to be very nice.*

Bobo: *A fruit-bearing plant; place of sunsetting; a little child asleep during the heat of the sun, in the shade of a tree.*

If nothing else the paintings demonstrate a profound know-ledge of desert flora. If the children were too young to hunt they were certainly taken out foraging. Trees and bushes are labelled to distinguish their roots, fruits and flowers and the age of the plant; the boys explained how the roots of plants they drew were prepared, how the fruit tasted, and in the case of the *maiga*, the sex of the plant.

!Nanni drew *a dark coloured bird which catches young antelopes. Its head is represented out of its day nest,* which was a circle like a dark sunflower with elongated petals. He also drew its *night nest* in the trunk of a tree, containing its eggs.

In January 1880 he drew a grave in great detail.

1 *!korro: grave*
2 *ya: earth*
3 *!kari: tree*
4 *!nue: bag (the dead man's bag which is placed underneath his head)*
5 *//ke: the dead person*
6 *//gabbe: the little chamber or hole at the side of the grave, where the body is placed*

He went on to draw a picture in soft black pencil resembling a map of the night sky but actually depicting a funeral. Numbers eight to eleven are *mouth of the grave, mound of earth and stones, stones (large), stones (small).* Number one is *food (i.e. cooking fire)*; number six is ≠*gau (!Nanni's little house).* Number five is *fire at which !Nanni and his brother cried.* Number seven is *my sister Karuma (the corpse).* Number fifteen is *gravemouth (closed).*

For all the colourful detail in their pictures and descriptions the children were too young to provide Lloyd with much information about the !Xun as specific as the material /Hang≠kass'o gave her about the /Xam-ka !ei. He described daily life in /Xam-ka !au and cultural practices unique to his people with perhaps the most clarity of any of her informants.

He gave Lloyd specific information about the uses and the construction of tools such as the */khu*, for example, a stick with a brush on the end used for eating soup, and the *!au*, a shaped rib-bone used for eating the flesh of some kinds of roots. He described how the rattles tied to the ankles, pictured in so many rock paintings, were made from the ears of springbok, and how the *!goin!goin* – a musical instrument like a bull-roarer – was made and how it could be played to ensure that the bees and their honey were abundant; he explained the individual markings of arrows and how the sections of an arrow were fixed in place with adhesives made from the poisonous juices of the *//kuarri* plant heated over a fire in a tortoiseshell.

Ritual pervaded the lives of the /Xam, /Hang≠kass'o explained, from the manufacture of arrows to the disposition of a cooked animal's bones by way of the hunt itself.

The success of the hunt depended on the observation of *!nänna-sse* – the rituals that influenced the connection between the hunter and the game. Once a hunter had struck an animal with his arrow there was a connection between the two of them and the man would have to watch what he ate, what he heard and how he felt. He certainly would not eat the meat of a fast-running animal, for example, and if the hunter had shot a gemsbok he would not touch springbok flesh because the poisoned animal would run all night before it died. Springbok did not sleep.

The springbok is wont to do thus: when the sun has set for it in one place, the sun arises for it in a different place, while it feels that it has not slept. For it was walking about in the night.

Once the trackers had brought an animal's carcass back to the camp, the rituals of *!nänna-sse* still applied. The way the animal was butchered, the order in which the meat was served and the placement of the creature's bones once all had been fed were of great importance. Generally the bones would be placed before the shelter of the man who shot it, apart from its shoulder blade, which would be hidden so that the dogs would not chew it, causing the hunter to lose his aim. Children were not allowed to play on a springbok's skin.

The springbok are in possession of magic arrows. Therefore we are ill on account of the springbok. Therefore we do not allow the little children to play upon the springbok skin. For the springbok is wont to get into our flesh, and we become ill.

So we do not play tricks with the springbok's bones; for we put the springbok's bones away nicely, while we feel that the springbok is wont to get into our flesh. The springbok also possesses things which are magic sticks; if they stand in us, we, being pierced, fall dead.

It is thanks to /Hang≠kass'o too that we know the signs of grass and branches made by someone leaving the camp to let everyone know that he or she had left and where he or she intended to go, and how a man overtaken by the heat of the day would throw dust into the air to let those waiting for him know that he was in trouble. The man's wife would see the dust, /Hang≠kass'o explained, and would know that the sun was killing his heart. Someone would run to him with water to cool him.

And he first sits up (he was lying down on account of his heart) to remove the darkness from his face; for the sun's darkness resembles night.

Jolly wrote to the Committee to withdraw his candidacy. Then in the second week of December 1879, four and a half years after Wilhelm Bleek's death, Lloyd received a copy of the Minutes of a meeting of the Committee of the South African Public Library informing her that

in view of the impending appointment of a Custodian of the Grey Collection the Committee of the Public Library regret to inform Miss Lloyd that they are not in a position to continue her temporary services beyond the 29th of February next.

This would have been excellent news had not the frontrunner for the post of custodian been Theophilus Hahn, whose influential friends, the attorney general among them, had been active on his behalf.

Within days /Hang≠kass'o left Mowbray for /Xam-ka !au to try and find his son. He was the last of the prisoners from the Breakwater, and the last of Bleek and Lloyd's principal informants, to stay in Mowbray.

Like them, he had spoken on behalf of an entire people. Thanks to him we know how the first people of South Africa greeted each other in the early evening:

It is the mouth of coolness.

We know what they said to each other when they were angry:

Grave man! Departed one!

We know what a hunter called !Kuarra//kau said when he accidentally pierced his foot with a poisoned arrow and refused to be cut to bleed out the poison:

My heart stands in the hill.

None of these things are any less important to have recorded than the name of the Rain and what /Kaggen did with the honey and the shoe at the waterpit.

Throughout the very distressing months that were about to come, in which Lucy Lloyd's health was to suffer terribly, the Bushman Work continued.

The !Xun children drew pictures of a mythological figure called /Xué for her. In April of 1880 Tamme drew /Xué and his father //N'u, a partially inflated stick man with his hands out, his fingers like roots. !Nanni drew /Xué himself with a quiver, woodpigeon's feathers where his hair should be and vegetation growing out of his teeth.

/Xué was water; and the water was in the shadow of the tree. And the woodpigeons ate the fruit of the /kui. And /Xué was a lizard, and lay in the dead leaves of ge /kui. And he saw the woodpigeons, and was water.

He was not a large water, but was a little water, a waterhole.

And the woodpigeons saw the water, and settled upon the water's edge.

And /Xué worked large grass, like reeds, and it took hold of a woodpigeon.
And the woodpigeons came to drink water, and the grass came near, and bit
the woodpigeon's bill, and the woodpigeon cried out; and the other wood-
pigeons flew away.

And /Xué was /Xué, and rose up.

/Xué was capable of transformation, fond of assuming the
form of tree by night, and could turn himself into fire, water,
an elephant, a fly or a lizard. His wife beat him with a
knobkerrie when he made her angry. Infuriating, unpredictable, powerfully creative and quintessentially *human*, /Xué
recalls /Kaggen of the /Xam people; his stories, set in a distant
mythological time and referencing Bantu-speaking people
displaced by the movements of the Boers, reminded Lloyd of
the /Xam stories she had recorded. The children's *kukummi* (to
use the /Xam word) meander wildly, as if half-remembered, or
as if the narrators had not yet had the opportunity to develop
their skills. Lloyd filled fifteen notebooks with !Xun testimony, some 2,466 pages, of which she translated four-fifths.

When her notice expired in February 1880 the Committee
refused to extend Lucy's term even though they had yet to
make an appointment. They were now willing to leave the
Grey Collection without any kind of custodian at all if it
finally meant the removal from the library of the woman who
had made Dr Dale and the Committee he chaired appear so
foolish.

Lloyd staged a sit-in the Reference Room, forcing the
personal intervention of the Prime Minister, whose influence
gained her a temporary extension of her position and a temporary guarantee of the collection's safety. Dr Dale decided that

this was to be his final humiliation. Realizing that the only solution would be to make an appointment, he finally wrote to Theophilus Hahn to offer him Lloyd's job.

The Trustees and Lloyd decided they would not let Hahn have the keys: Dale had not consulted them, and this gave them grounds, they believed, to contest the appointment in the law courts a short walk from the library across the company's gardens. A summons was served in February but the Committee managed to delay the hearing until 20 May, when representatives of the Committee and the Trustees appeared before Justices Dwyer, Jacobs and Smith at the Supreme Court.

It is entirely coincidental of course, given the delays brought about by members of the Committee, that Justice Smith of the Supreme Court of South Africa had been elected a member of the Committee of the South African Public Library a week before the hearing.

Three months later, a tactical abstention on Smith's behalf saw Theophilus Hahn become the Grey Collection's new custodian.

No texts of *traditionary literature* in the National Library of South Africa today appear to have been added to the Grey Collection by Theophilus Hahn. In 1881 he published a fascinating, if fanciful, philological treatise dealing with the culture, myth and language of the Nama Khoe people, his favourite and apparently his only linguistic subject, and in 1882 he published the text of an address on the scientific study of language. These were his two major contributions to the field of philology in his time at the library.

He resigned in 1882 following *objections to his behaviour*. His catalogue was not published for a year after that, the printers having repeatedly declared the manuscript impossible to print. The Committee made no appointment after his resignation.

Kumm:

The broken string

Dia!kwain's father Xättin, Clay Hand, learned about the *Rain's things* from a man called !Nuin /kuïten, a skilled rain-maker who sometimes took the form of a lion.

!Nuin /kuïten knew that he was not a patient man, Xättin told his son, so when he went about as a cat, *shod with lion's hair*, it was only after dark: he knew that it was safer for his people that way. He patrolled the night looking for those who meant his family and friends harm and you might see his tracks the next day.

– A big man has passed this way in the night, you might say when you saw his tracks in the morning, walking on lion's hair.

!Nuin means bowstring and !Nuin /kuïten would strike a taut bowstring with a stick when he wanted to bring rain. The sound rang everywhere; it passed through everything, filling the sky.

He was in his lion's body when he took an ox and killed it to eat. The farmers who owned the animal came looking for him and there was a fight. Eventually the men fled, but when it was over !Nuin /kuïten hardly had the strength to make it to Xättin's shelter.

He had been shot. He was dying, he knew – and there were so many important things he had to tell his pupil before he died.

That was why he spoke to Father about it, for he did not know whether Father would see him again; for it seemed as if he would die without Father seeing him again. For he felt as if he should soon go, leaving Father. Therefore he told Father about the pain he was suffering; things felt as if he were suffering; things felt as if he must soon go, leaving Father.

He had not had time to pass on all he knew and now it was too late.

For he wanted to take Father with him, to teach Father about his magic, which he worked. Then Father would know the things which he had taught him, he would not forget them, he would go on thinking of them, where Father walked among them.

Once he had asked /Xättin to remember the songs he had taught him he would have continued speaking, but in the middle of his last sentence a wind was already mustering itself to blow across the hot flats and *brinkkops*.

Xättin remembered his teacher and sang about him.

> *People were those who*
> *Broke for me the string.*
> > *And so*
> *The place became like this to me,*
> > *On account of it.*
> *Because the string was that which broke for me.*
> > *And so*
> *The place does not feel to me,*
> *As the place used to feel to me,*
> > *On account of it.*
> > *For,*
> *The place feels as if it stood empty before me.*
> > *Therefore,*
> *The place does not feel pleasant to me,*
> *On account of it.*

14: //Kabbo: a portrait by William Schroeder from a photograph now lost. In plate 6 he was photographed as an anthropological specimen, in circumstances that allowed him little dignity; this portrait suggests the esteem in which he was held during his time in the Bleek and Lloyd household.

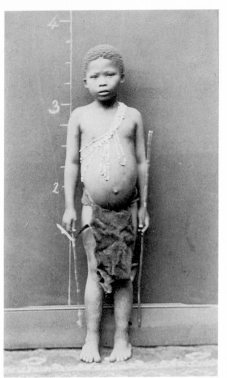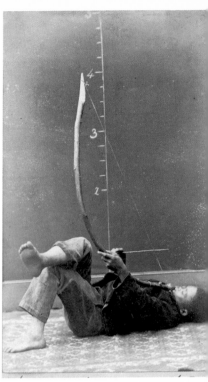

15, 16: Da and Tuma photographed with musical instruments, a bullroarer (in Da's right hand) and a musical bow – one of the world's few percussive wind instruments.

17: The view of a farm from the top of a *brinkkop* in what was once /Xam-ka !au, boulders of dolerite in the foreground.

18: !Kweiten ta //ken, Dia!kwain's sister, with two of her children, June 1874 – January 1875.

19: /Hang≠kass'o (Klein Jantje), son-in-law to //Kabbo: another portrait by William Schroeder. Like Schroeder's portrait of //Kabbo, this picture was published in *Specimens of Bushman Folklore.*

20: !Kweiten ta //ken in the garden of Charlton House with one of her children.

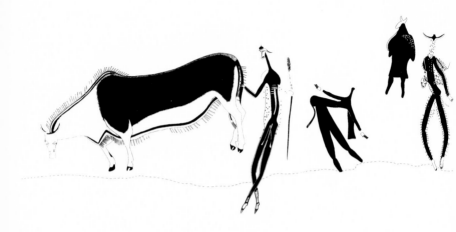

21: Detail of a painting showing shamans and an eland. As if it has been poisoned, the eland's hair is on end, its head is lowered and it is stumbling; in the 'death' of trance, the man holding its tail, with hooved feet and the scalp of an antelope, is stumbling too. To his right, a shaman stands bent double, his arms raised. The top of the head of the man on the extreme right is that of an antelope.

22: A 'procession' of dancing shamans. Four of the men are bleeding from the nose, something associated with trance and the dance that produces it, as are the sticks others carry to support their weight. The lines emerging from the head of the man on the far right probably represent the movement of *!gi* (*power* or *force*) or sickness removed from the person they are healing, who is not shown.

23: The front of Charlton House, with Jemima and children in the garden, *c.* 1880.

24: From left to right: /Uma, !Nanni, Tamme and Da, before their shelter of 'gum boughs' in the garden of Charlton House, 1880–81.

25: Dorothea Bleek took this photograph, recording the existence of a /Xam man called Tsoinxa, in the Northern Cape town of Kenhardt, forty years after /A!kungta came to The Hill.

26: Another of Dorothea Bleek's photographs of /Xam people, taken in Eyerdoppan, Northern Cape, in *c.* 1910, showing a shelter and a windbreak covered with ragged fabric and sheepskins.

27: *Left*: Lucy Lloyd on the receipt of her Honorary Doctorate from the University of the Cape of Good Hope, 1913.

28: Dorothea Bleek, who continued the work her father and her aunt began in the 1860s, pictured here in the 1920s as the world's pre-eminent expert on the language and culture of the San people of Southern Africa.

29: Hei//kum people of Ovamboland, Northern Namibia, 1936. The women are seated, the men prepared for hunting.

'This is no Bushman painting. This is Great Art'

Namibia's highest mountain came to its names on account of the desert light. The Afrikaners called it the Brandberg, which means 'burnt mountain', as does its Khoe name Dureb, while the Herero people call it Omukuruwaro, meaning 'fire mountain'. At dawn and dusk it glows warmly, one of the Namib desert's most spectacular sights.

In a north-facing rock shelter in the mountain's Tsasib Gorge is a panel some eighteen feet long and seven feet high where more than fifty human figures and some forty animals (oryx, mountain zebra and lion amongst them) have been painted. Near the centre of the panel is the White Lady of the Brandberg, perhaps the most famous of all southern Africa's rock paintings, walking from left to right across the granite, leaning forward slightly from her hips and holding a flower.

She was first copied one morning in 1917 by a cartographer called Reinhardt Maak who had stumbled into her shelter the evening before, exhausted and thirsty and looking for somewhere to spend the night out of the cold desert wind. He did not see the paintings until the morning, when, dumbstruck, he reached for his sketchbook, having immediately recognized *the Egyptian-Mediterranean style of all the figures* about the White Lady, clearly the focal point of the panel.

Like the grander of the figures about her, she has been painted with her face in profile and her shoulders and arms from the front; if it were not for what she is wearing she could almost be walking across the walls of a Pharaoh's tomb. Clearly these figures should not be here – and the painting's style is not the only thing that tells us this. The hairstyles and the robes of the Lady's cortège alone are enough to distinguish the artists as southern European or North African.

It was the Abbé Henri Breuil, a French priest and celebrated specialist in the rock paintings of Palaeolithic Europe, who recognized the provenance of the clothes that identify the woman's origin. She is wearing a short-sleeved jerkin and a beaded headdress held in place by a strap under her chin. Carrying a bow, an arrow and a flower, wearing an archer's gauntlet and flesh-pink tights, she is dressed identically to the female bull-jumpers of the Palace of Minos in Knossos.

Of course, this beautiful painting could not possibly have been made by the Stone Age hunting and gathering people of southern Africa. It was painted by the survivors of a party of shipwrecked Mediterraneans who trekked eastwards from Cape Cross on the Atlantic coast towards the dry heart of the Namib. Given their innate superiority it was inevitable that they should subjugate the people they found there. They painted those short, yellow-skinned people bowing in deference and offering up their children.

In 1947 the Abbé visited the Transvaal farm of General Jan Smuts, then Prime Minister of South Africa, to show him the copies he had made. There was silence as Breuil unrolled more than twenty watercolours one after the other before the general and his wife, and then a pause. Smuts, as dumbstruck as the cartographer Maak thirty years before, needed a few moments to collect himself.

You have upset all my history, he eventually told the Abbé. *And you think you are going back to Europe! Well, you are not; you will go out there again and put history right; for, when you publish these paintings, you will set the world on fire and nobody will believe you.*

When Breuil returned to the Brandberg to see the White Lady again he went in the company of Colonel Hoogenhout, the administrator of South West Africa. Hoogenhout shared Smuts' opinion.

This is no Bushman painting, he said. *This is Great Art.*

Dorothea Bleek, third eldest daughter of Wilhelm and Jemima Bleek, was shown Breuil's copy soon after it was made. She had published her *Comparative Vocabulary* of San languages twenty years before the Abbé had first visited Namibia and had gone on to publish a study of the Nharo San people of the central Kalahari researched over many months in the field, notes and prefaces for four books of copies and photographs of San paintings, one of which was a selection of the copies that George Stow had sent her father, and was completing both her own book of reproductions of San paintings and the *Bushman Dictionary* her father had been sorting through on the evening of his death some seventy-two years before. She believed she knew what was on the rock too.

It is a Bushman painting with face and limbs smeared by pink clay, she said.

The White Lady of the Brandberg, painted beautifully, bending slightly forward from her hips as she strides from right to left across the granite, is naked, and despite the Abbé's best efforts it is not particularly difficult to tell that she is male.

/Uma left Mowbray in December 1881. As they had been promised, !Nanni and Tamme were returned to the desert at the end of March 1882. The youngest of the !Xun children, Da, left two years after that in March 1884. He must have been about ten. As hard as she had tried over the years, Lloyd found it impossible to trace his family and so he was *found employment* somewhere in the Cape Colony. We do not know if the elder children found their families or what became of Da.

The Bushman Work did not end with their leaving Charlton House, however. A group of /Xam-speaking people relocated by the government from the Northern Cape to Salt River (a little town long-since absorbed by metropolitan Cape Town) soon visited and one of them, a woman called /Xaken-ang, spent a few months in the Bleek and Lloyd household in 1884 when Dorothea was nine and Edith nineteen.

Still particularly keen to discuss George Stow's rock paintings, Lucy Lloyd had invited some of the older men and women to the house. When they came they brought the entire band with them. Clearly very pleased to be among *friendly people*, it would have been very rude to have sent them away, Lucy Lloyd thought; they were starving, and instead of sending them back to their shelters she gave them roast meat and read them *kukummi* from the notebooks once they had been fed. All knew the stories they heard, and when Lloyd left off they continued in practically the same words used by //Kabbo, /Hang≠kass'o and Dia!kwain years before.

/Xaken-ang would not stay at Charlton House any longer than the few weeks she had originally agreed. She found the damp and the cold of the Cape difficult and soon went back to Salt River to stay with her relatives and friends, who disappeared *en masse* not long afterwards. Dorothea Bleek discovered what became of them twenty years later.

In 1887 Lloyd collected some information from a boy from the Lake Ngami region, and then a little more from a young woman from the same area in May the next year, and their voices were the last of the *collecting* work she had begun in earnest with the arrival of /A!kungta seventeen years earlier. Now she turned to the *working out* and *publishing* her brother-in-law had requested of her.

In the twelve years since Wilhelm Bleek's death, Lloyd had produced 9,068 pages of material in fifty-four notebooks and laboured without reward to defend his legacy at the South African Public Library. It had been difficult work and the effort had left her ill. When she left South Africa for Europe in 1889 it was partly for treatment and partly to consolidate the Bushman Work near Europe's publishers and academics.

Jemima Bleek let Charlton House and moved to Berlin with her five daughters – Edith, Dorothea, Mabel, Margaret and Wilhelmine – to be near her late husband's family. Lucy Lloyd went first to Britain, staying for a time in Wales and in London, and then joined her sister in Germany.

On the death of her father Dorothea Bleek had been two years old. She was fifteen when she left South Africa for schooling in Germany and Switzerland but her Aunt Lucy had already inspired in her a fascination with San languages that was to take her back to the continent of her birth and see the Bushman Work continue for another generation. In 1904, at the age of thirty-one, having studied African languages in the same university faculty attended by her father in the 1850s, she went back to South Africa.

Jemima Bleek went with her and rented an elegant colonial house in Sir Lowry's Pass, a village at the bottom of the bright mountains an afternoon's journey by coach from Mowbray.

Closely following the career path plotted by her Aunt Lucy, Dorothea began her career as a teacher and then became the world's foremost expert on San cultures and languages. She lived for a while in the Karoo town of Cradock, teaching at a girls' school, before leaving to spend a year looking for rock paintings in the mountains of the Eastern Cape and the Orange

Free State. Soon after that she made for the Northern Cape and after that the deserts north of the Orange River. In the following years she crossed Africa by wagon to spend time in what would become Tanzania, Botswana, Namibia and Angola, studying the culture and languages of the San in the field.

Lucy Lloyd stayed in Europe hoping to find sponsors for the publication of the copies of rock art George Stow had sent to her brother-in-law nearly thirty years before, all the while doing her best to bring the 12,000 pages of /Xam testimony in her care to the attention of the world's scientific community. Her health was poor, but her obligation to *work well out* the Bushman Work endured in the face of almost complete indifference from science and incomprehension from the publishers of Europe.

These were difficult years for Lloyd. On the collapse of her health she had been informed by specialists in London that she *must not expect to be really strong again* but that she could *hope to go on for some time, and do some good work, still* if she took things *quietly* and did not *drive* herself, advice she did not believe she could afford to take. She stayed in London to write the last of the *Reports* on the Bushman material collected in the years following Wilhelm Bleek's death, taking meticulous care to write herself out of the story it told: in it the only real evidence of the decades she gave to the research is the letter L. On seeing the printer's proofs in 1889 she even asked the typesetters to make her name on the title page smaller.

From London she moved to the Charlottenburg district of Berlin, where she worked to complete the manuscript of a selection of extracts from the notebooks, eventually published in 1911, forty-one years after /A!kungta's release from the Breakwater, as *Specimens of Bushman Folklore*. She was seventy-six.

Nowhere in the preface of this book – irrefutably a classic of world literature – does Lucy Lloyd admit to having made the greater part of the transcriptions it contains, instead referring in passing to the *other collector whose poor ear was accustomed to English sounds*. With its parallel English and /Xam texts, numbered lines and intriguing annotations it is a distillation of all the creased pages of handwritten *kukummi* in the notebooks, constantly surprising, confusing and intriguing. Here, however, following a narrative through to its end is not a question of going from book to book, skipping pages and noting line numbers, and nor do you have to negotiate Wilhelm Bleek's awful handwriting.

The portraits of //Kabbo, /A!kungta, Dia!kwain, !Kweiten ta //ken and /Hang≠kass'o that Lloyd chose do not only show *subjects* but collaborators; Dia!kwain, for example, stands in a suit holding a hat and his flute, showing his brass ring to the camera, while //Kabbo appears in a colour chromolithograph wearing a greatcoat and earring. Their voices are clear and quickly distinguishable: Dia!kwain imaginative, loquacious, /Hang≠kass'o precise and poignant, //Kabbo allusive and profound, curiously spare even when speaking at length.

Shortly after the publication of *Specimens of Bushman Folklore* Lloyd moved back to South Africa where she became the first woman to receive an Honorary Doctorate from the University of the Cape of Good Hope in belated recognition of her remarkable skill with languages and for her efforts to record South African folklore.

A year after that, on 31 August 1914, having driven herself against doctor's orders for a whole sixteen years, she died at home in Charlton House at the age of seventy-nine.

Ten years later Dorothea Bleek published a second book of extracts from the notebooks under the title *The Mantis and His Friends*, printed from a manuscript she had begun in collaboration with her aunt. The book, concentrating on the cycle of stories about /Kaggen, was intended for children and so Dorothea Bleek made an attempt to clean the material up a bit. Despite her best efforts at bowdlerization – the character renamed Foulmouth lost his propensity for evil farts and began instead to suffer chronic halitosis, for example – it is a very unlikely children's book. The stories are confusingly surreal and apparently plotless, full of impenetrable cultural references and have for a hero an abject coward whose moral compass always points to his stomach.

The Mantis and His Friends, however, does tell you the correct things to do once you have shot an eland in the harsh Northern Cape in order to ensure the safety of your person from damaging spiritual intervention, and this is worthwhile knowledge at any age.

Lucy Lloyd would have published George Stow's copies privately had she had the funds, and on her death in 1914 she deeply regretted they were better known to the publishers who had rejected them than to science and art history. In 1930 Dorothea succeeded in seeing seventy-two of the plates published. For the text to accompany the facsimiles she travelled thousands of kilometres searching for the sites Stow visited in the 1800s so that she could give a description of each location and remarks on the quality of the copy. Her texts were printed alongside explanations and comments given by Stow, Dia!kwain and /Hang≠kass'o.

Besides the copies, Dorothea inherited the notebooks. She began to fill the incomplete columns facing the /Xam transcriptions with English translations, later editing extracts for publication in South African anthropological journals with the aim of bringing the beliefs and world-view of the /Xam-ka !ei to wider notice. Her aims and her methods were much the same as those of her aunt, although it is perhaps true to say that Dorothea found it more difficult than Lucy Lloyd to transcend the prevailing racist climate of the South Africa of her day.

In completing the translations she did not have the benefit of native /Xam speakers to help her in any practical way. She did, however, have a useful perspective afforded her by her knowledge of several San languages spoken in the Kalahari, particularly those of the Ju/'hoan and the Nharo.

By the time she had moved to her rambling house in the Cape Town suburb of Newlands, with its unkempt garden and walls lined with books, she was the world's pre-eminent expert on San languages and culture. A matter of weeks before her death in 1948 at the age of seventy-six, Dorothea Bleek completed, with neither funding nor the promise of publication, the *Bushman Dictionary* her father had begun in the 1870s and was compiling on the last evening of his life. It was finally printed in 1956, eight years after Dorothea Bleek's decease and a century after her father first came to South Africa with the bishop of Natal.

Wilhelm Bleek's huge personal library was eventually donated to the University of Cape Town, where his scruffily signed philological texts and grammars, complete with annotations and cryptic marginalia, are still on the shelves.

The notebooks disappeared.

Kumm:

The Bushman dies, he goes to this place

The Bushman dies, he goes this place.

The old man becomes lean, he dies, he goes to this place.

The old woman becomes lean, her flesh vanishes away; she dies, she dies, she goes to this place.

The very small child, it dies, it goes to this place.

A man shoots another with an arrow, the other dies, the other man goes to this place.

Another man shoots another with poison; the other dies from the poison, the other goes to this place.

Another man stabs another with a blade, the other one dies, the other goes to this place.

A man shoots a woman with an arrow, she dies, she goes to this place.

A man shoots another with an arrow, the other man dies, he goes to this place.[1]

A Bushman shoots another with an arrow, the other Bushman dies, he goes to this place.

A Bushman knocks down another man with a knobbed stick; the other dies, the other goes.

Another Bushman stabs down the other with an assegai; the stick's knife. Another man cuts the other with a knife. The other goes.

The very old man, his head becomes white, he dies of hunger, he goes.

The old woman very, her flesh is dry, she dies of hunger, the young man shoots amiss, he dies of hunger, he shoots amiss.

---

[1] *An opening/mine must be what he speaks of. The people call it 'grave'.*

*He shoots his fellows with the arrow; the other man shoots another
    with an arrow. The other, he dies.*
*Many folk together go to fight many other folk. They fight one
    another. The other man fights and dies.*

Where Is /Kaggen?

In the early 1970s, a PhD student called Roger Hewitt applied to the librarian of the Jagger Library at the University of Cape Town for permission to study Bleek and Lloyd's Bushman notebooks. The librarian replied that they had probably been destroyed. If they had not, Hewitt discovered, it seemed likely that Lucy Lloyd had taken them to Wales or Berlin or that they had been lost after Dorothea's death. Certainly no one had seen them for decades.

Hewitt continued to look for them, eventually happening across a *small, inexplicit reference to some unidentified notebooks* in a book by a former librarian at the university and, convinced that these were the notebooks he was looking for, wrote to the librarian for a third time to convince her to employ people on his behalf to search the shelves.

Within two weeks I had a letter back. The people employed had indeed found the Bleek and Lloyd notebooks – one hundred and eighteen of them.

Today the material on the lined, creased pages of these hardbacked notebooks forms the most important part of a splendidly rich resource known as the Bleek and Lloyd Collection, an archive comprising nearly a century's worth of correspondence, notes, fragments, drafts, paintings and photographs.

Wilhelm Bleek had expected that the words he and his sister-in-law took down would be consulted by philologists looking to answer questions concerning the history of our species and the origins of language. A hundred years after his death, however, it was archaeologists, anthropologists and art historians who turned to the nearly forgotten words of //Kabbo, /Hang≠kass'o and Dia!kwain – and they were not necessarily looking to solve the problems he had anticipated.

Downstream from the confluence of the Qaqa and the Senqu, nearly a hundred kilometres from the highlands of Lesotho, there is a cave under a waterfall at a place called Pashuli's Hoek where George Stow copied a rock painting in the first years of the 1870s. By the time Dorothea Bleek came to visit the panel in the 1920s the walls of the cave were badly flaked and the pictures very faded, but she still was able to make out at least twenty-two figures, among them an ostrich, a baboon standing with the legs of a man and a tall, *kaross*-clad figure with the head of an antelope; to the right was a striding man with the head of a hartebeest, his quivered arrows showing over his shoulders.

Almost all the figures in Stow's copy have the heads or limbs of birds or game, feathered and antlered. Some have been stretched unnaturally tall and thin. One of the two essentially human figures in the copy is bent almost double and holds aloft a stick with a divided end, almost certainly a flywhisk, possibly aromatic leaves of *buchu*, the only thing that could pacify a rain animal that did not want to be caught.

When Dia!kwain was shown the copy in 1874 he explained:

These are sorcery's things. I think that one man, to the right of the spectator, having killed a hartebeest, becomes like it with his companions. The Mantis going with them. The others had helped him. They become Mantises.

The Mantis is not there.

/Kaggen, he said, is going with the men who are companions to the hartebeest man, and they become mantises – but *I Kaggen is not there.*

Where is he?

It is a fact that you will not find him painted or engraved on any rock face in South Africa. Not one single picture of the trickster-creator of the /Xam-ka !ei has been identified – and as for his family, if there are pictures of *them* then their numbers are vanishingly small.

Over a campfire in Lesotho in 1874, a man called Qing pondered the question of the Mantis's whereabouts. *Where is /Kaggen? We don't know, but the Elands do*, he said.

If the elands could actually tell us where he is it would be difficult to decide which one to ask: there are thousands still to be seen in southern Africa, painted in skilfully shaded polychromes, in black and red monochromes, in stamped and incised engravings. They are as often depicted with almost photographic naturalism as with symbolic exaggeration, from the side, from behind, even from above, sometimes with great detail and sometimes with the sparest and most elegant of lines. There are male eland, female eland, eland painted to show their age and their seasonal coats.

Maybe there are other animals who know where to find /Kaggen. Eland are not the only animals depicted, after all, and although other antelope such as gemsbok, reebok and kudu are particularly common, you might find rhinoceros, giraffe, lion, fish and birds – in some regions of South Africa you will be lucky to find any eland at all.

It depends where you look, but most of the animals pictured are game animals rather than the porcupines, ground-squirrels, tortoises and hyraxes that played the most important part in the everyday diet of the /Xam people. This tells us that certain animals were important in some way that did not necessarily have anything to with nutrition, and contrary to the expectations of the Abbé Henri Breuil, depictions of hunting are so rare as to be unusual. This alone broadly scuppers the sympathetic magic hypothesis.

Instead of hunting scenes you might see a snake slithering along a rock face having emerged from one crack to disappear into another; you might ask where it could be coming from or to where it might be returning. You might see creatures that have never been hunted anywhere in the wild, since they have never existed, or rows of dots and patches of pigment, geometric shapes and zig-zag lines that in some places have been painted with no representational picture near by and in others seem to connect animals and people. These lines might emerge from the heads or the hands of a human or partly human figure.

You will find people easily since there are twice as many pictures of human beings as there are of animals, and it is easy to tell that there are more men than women depicted since more often than not they are naked; if they are dressed, and often even if they are not, women often carry sticks weighted with pierced stones used for digging, or gathering-bags of animal skin; men will often be carrying hunting equipment. People might be painted standing, running across the rock, upside down, connected to dozens of others in conjoined procession or with the proportions of their limbs and bodies distorted.

Bridging images of humans and animals are the zoomorphic figures known as theriantropes: people with the heads and hooves of antelope, fish tails for legs, wings for arms. Since /Kaggen is nowhere to be found among them, we should not necessarily expect to be able to read the paintings as illustrations of myths. They are not 'like' the carvings in an Indian temple, say, where we might expect to see Hanuman summoning his armies on behalf of Rama to bring Sita home.

It does not take too long to find !Khwa, however. You might see him walking on his columns of rain for legs, or with the legs of an antelope or an elephant, perhaps being led by a thong towards a drought. Evidently we can expect to see *certain* figures from San myth, but whatever the painters and engravers had in mind when they made their art, it seems that simple illustration was not it.

From this most cursory study of the rock art of the Southern San it would appear that sympathetic magic or illustration are not the 'solutions' we are looking for. The problem is where to start looking for a better one.

First of all, it is probably best to consider what the pictures are actually *of*, and this not simply a question of staring at them to identify what is 'in them'. No Stone Age hunter would be able to 'read' the portraiture of seventeenth-century Europe without some understanding of the visual language of the art or the culture and the religious beliefs of the people that produced it, and in making sense of the paintings and engravings of the Southern San we are dealing with a body of art that is every bit as subtle and complex but made by a people who perceived the world in a radically different fashion from anyone with a farmer or a baker in their family tree – which is most of us alive today.

Another consideration must be *where* the paintings and engravings are made, because it is obvious that they are not always to be found in places used for shelter. Some are found in locations very difficult to reach. There are paintings on ledges along the walls of steep *kloofs* or in recesses in cliffs which can be scaled only with difficulty, sometimes within metres of a far more 'suitable' spot.

It seems that the /Xam-ka !ei were prepared for meaning to emerge almost anywhere and used ritual as nothing less than a survival tool, so it would seem unlikely that something situated so carefully and so time-consuming in its production would not have some kind of purpose.

At first sight it seems terribly difficult to untangle, but we can assume that the 'solution' to the art, in the absence of anyone who can explain it to us directly, must lie somewhere between the myth, the ritual culture and the understanding of 'place' of the people who made it.

/Kaggen does not love us if we kill an eland.

What happens to an eland when you hit it with a poisoned arrow?

It will start and you will follow its spoor. As the poison in your arrowhead begins to work it will begin to slow and to stumble, losing its balance. Sweating, its lowered head swaying, it will try to lift its muzzle to let breath pass through nostrils blocked with blood and mucus. Its hair will stand on end; it will tremble and bleed from the nose. With its muscles in spasm, it might attempt to run with one of its legs held out behind it, obviously in pain. Eventually it will die.

What happens to a *!gi:xa* in the circular dance of the *!gi:ten*?

As he nears trance he will begin to slow and to stumble, losing his balance, moving as though exhausted and on the verge of consciousness; he will sweat, his hair will stand on end and he might shiver. He will bleed from the nose and his muscles will spasm painfully. Eventually he will die.

The eland's death is permanent. The shaman's death is temporary, a *half death*, as the Ju/'hoan people of the Kalahari call it. Unlike the eland he or she will be able to describe the experience and the journey underground, through the water

or the rock face to the world of the spirit; he or she will 'die'
to visit the dead dwelling in the past with the Early Race, to
fight those who shoot their arrows of sickness into the living
or to ask the assistance of deceased *!gi:ten* with sway over the
rain or the herds. Maybe he or she will travel long distances
to visit relatives, transformed into one of the animals of the
veld or passing through the air at a great height.

There is a link to be made between the 'death' of a shaman
and the death of an eland. You can still see it on the rock face.

Dying antelope, very frequently the eland, are depicted in
great detail, stumbling, their hair on end, bleeding or foaming
from the mouth or nose and with their heads lowered. 'Dying'
shamans are depicted equally meticulously in the positions
associated with the explosion of *!gi* – power – and the onset
of trance, wearing rattles on their ankles and carrying sticks to
support their weight, bent double at the waist with their arms
held out behind them: the position dancing San shamans still
take to help them produce or summon *!gi*. In many paintings
you will see blood coming from their noses, sometimes spread
over their cheeks by their fingers, or stumbling with others
supporting them. They will be for the most part men, touching
their faces and often sitting with one leg up; women will very
frequently be painted sitting near by, clapping. You might see
the circular furrow they have danced into the ground.

Often dying antelope and dying shamans will be painted in
the same panel.

There is famous painting from the mountains of Lesotho in
which an eland stands in profile with its head down, swaying
so that its face is towards the spectator. Its hind legs are crossed
as it stumbles and its hair is on end. Holding its tail is a man
whose head is more antelope than human; his hoofed legs are
crossed in an identical fashion to those of the animal he is

coming to resemble and he is covered in dots and lines. Beside him the artist has drawn another man bent double at the waist with his arms held up behind and above his body.

Like many other similar paintings, this picture describes the link between death, trance, the *!gi* of a powerful animal and the transformation of the shaman. It shows a trance dancer using the *!gi* released in the death of the eland to propel him from the material world into the world of the spirit. He is so full of the power of the eland that he comes to resemble it. At the consuming, hallucinatory apex of the trance dance he really does *become* an eland.

I think that one man, to the right of the spectator, having killed a hartebeest, becomes like it with his companions.

Looking at the art of the Southern San we should expect to see a shaman's-eye view of the universe in which the visionary and the everyday have equal weight and value and nothing is necessarily 'real' or undiffused through symbol and visual metaphor. The eland or the hartebeest is not even necessarily killed in the literal sense.

People with the heads, horns, hooves and pelts of springbok, hartebeest and gemsbok are *!gi:ten* who derive their power from animals other than the eland. Pictures of human figures trunked and tusked, feathered and winged, or with the buttocks, bent tails and jaws of baboons, reflect a shamanic relationship with the animal from which each *!gi:xa* derives his potency, while the appearance of wings and the heads of birds are metaphorical representations or visual descriptions of the sensations of flight brought on by the experience of trance.

According to //Kabbo, Dia!kwain and /Hang≠kass'o, the /Xam-ka !ei clearly believed that living *!gi:xa* could adopt the forms of creatures indistinguishable from the creatures of the veld and travel to visit people in much the same way as the dead *!gi:xa* returned to the world of the living in animal form. This transformation often occurred in trance, as the pictures show. Paintings of fish and fishy theriantropes offer more evidence that the art is to do with trance: sensations of floating and moving underwater have been described by San healers in the Kalahari, one of whom even told a South African anthropologist that that was where he was taught to heal.

Water served as one of the most important passages to the world of the spirit. When Qing explained to the magistrate J. M. Orpen on their mission to find Langalibalele and the Hlubi that the paintings of men with reebok heads they saw on their way were *men who had died and now lived in rivers, and were spoilt at the same time as the elands and by the dances of which you have seen paintings*, it seems he was referring to living shamans. They had 'died' in the dance, they lived underwater – a metaphor for trance – and they were 'spoiled', in the same way the Meerkats 'spoiled' the first eland, by the dance that killed.

In one of Orpen's copies there are six men and two red creatures that resemble rhinoceros. Four of the men lead the lower of the two creatures by a cord of some kind which seems to be fixed somehow above its mouth. Qing said of the picture:

/Kaggen gave us the song of this dance, and told us to dance it, and people would die from it, and he would give charms to raise them again. It is a circular dance of men and women following each other, and it is danced all night. Some fall down, some become as if mad and sick; blood runs from the noses of others whose charms are weak, and they eat charm medicine, in which there is snake powder.

When a man is sick, this dance is danced around him, and the dancers put both hands under their armpits, and press their hands on him, and when he coughs, the initiated put out their hands and receive what has injured him – secret things.

For the /Xam-ka !ei in the parched Northern Cape, the waterpit or *vlei* took the place of the rivers of Lesotho, Qing's country.

In one of Stow's copies there is a picture of four realistic kudu crossing a *vlei* represented as a series of nested U-shapes. Across the bottom of the picture are two long rows of dots. You do not necessarily have to travel to the southern African subcontinent to see forms like U-shapes and dots. These simple shapes provide yet more clues to the link between shamanism and rock art.

Trance brings hallucination, and at the beginning of every hallucinatory experience you will 'see' certain shapes and patterns known as entoptic shapes. Dots, lattices, horseshoes and circles are some of the most common. They have nothing to do with your expectations or your culture and everything to do with your central nervous system; they are latent, predictable, and as familiar to anyone who has ever taken hallucinogenic drugs for recreational purposes in the West as they are to those who ritually eat *dream fish* caught off Norfolk Island in Melanesia or the right kind of narcotic bamboo grubs in the Amazon.

Entoptic shapes are found in the art of shamanic cultures on every continent. For the Huichol Indians of the Mexican Sierra Madre, for example, spirals and concentric circles are pictograms, a visual shorthand signifying *yagé*, the hallucinogenic plant *banisteriopsis*. Its coded presence in a painting specifically says *this is an hallucinated vision*. There are many other examples across the world, from the geometrical figures and 'symbols' in the beautifully pointillist rock art of Australia to 'lightning' in the rock art of the first people of North America.

Dots, grids, zig-zags and nested horseshoe shapes are everywhere in the art of the Southern San. Snakes, antelope and people are frequently made up from them and this is to be expected, since in the advanced stages of hallucination an overwhelmed brain begins to interpret entoptic shapes as recognizable forms.

As common as the sight of entoptic shapes as you enter a state of trance are hallucinations of physical sensation, often experienced as a tingling or a crawling on the skin. Modern San shamans describe feelings of height, tingling and the movement of *!gi* – energy or potency – up their spines from their bellies into their heads as they enter trance. Paintings where dots and zig-zags cover the spines and limbs of trancing *!gi:ten* visually describe those feelings.

Zig-zags issuing from the heads and hands of dancers represent the so-called *lines of force* visible, according to the Ju/'hoan people of the central Kalahari, only to others in a state of trance. These *lines of force* are entering the shamans' bodies, or leaving them to continue on into the world of the spirit, behind the rock face, through the waterhole, or out into the veld. Sometimes they link people and animals, making the connections and the movement of *!gi* explicit.

A combination of ethnology and neuropsychology lets us 'decode' the painting copied by Stow in which four kudu cross a waterpool made up from nested U-shapes. Shamans from cultures across the world speak of descent into the 'world of the spirit' through 'tunnels' and often depict the passage itself with spirals, mandalas or entoptic shapes. Stow copied a painting of four powerful animals, or a visual metaphor for the power contained in those animals, and the point of entry to the 'spirit world', the place of the dead, painted by someone with first-hand experience of trance.

/Xam-ka !au's waterpits were one of the most important routes you took when you left your body behind. In other places it was rivers and the painted rock face itself: if antelope and snakes can emerge from cracks and crevices, a shaman can just as well disappear into them. Paintings mark portals.

For all the hallucinogenic imagery in the notebooks and in the rock art of the Southern San, it appears that Lloyd and Bleek did not record anything about hallucinogens, but it would be surprising if the /Xam-ka !ei did not know of any. Hunting and gathering peoples are famously and necessarily experts on the plants and animals around them, and southern Africa has its share of psychoactive fungi and root nodules.

Regardless of whether or not the San south of the Orange River used hallucinogens, the dances depicted so frequently in southern African rock paintings were enough to induce altered states of consciousness. If they were in any way similar to the dances performed by surviving San communities that still preserve those traditional aspects of their culture, then hyperventilation, repetitive movement and extraordinary concentration over hours is enough to do the trick. It takes practice, training and skill to be able to control the degree of immersion into trance and the experience of the journey can be terribly frightening, while manufacturing what the /Xam-ka !ei called *!gi* is very painful. It boils in the stomach, causing excruciating cramps, and its passage through the body to the head causes painful cramps and spasms on its way.

Some of the best evidence that San rock art is to do with trance and its benefits, chiefly healing, rain-making and control of the herds, are the accounts of rain-making in the Bleek and Lloyd Collection.

!Khwa, the Rain, shown as a creature something like a hippopotamus or a somewhat amorphous ox, more often than not with features reminiscent of the cloud formation *cumulus mammatus*, was hunted in trance. Shamans with animal features and in postures associated with the trance dance are depicted leading the rain animal by a thong thrown over his head and horns, just as Dia!kwain or /Hang≠kass'o described it:

The men go near the place at which there is water (a spring in a deep hole), for they know that the rain animal is in that water. Then they feel where the wind is, lest the rain animal smell them, they mean to go the water without it being aware of them; they will lie in wait till it goes to graze and approach the water while it is grazing.

There are 'cuts' on the engraved rain animal at !Kann, a place Dia!kwain's father Xättin must have known well. The *!gi:ten* would cast the flesh and the blood of the rain animal where they needed water, plants, and grazing for game.

Then the wild onion leaves sprout for the people, and they dig and feed themselves with them. The people who are at home see the rainclouds and say to each other 'The !gi:ten *really seem to have their hands upon the rain animal, for you see that the rainclouds come gliding along. For the rainclouds are fine, and it looks as if they are truly going to make rain fall for us.'*

Rock paintings, then, were made by shamans recording their experiences, marking powerful places and fixing their animal-derived potency on the rock face with plant matter and animal blood rich in *!gi* for the future.

This is not the whole story. Shamanism does not answer all the questions we have about rock paintings. For a start, we cannot be sure that all theriantropes – zoomorphs – are always *!gi:ten* in trance.

Transformation was not the exclusive province of the trancing healer, rain-maker or master of the herds. In the *kumm* of the man who was transformed into a tree by the glance of a 'young maiden' on the cusp of womanhood, the poor petrified man *still has his nails, he still has his eyes, he still has his nose, his eyes remain, he is a tree, he has his head, he has his head hair, he talks, he is a tree.*

Things share states. Reading the notebooks it is too often quite impossible to tell whether someone or something referred to is dead or alive, animal or human, conscious or not – and this is true not only of the myths but of the accounts of everyday life. A perception of the liminal nature of things and a readiness to accept the possibility of transformation were hallmarks of the culture of the /Xam-ka !ei.

The 'Bushman's letters' so eloquently described by //Kabbo were a kind of transformation:

We have a sensation in our feet, as we feel the rustling feet of the springbok with which the springbok come, making the bushes rustle . . . We have a sensation in our face, on account of the blackness of the stripe of the springbok; we feel a sensation in our eyes on account of the black marks on the eyes of the springbok . . .

Hunter and quarry were linked long before a poisoned arrow had struck its target. Through the web of ritual hunting observances called *!nänna-sse* and what //Kabbo called */Xam-ka-!ke-ta !gwe* – the *letters* that *tapped* in the body resembling *the letters of books which take a message or an account of what happens in another place* – the hunter came to embody the creature he was hunting. We could think of it perhaps as a sort of 'tuning' in which the hunter prepared for the hunt by developing a kind of complicity, or at least a sympathy, with the animal he was tracking. It is a hunting technique that allows the hunter to make decisions based on the most subtle information he has ever learned and it works extremely well.

The springbok, when coming, scratches itself with its horns, and with its foot; then the Bushman feels the tapping.

//Kabbo did not need to be in a state of trance produced by hyperventilation, concentration and movement to syncopated rhythms to feel himself springbok. It seems a little bold to say that *all* theriantropic figures were painted by shamans remembering, fixing or celebrating their animal-derived potency in pigment when hunters were able to think themselves into their quarry to the point that they practically left themselves behind.

While we are considering painted theriantropes and transformation we must also take into account the recently dead. !Nanni told Lucy Lloyd in 1881:

a snake which is near a grave, we do not kill, for it is our other person, our dead person, the dead person's snake. When we see an antelope, an antelope near our other person's place, that place where our other person has died, we respect the antelope, for the antelope is not a mere antelope. Its legs seem small, it is the person who has died, and is a spirit antelope.

Spirit animals were not 'real' animals even though they were 'there' as much as any creature of the veld. They were not conjured or perceived during a state of altered consciousness but a part of the tangible physical world.

The dead were clearly present for the /Xam-ka !ei. Could

they perhaps be in the rock paintings too? Death meant a passage
to the 'past' and this was where the First at Sitting People were.
These families of animal-people had recognizable habits;
trunked, clawed and feathered, they hunted with weapons,
married with ritual and cooked with pots. They were simultaneously human and animal – how would they be depicted?

The lion goes, for he goes above in the heaven. Therefore he does
firm stand above in the sky. He is a lion who talks, he eats people,
he talks, he is a lion, he is a man, he has hair, he is a lion, his hands
are a man's.

Spirits of the dead, ill-working *!gi:ten*, were responsible
for illness and death. They were greatly feared. When Qing
explained to Orpen that the men with the heads of antelope
in the paintings they had seen were *men who had died and now
lived in rivers, and were spoilt at the same time as the elands and by
the dances of which you have seen paintings* he was not necessarily
talking about living shamans at all. Perhaps he was simply
talking about the dead; perhaps he was talking about the First
at Sitting People. The dead were certainly believed to live
'underwater', since if you wanted to visit them in trance you
would have to go through rivers, waterpits or *vleis*. What is
more, Dia!kwain and Qing quite independently identified the
same picture of theriantropes as a painting of the people of the
Early Race. Dia!kwain even said that they were *the ancient
Bushmen, . . . the race preceding the present Bushmen . . . who it is
believed killed people.*

The dead *killed people* with their attacks on your family and
your neighbours – the living.

Qing told Orpen that when the first eland was killed it
provoked /Kaggen to create the first herds and turned those
that wanted to eat them into hunters: *'Go and hunt them and*

try to kill one, that is now your work, for it was you who spoilt them,' said /Kaggen. *That day game were given to men to eat, and this is the way they were spoilt and became wild.* Since the antelope-headed people were *spoilt at the same time as the elands,* Qing meant that theriantropes are quite simply the most ancient of people – the Early Race.

If death were a place, 'the past', and you were joining them there, you would not necessarily be able to take with you the customs, manners or even the morphology of the people of the present. To die would be to resemble the people of the past.

These dead people were *spoiled by the dances of which you have seen paintings* when living shamans danced to conjure *!gi* to fight off their attacks or to enter trance so that they could go to the past and fight them hand-to-hand. Many 'war scenes' in which arrows fly back and forth across the rock face are not intended to be realistic portrayals of actual battles.

There is a painting on a red sandstone panel in a place called Beersheba near the Natal town of Underberg in which two groups of men are roughly divided by a column of cattle and pale calcified stone. The men on the right of the divide have horses, and one or two of them cross the lighter rock, threatening to encircle the group of men on the left.

The men to the left of the cattle are naked and have their legs at right-angles to their bodies with their leading feet on the ground and the soles of their trailing feet pointing upwards, a convention used to imply movement at speed. They are armed with bows and arrows and they are running away from the men on horseback, who are firing their rifles after them as they run. The men with guns wear hats, trousers and shirts and their feet are in stirrups.

At least four of the riders have climbed down from their horses to fire standing. They have powder flasks at their hips, one of which has the definite curve of a horn, and there are flashes where the hammers of their flintlock rifles have struck. The white-painted lines emerging from the barrels of the firing weapons indicate the travel of a ball. One of these lines ends where it meets the body of a running man who stumbles, unless the artist has him flat on his back and dead or dying already, in which case the two lines coming from his head are blood seeping from his skull, presumably where it has been split by a rifle ball.

Above him and to his left is another man who looks as if he has been struck in the back, painted so that the top of his body leans angularly behind him and his face is towards the 'sky'. Maybe he is looking over his shoulder at the men firing at him, as the man immediately above him seems to be. Three arrows fly from left to right, answering the rifle balls.

This picture records events – very possibly something that occurred on one specific day sometime in the early nineteenth century, given the level of the detail – but this 'war scene' is not as self-explanatory as it may appear and nor is it merely a pictorial narrative of those possible events. The /Xam word /a meant 'curse', 'harm' and 'fight' and there is plenty of that in this picture, but of course it also meant 'a concentration of power', the kind that could knock you over if a *!gi:xa* nearing trance were to point his finger at you. This kind of power, the same sort of /a that /Kaggen battled when his eland was butchered by the Meerkats, is also being generated in the picture.

On the extreme right, behind the horsemen and about half-way up the panel, a man is painted sitting with one of his knees bent, a position used by artists to show a *!gi:xa* entering trance. Two curious feathered antennae issue from his head, like the long 'tail' emerging from the base of his spine unlikely to represent anything visible in the physical world. He has his hand to his nose, which seems to be bleeding.

He may be a malevolent ambassador of the dead, urging forward the commando he has summoned. He may be fighting it. The artist may simply have him there to introduce a spiritual significance into an awful massacre so as to 'make sense' of it, to give these deaths dignity or a purpose in the face of a violent intrusion that amounted to an attack on a way of making sense of the world.

The people who painted this picture understood the carnage visited on them by the settlers as an attack of a spiritual kind. The consequences of the onslaught were metaphysical, whether or not the commando was summoned or protected by the dead.

In the last few decades the notebooks in the Bleek and Lloyd Collection have afforded us many subtle insights into the rock art of the Southern San, although there is still much to be understood. What researchers *have* discovered has already been very useful to our understanding of rock paintings well beyond the southern African subcontinent, however, and has shed some new light on the paintings and engravings of Australia, the Americas and Palaeolithic Europe too.

In the Chauvet Cave in the Ardèche valley of France, for example, there are very few human figures among the exquisitely rendered rhino, lions and cave bears. One of them, 31,000 years old, is of a man with powerful human thighs and the head and the neck of a bison.

We know that we should not interpret this image as some long-forgotten Bison God presiding over the cave. It is far more likely to do with the profound wealth of knowledge the hunting and gathering people who painted it had of the animals they lived amongst and of the unique power they considered some of them to possess. We can assume that the painting is the product of a culture that had no problem with the idea of transformation and hunters who 'thought themselves' into the animals they were tracking; whoever painted this man-bison in an interglacial period of the last Ice Age could well have had first-hand experience of transformation through shamanic ritual practice.

At the cave called Les Trois Frères a man with horns and a bison's belly stands with a bent knee and his hand to his nose. Twenty thousand years later this was called a *!gi:xa* in southern Africa.

If the people of the European Upper Palaeolithic had their equivalent of *!gi:ten* then they had someone very much like /Kaggen, too, we can be sure. We will never know what they called him, of course, because the agriculturalist people who had migrated from the Middle East into Stone Age France did not record the beliefs of the culture that they eventually wiped out.

The people who painted in the Chauvet cave, the first people of northern Europe, had no one to do that but themselves and they lived some 29,000 years on the wrong side of the invention of the alphabet.

So where *is* /Kaggen then?

We should forget the rock paintings and engravings for a moment and start looking in a certain *vlei* where reeds grew in the time of the First at Sitting People and where an old man put honey on a stone for a shoe to eat.

/Kaggen was a powerful *!gi:xa* and he poured himself into his work creating the first eland. To give the old man his due he was a genius of improvisation and this time he surpassed himself. By any measure a fully grown eland is an awesome creature. It can weigh as much as a ton; the lustre of its skin is startling; despite its huge size it can leap over your head.

When the old man's eland was killed without his permission, /Kaggen could not even use his arrows to hit the people butchering it. The Meerkats, sitting in the honey-scent of its cut fat, were in control of its potency, having killed it.

He made his eland at the waterpit, a place both of transformation and resurrection and of passage into the past, where the dead and the people of the Early Race lived. It is no wonder the eland is so powerful. With the death of the first eland came the creation of the first hunter, and this is why the eland is the animal of a man's initiation: a youth's first eland kill, making him a hunter, recreates him as a man.

When /Kaggen made the first eland he rubbed a shoe with something powerful, honey, and he sang to it. The creature was full of power; it was possible to release it and to use it. The rock face on which it was so often painted in ground ochres, ash, haematite and blood was a stiff meniscus between this world and the world of the spirit; the snakes slithering in and out of cracks are travelling between the two.

The eland was an emblem of plenty, a visual metaphor for power and sometimes a *reservoir* of power for those enacting rituals before its painting. On a rock face the eland served to remind people of the role that the animal played in allowing passage from one world to another; it stood for social stability and times of ease when game was plentiful after the rain. Remembered in the rituals of initiation and marriage it stood for the *customs* that distinguished the San from the people of the Early Race and the animals about them.

The eland, the acme of game animals, symbolized a universe that was above morals and obligations, a pitiless, beautiful and unpredictably generous place where transformation was everywhere.

Where is /Kaggen?
We don't know, but the Elands do. Have you not hunted and heard his cry, when the Elands suddenly start and run to his call?
Where he is, Elands are in droves like cattle.

/Kaggen is with the eland.

Kumm:

/A:kumm and the lion

//*Khe*//*khe* meant 'beast of prey'. It was an oath, like 'damn it' or 'for God's sake', and most of the time you had the lion in mind when you used it. Lions were dangerous, powerful creatures that had the power to make you sleepy and then hasten dusk. Good creatures to swear on.

Our parents used to say that he is a thing which dreams when he lies asleep that people have seen his footprints, people have made free with his name. Whenever he dreams, he believes his dream.

The lion could even tear your waterbag from a distance and catch you while you were absorbed in making the repair. Children never called a lion by its real name, //*kha*, the first word in Lucy Lloyd's first notebook. Instead it was /*kerre-*/*e*, 'lighting in', or *ts'á a* /*na* /*hoken e*, 'the thing whose head is darkness', since dusk was the lion's shadow. If a boy or a girl saw his spoor they should never say – look, lion prints! because the flies living in the animal's armpits would report back to the owner of those armpits that a child had been making free with its name. If a child tried to shift a fly from his face by blowing through his nostrils then that fly would go back to the lion and tell it that the child had been making mock of its smell. You had to be careful.

How big is he? the lion would ask the fly, who would reply *he is a child.* The lion would ask *is he big?* and the fly would reply *he is little.*

Leave him alone, the lion would say, *he will grow big.*

Lions had long memories; they would wait for the boy to grow and come to the hunting ground as a man before they would stand in front of him to ask: do I still look like a plaything to you?

Then our mouth is black with fear, with terror, with alarm. Our mouth is not light on account of our terror.

It was not until you were grown that you could call a lion by name.

Dia!kwain's elder sister /A:kumm, Fight Story, knew about the power of lions. She was walking home one evening after a visit when an owl swooped down out of the sky at her.

An owl did as follows to my elder sister /A:kumm as she was leaving Kenhardt. When she was half way the owl saw that the sun was about to set and snatched her, it tried to catch her.

Then it flew away. /A:kumm remembered that when an owl tried to catch you like this it meant that a beast of prey was near by. Her life was in danger and she was only half-way home.

She lit the biggest fire she was able. The creature would still be slinking towards it while /A:kumm made a dash for her family, she hoped; if the fire were to waylay the animal coming for her for a few minutes she might just make it to safety.

When she reached the hills that lay between her and her home she saw a lion sitting on the broken dolerite. Now it was getting very dark, and this was probably the lion's fault too. /A:kumm carried on in the direction of her family, willing herself invisible and scentless.

And my sister went evading him as he sat there. And the lion came to the fire and missed her at the fire. And the lion found her footprints and followed them. And as she went along she heard the lion roaring as it sought her.

It was almost night as she heard the animal roaring behind her and so she made towards the hills to hide herself among the quiver trees and boulders: it was either that or a race against a beast of prey through the dark, and that was far too dangerous. If she could find somewhere on hill to hide she might at least have a chance.

I will climb onto a rock in the dusk, I will go to lie down up on the ridge of rock, she thought.

And she climbed up onto the rock in the dusk, and she lay down on the ridge of rock. And she lay waiting. She slept.

And she slept until the lion woke her. It was calling her name.

/A:kumm:we! A xa de? shouted the lion. *Oh, /A:kumm! Where are you?*

Having tracked her across the dust the animal had lost her spoor at the boulders. It had obviously lost her scent, too, because now it had resorted to human speech.

/A:kumm said nothing. She knew that it could not be a man calling for her because no one but the lion knew she was there. *The old women have often told me that a lion will call sounding like a man when he wants us to answer. He is doing this because he wants me to think that a person is calling me, and go to him*, she thought to herself. If the lion had resorted to speech it had to be desperate. She said nothing.

Carry on shouting, she thought. – I know what you are but you don't know where I am. Carry on.

The lion called her again. '*/A:kumm-we!* – Oh /A:kumm! Where are you? Your footprints stop here and I can't see you anywhere. I could've sworn you'd be sitting here, but you're not.' *Do pull me up,* he went on. *Why do you let me call seeking you, when I am sure you are sitting there?*

She was silent.

Then my sister remembered that Mother had told her that a lion will put his tail in his mouth and call seeking us with his tail in his mouth, when he wants to sound like a man, so that we do not hear that he is a lion. That is why he puts his tail into his mouth.

She said nothing.

!Kau-/nunu:

Kenhardt

*As to Kenhardt, at the time when the lion acted like this towards my sister,
the homes of the white people were not yet there. But Bushmen were living
at Kenhardt.*

A photograph of an old woman called Som:ang and her
husband !Kommanan-!a.

Their Dutch names were Lenki and Klaas and they both
wear rags. Som:ang was four feet six inches tall, her hair was
short and white, she carried a stick, and she was still a girl
in 1868 when Kenhardt was founded at a 'Bushman water'
called !Kau-/nunu with the arrival of the magistrate who
sentenced //Kabbo and his family.

It was on her journey home from !Kau-/nunu that
Dia!kwain's sister was pursued by a lion that put its tail into
his mouth to speak with the voice of a man. She might even
have been visiting Som:ang's family, as many as twenty years
before Maximillian Jackson, the magistrate who sentenced
//Kabbo and his family in Victoria West, came; perhaps fifty
before the photograph was taken.

As a girl, Som:ang had been at school learning to speak
Dutch when the Koranna came and everybody ran away
to //Ka//kammi, today known as Kakamas, about eighty
kilometres west of the town of Upington along the Orange
River. Both she and her husband !Kommanan-!a were born
at a place called the Bitterpits, //Kabbo's place.

This was once a Bushman water, Dorothea Bleek records in the notes on the reverse of the photographs.

Mrs Bernardi, née van der Westhuizen, said that when her father bought the place in 1874 there were 42 Bushmen there. Most of them moved away, but one family remained in her father's service till his death, then went with her brother. !Kommanan-!a said that at their home they ate ants' eggs, bitter oinkies, tortoises, porcupines, and game, chiefly springbok, ostrich and springhare.

The photograph was taken in 1910. !Kommanan-!a was probably one of the Bushmen to move away when the farm was sold. Wherever he went it is unlikely that he was able to eat ants' eggs, bitter oinkies and springbok and by the time that Dorothea Bleek took his picture he was surviving on *magistrate's rations*.

Between 1910 and the late 1920s Dorothea Bleek travelled all over southern Africa, visiting present-day Namibia, the Bechuanaland Protectorate, Angola and Tanzania, recording as much of the threatened San culture of these places as she could by making photographs, transcriptions and audio recordings on wax cylinders recently rediscovered in the archives of the University of Cape Town. The first place she visited was the Northern Cape, looking for the *children and nephews* of the people her father and her aunt had interviewed in the last decades of the 1800s. This was where she took the photograph of Som:ang and her husband !Kommanan-!a.

In Kenhardt she discovered what happened to /Xaken-ang, the old woman who left Charlton House in 1884, and to the other /Xam people who disappeared from Salt River all those years before. They had asked a policeman for directions, he had shown them the way and they all walked back home.

Among the other pictures she took in Kenhardt and the nearby towns is a photograph of Sonkia-bo, an old woman sitting behind an iron cooking pot. Like Som:ang she is wearing rags. Her hair is knotted into short dreadlocks and she sits before a shelter made from dry branches and sacking. She was a little girl when the Koranna came to Kenhardt *from the north of the river, or from the other side of it*. She told Dorothea that when they fought the Bushmen, and killed them, the ammunition in their guns was made from steenbok horn. Her cousin's grandmother had been shot in the thigh but she did not die.

The Koranna came first from the north and killed many Bushmen and women. Then the white men came from the south and killed many more. When they were children, *only* Bushmen were in the country, many Bushmen.

The dry flats and *koppies* behind Dorothea's subjects stretch off indistinctly. There is woodsmoke, and dust, strips of torn cotton caught up in windbreaks made of bushes. The only stories the people have to tell are of dispossession and expulsion; the landscape behind them is bereft of herds other than the stock belonging to farmers of European descent.

An old man called !Nuren /a xwaiten stands with the aid of a stick, his legs apart to accommodate the hernia in his belly, his chest a mass of wrinkles. He has a sad frown.

Fifty years ago, every adult Bushman knew all his people's lore. A tale begun by a person from one place could be finished by someone from another

place at a later date. In 1910 I visited the northern parts of the Cape Colony and found the children, nephews and nieces of some of the former informants still living there. Not one of them knew a single story. On my reading some of the old texts a couple of old men recognised a few customs and said 'I once heard my people tell that.' But the folklore was dead, killed by a life of service among strangers and the breaking up of families.

Where is /Kaggen?

/Xam-ka !au, the dust of the /Xam, was never a world of ease and plenty. Apart from a few weeks after the rains when the herds came and the leaves were plentiful it had never been anything other than terribly difficult, unforgiving and harsh. The ancestors of the people in Dorothea Bleek's photographs, all descended from the very first people ever to inhabit the land, had always lived in shelters and behind windbreaks with neither money nor security and with few possessions – but they had never been *poor* like this.

/Kaggen is not here. He is with the elands and he took something that used to insist itself in myth and ritual with him when he went. He is not here because poverty is predictable; it explains itself. Here the only ritual necessary to survival is labour, best explained by the story of constant hunger.

The people in these pictures are shown standing, if they are able. The children seem pleased to be photographed. Everybody else is generally indifferent, with the exception of a very old woman called /Gara-ang, known as Cinna, who sits with her knees up, dressed in rags. She was less than four feet tall. Dorothea could not speak to her since the old woman was too deaf, so whatever she had to say was never written down. In one picture she sits with her blanket over her shoulders showing the photographer her profile, set in a kind of scowl. In another she tries to hide her face from the camera with her blanket.

An old man called Tsoinxa stands before his shelter, a rough hut made covered with dried grass and old sacking, with his hands in the pockets of the remains of an old raincoat. It is difficult to read his expression, simultaneously frown and smile. The only language he spoke was /Xam, and he was born in the town of Vanwyksvlei, or /Oggen-/oggen as it used to be known before the van Wyks founded their sheep farm beside the spring there.

There were many lions there; they killed three, then left the place.

This must have been decades before Jackson came to Kenhardt.

He had lived at Sklip-gat and Bitterpits, then had come to Klipdam and grown old under his master there.

The Bitterpits used to be a Bushman water.

Author's note

Neither 'San' nor 'Bushman' was a positive term.

San – 'cattleless' – was a denigrating word used by a people for whom cattle were everything, the Khoekhoen, for others who had none. It has, or had, a meaning somewhere between 'tramp' and 'outside of the law', but the most frequently used alternative, Bushmen, held terribly racist connotations of its own. It is a fact that the first people of southern Africa had no name for themselves as a whole.

For many the term 'Bushmen' has new connotations to do with resistance and nationhood, but the consensus is that San, free at least of colonial overtones, is probably the better of the two. I have tried to avoid either term by using /Xam-ka !ei where I can, but this has not always been possible when speaking of this people and their relatives together. Then I normally use San.

I have also used the more accurate Khoekhoen instead of Khoikhoi.

The South African San Institute (SASI) is a non-governmental organization seeking to address issues of land rights, language, health and income-generation for the benefit of the San people of southern Africa. Its aim is to ensure them permanent control of their own lives and resources. SASI can be contacted at www.san.org.za/sasi/home.htm

For those interested in efforts being made towards the understanding and the preservation of San rock art, the Rock Art Research Unit of the University of Witwatesrand can be visited at www.wits.ac.za/science/archaeology.

Acknowledgements

Thank you to Lucy Jago first of all, who thought that this should be a book. Thanks also to Stephanie Cabot at William Morris and Eleo Gordon, my editor at Penguin, for the opportunity to write it and the advice I needed to see it finished.

Thank you to Mervyn, Geraldine and Paul Bennun and to Serena Bobowski.

I am not an anthropologist by training and in writing this book I have drawn on research published by archaeologists and anthropologists who have made the study of rock art, the material in the Bleek and Lloyd Collection and the San people of southern Africa their lives' work. I am particularly grateful to Hugh Brody, Janette Deacon, Thomas Dowson, Marius Guenther, Roger Hewitt, Richard Katz, David Lewis-Williams, Anne Solomon and Robert Thornton.

Thank you to Sheila Menon, whose assistance made the research in the Northern Cape possible and whose company made it such a pleasure, and to Kester Thompson, whose /Kaggen at the Gate Theatre in London makes an extended appearance here.

Thanks also to Colin Bennun, Ania Dabrowska, Jagoda Przybysz, Tanya Barben of the Rare Books and Special Collections Department of the University of Cape Town Library, Lesley Hart, Janine Dunlop, Yasmin Mohamed and Isaac Ntabankulu of the Manuscripts and Archives Department of the University of Cape Town Library, Chris Philips, Nabil Elouhabi, Eugenie Furniss and Jamison Stoltz at William Morris, Ahmed Sidki and Cath Trant, Julie Duffy at Penguin, my copy-editor Trevor Horwood, Marius and the staff of the National Library of South Africa in Cape Town, Ted

Hopkins, Colin Campbell, the van Wyks of Cape Town and Pap-kuilsfontein, the staff of the British Library, Pani Ahmadi-Moore, Heather Uprichard, Mark Watkins, Huffie Strauss at Traveller's Rest, Annie Peel, Olivia Funnell, Paul Bradshaw, Andrew Gideon Thomson, Brian Coleman, Corah Clarke, Capoeira Cearà, Manoel dos Reis Machado, Michael Uwmedimo, Katlego Moteno, Miguel Arnedo, Alex Lloyd and everybody at Arbeidsvreug.

Don Pinnock first introduced me to the rock art of the Southern San in the course of a journey that began at the source of the Orange River in Lesotho and ended here. Thanks to him and to Patricia Shonstein Pinnock for their excellent advice, their hospitality and their support.

Visiting rock art sites

I have intentionally disguised the whereabouts of the rock art sites in this book since they are nearly all on working farms where people value their privacy or in unprotected places where the engravings and paintings and the environment around them are at risk.

There are many very atmospheric and important sites in southern Africa that can be visited without trespass or the danger of damage to the art on the site. It is better by far to visit rock art sites with a guide: he or she should be able to explain the pictures to you and point out details and figures that you might otherwise have missed.

San rock art is a priceless resource and no one will ever make any more. Places which should be designated World Heritage sites are unprotected and susceptible to vandalism and 'accidental' damage. If you choose to visit them it may well be your responsibility to play the part of the curator; you should take the responsibility very seriously.

Taking rubbings of engravings is extremely damaging as it destroys the patina on the rock for good. Take photographs instead. Never walk on engravings and do not touch rock paintings. Take great care with liquids of any kind near paintings; water alone is enough to damage pigments permanently.

/Xam and !Xun names

A guide to the pronunciation of the special characters can be found on page 391.

/A:kumm   Sister of Dia!kwain. The name means 'Fight Story'.

/A!kungta   Klaas Stoffel. /Xam man resident at The Hill from 29 August 1870 to 15 October 1873.

Da   !Xun boy from the north of present-day Namibia resident at Charlton House from April 1880.

Dia!kwain   David Hoesar. /Xam man resident at The Hill from 29 November 1873 to 18 March 1874 and 13 June 1874 to 7 March 1876.

Du-//hu   Wife of Dia!kwain's brother K'obo.

//Goo-ka-!kui   //Kabbo's son. The name means 'Smoke's Man'.

/Hang≠kass'o   Klein Jantje. /Xam man resident at The Hill between 22 June and 28 July 1871 and at Charlton House between 10 January 1878 and December 1879. Married to //Kabbo's daughter Suobba-//kein, known as Sara.

!Hu!hun   Son of /Hang≠kass'o and Suobba-//kein.

/Huntu!katt!katten   /Kaggen's wife, the Dassie, Hyrax, or Rock Rabbit.

Jantje Tooren   //Kabbo's Dutch name.

//Kabbo   Oud Jantje Tooren. /Xam man resident at The Hill from 16 February 1871 to 15 October 1873. Married to !Kwabba-ang (Oude Lies.) //Kabbo means 'Dream'.

/Kaggen   The Mantis. Old man, trickster, eland-creator, coward and hero.

≠*Kamme-ang*   Dia!kwain's mother. ≠Kamme-ang was her *little name*, that given her by her parents. She was better known as /Ko:ang, which means 'Start Back'.

≠*Kasing*   Klaas Katkop. /Xam man resident at The Hill between 1 November 1873 and 18 March 1874 and 13 June 1874 to 13 January 1875. Married to Dia!kwain's sister !Kweiten ta //ken.

/*Kaunu*   New Grass Leg. A rain-maker who taught //Kabbo.

!*Khwa*   The Rain or the Water. !Khwa-ka xoro was the rain animal.

!*Khwe //na s'o !kwe*   *The First at Sitting People.* The Early Race.

/*Ko:ang*   *See* ≠Kamme-ang.

K'obo   Dia!kwain's elder brother. His *little name* (the name given him by his parents) was //Xwa:gan-te.

!*Kwabba-ang*   Oude Lies. //Kabbo's wife.

!*Kwammang-a*   /Kaggen's son-in-law: the red in the rainbow, possibly the rainbow itself.

!*Kweiten ta //ken*   Rachel. /Xam woman resident at The Hill between 13 June 1874 and 12 January 1875. Dia!kwain's sister. Married to ≠Kasing.

!*Nanni*   !Xun boy resident at Charlton house from 1 September 1879.

/*Ni*   /Kaggen's grandson, the Ichneumon (mongoose).

!*Nuin /kuïten*   Celebrated rain-maker; taught Dia!kwain's father Xättin about the *Rain's things*. !Nuin means 'Bowstring'.

Oud Jantje Tooren   *See* //Kabbo.

Oude Lies   *See* !Kwabba-ang.

Suobba-//kein   Sara. Married to /Hang≠kass'o. //Kabbo's daughter.

Tamme   !Xun boy resident at Charlton House from 1 September 1879.

/*Uma*   !Xun boy resident at Charlton House from April 1880.

Whai:ttu   Dia!kwain's sister. The name means 'Springbok Skin'.

/Xam-ka !au   The Dust/Earth/Soil of the /Xam.

/Xam-ka !ei   The indigenous people of South Africa's Northern Cape province.

Xättin: Dia!kwain's father. Xättin means 'Clay Hand'. His *little name* (the name given him by his parents) was ≠Gwai-/ka.

!Xo: /Kaggen's adopted daughter, the Porcupine.

!Xun   The San people of north-central Namibia.

Glossary

/a (/Xam) 'Fight', 'curse', 'harm' or 'a concentration of magical power'.

assegai A broad iron spearhead with a pointed tip introduced to southern Africa by Bantu (siNtu) speaking people such as the Zulu and the Xhosa.

brinkkop (Afrikaans) A corruption of *bruin kop*, meaning 'brown hill'.

!gi (/Xam) Force; spiritual power.

!gi:ten The plural of *!gi:xa*.

!gi:xa (/Xam) 'Possessor of power'; a shaman, usually, or spirit.

Hottentots Pejorative word used by European settlers in South Africa for the Khoekhoen.

Khoekhoen Formerly spelled Khoikhoi. Herding people related genetically and linguistically to the hunting and gathering people they called San, Soaqua and Sonqua (the so-called Bushmen).

kloof (Afrikaans) A ravine.

knobkerrie Throwing stick used in the hunt and as a weapon.

koppie (Afrikaans) A little hill.

kukummi (/Xam) The plural of *kumm*.

kumm (/Xam) Something told; a story, a piece of history, a myth, news.

!nänna-sse (/Xam) Rituals enacted to show respect to a hunted animal.

/nu !ke (/Xam) The dead; spirits of the dead.

San (Khoe) 'Cattleless'; used by the Khoekhoen for the hunting and gathering people of the Cape interior.

spoor The tracks left by an animal (or person).

stoep   (Afrikaans) A verandah.

veldkos   (Afrikaans) 'Food of the veld'; roots, leaves, seeds, tubers, larvae, etc.

vlei   (Afrikaans) A pool of standing water.

A guide to pronunciation

/ – the dental click.
/ / – the lateral click.
! – the guttural (alveolar-palatal) click.
≠ – the palatal (alveolar) click.

The dental click, /, is made by pressing the tip of the tongue against the teeth and then withdrawing it. The palatal click, ≠, is made by pressing the front part of the tongue on the roof of the mouth and quickly removing it. The lateral click, //, is made with the tongue in the same position as the palatal, ≠ by releasing air along the sides. The guttural (alveolar-palatal) click, !, is made at the very back of the mouth.

The 'X' of /Xam-ka !ei is pronounced like the Afrikaans 'g', an aspirated guttural something like the 'ch' in *loch*. Hard consonants after the clicks are pronounced.

The dental click is almost identical to the sound of indignation, not unfrequently uttered by Europeans; and the lateral is similar to an interjection, by which horses are, in some countries, stimulated to action. The guttural click has been compared to the popping of the cork of a bottle of Champagne, and the palatal to the crack of a whip. (Wilhelm Bleek, 1867)

An apostrophe is used to indicate an arrest of breath, a colon to indicate a lengthened vowel.

In the Xhosa, Zulu and SeSotho languages, letters instead of symbols are used to designate clicks:

/ *is represented by 'c'*,
≠ *is represented by 'q'*,
// *is represented by 'x'*.
! *has no letter equivalent in these languages*

References and notes

There exists an enormous body of historical and ethnographic research pertaining to the work of Wilhelm Bleek and Lucy Lloyd, the material they collected from their /Xam informants and the San people of southern Africa. I have drawn on this research on nearly every page here; in many ways much of this book should be considered a survey of the broad consensus achieved through the decades' worth of work that went into the publications on the following list.

Morgan Bisele, *Women Like Meat: The Folklore and Foraging Ideology of the Kalahari Ju/'hoan* (Witwatersrand University Press, Johannesburg 1993)

Dorothea Bleek, *A Bushman Dictionary* (American Oriental Society, New Haven 1956)

Edith Bleek and Dorothea Bleek, 'Notes on the Bushmen', in Helen Tongue (ed.), *Bushman Paintings* (Clarendon Press, London 1909)

W. H. I. Bleek and I. C. Lloyd, Notebooks and papers in the Manuscripts and Archives Department of the University of Cape Town (BC151)

W. H. I. Bleek and I. C. Lloyd, *Specimens of Bushman Folklore* (George Allen, London 1911)

Hugh Brody, *The Other Side of Eden: Hunter-Gatherers, Farmers and the Shaping of the World* (Faber and Faber, London 2001)

Hilary Deacon and Janette Deacon, *Human Beginnings in South Africa* (David Philip, Cape Town 1999)

Janette Deacon, 'My Place Is the Bitterpits: The Home Territory of Bleek and Lloyd's /Xam San Informants', *African Studies*, 1986

Janette Deacon, 'Archaeology of the Grass and Flat Bushmen', in J. Deacon and T. Dowson (eds), *Voices From the Past: /Xam Bushmen and the Bleek and Lloyd Collection* (Witwatersrand University Press, Johannesburg 1996)

Jared Diamond, *Guns, Germs and Steel* (Vintage, London 1998)

R. Elphick, *Khoikhoi and the Founding of White South Africa* (Raven Press, Johannesburg 1985)

M. Guenther, 'Animals in Bushman Thought, Myth and Art', in T. Ingold, D. Riches and J. Woodburn (eds), *Hunters and Gatherers: Property, Power and Ideology*, vol. 2 (Berg, Oxford 1988)

M. Guenther, *Bushman Folktales: Oral Traditions of the Nharo of Botswana and the /Xam of the Cape* (Franz Steiner Verlag, Wiesbaden and Stuttgart 1989)

M. Guenther, 'Attempting to Contextualise /Xam Oral Tradition', in J. Deacon and T. Dowson (eds), *Voices From the Past: /Xam Bushmen and the Bleek and Lloyd Collection* (Witwatersrand University Press, Johannesburg 1996)

Roger Hewitt, *Structure, Meaning and Ritual in the Narratives of the Southern San* (Helmut Buske Verlag, Hamburg 1986)

R. Katz, *Boiling Energy: Community Healing among the Kalahari !Kung* (Harvard University Press, Cambridge, MA 1981)

Richard Lee, *The !Kung San: Men, Women and Work in a Foraging Society* (Cambridge University Press, Cambridge 1979)

David Lewis-Williams, 'A Visit to the Lion's House: The Structure, Metaphors and Sociopolitical Significance of a Nineteenth-Century Bushman Myth', in J. Deacon and T. Dowson (eds), *Voices From the Past: /Xam Bushmen and the Bleek and Lloyd Collection* (Witwatersrand University Press, Johannesburg 1996)

David Lewis-Williams, *Believing and Seeing: Symbolic Meanings in Southern San Rock Paintings* (Academic Press, London 1981)

David Lewis-Williams, 'A Dream of Eland: An Unexplored Component of San Shamanism and Rock Art', *World Archaeology* 19 (1987): 165–77

David Lewis-Williams and Thomas Dowson: *Images of Power: Understanding San Rock Art* (Southern Book Publishers, Johannesburg 1989)

Lorna Marshall, 'N!ow', *Africa* 27 (1957): 232–40

J. M. Orpen, 'A Glimpse into the Mythology of the Maluti Bushmen', *Cape Monthly Magazine* 9.49 (1874)

Nigel Penn, 'Fated to Perish: The Destruction of the Cape San', in P. Skotnes (ed.), *Miscast* (University of Cape Town Press, 1996)

Nigel Penn, 'The Northern Cape Frontier Zone 1700–c.1815', PhD Thesis, University of Cape Town, 1995

Nigel Penn, 'Pastoralists and Pastoralism in the Northern Cape Frontier Zone during the Eighteenth Century', in *Prehistoric Pastoralism in Southern Africa*, The South African Archaeological Society Goodwin Series, vol. 5 (South African Archaeological Society, Cape Town 1986)

Sigrid Schmidt, 'Lucy Catherine Lloyd', in J. Deacon and T. Dowson (eds), *Voices From the Past: /Xam Bushmen and the Bleek and Lloyd Collection* (Witwatersrand University Press, Johannesburg 1996)

P. Skotnes: 'The Visual as a Site of Meaning: San Parietal Painting and the Experience of Modern Art', in T. A. Dowson and D. Lewis-Williams (eds), *Contested Images: Diversity in Southern African Rock Art Research* (Witwatersrand University Press, Johannesburg 1994)

Anne Solomon, 'Meanings, Models and Minds: A Reply to Lewis-Williams', *South African Archaeological Bulletin*, June 1999

Anne Solomon, 'The Myth of Ritual Origins? Ethnography, Mythology and Interpretation of San Rock Art', *South African Archaeological Bulletin*, June 1997

Otto Spohr, *Wilhelm H. I. Bleek: A Bio-bibliographical Sketch* (University of Cape Town Library, Cape Town 1962)

Otto Spohr (ed.), *The Natal Diaries of Dr W. H. I. Bleek* (A. A. Balkema, Cape Town 1965)

Robert Thornton, 'This Dying Out Race: WHI Bleek's Approach
to the Languages of Southern Africa', *Social Dynamics*, 1983

Robert Thornton, *The Discovery of Southern African Literatures*
(University of Cape Town Press, Cape Town 1983)

Patricia Vinnicombe, *People of the Eland* (Natal University Press,
Pietermaritzburg 1976)

R. Yates, A. Manhire and J. Parkington: 'Colonial Era Paintings in
the Rock Art of the South Western Cape: Some Preliminary
Observations', in *Historical Archaeology in the Western Cape*, South
African Archaeological Society, Goodwin Series, vol. 7 (South
African Archaeological Society, Cape Town 1993)

David Lewis-Williams' *Stories that Float from Afar* (David Philip,
Cape Town 2000) is the first major publication of material from the
notebooks in the Bleek and Lloyd Collection since Bleek and
Lloyd's *Specimens of Bushman Folklore* in 1911 and contains different
versions of some of the material published in this book as well as
many other previously unpublished myths, personal histories and
descriptions. Its publication, which came when work on this book
was already well advanced, gave me the opportunity to compare
versions of previously unpublished translations with my own. It is
recommended to anyone with an interest in the Collection who
might find it difficult to locate *Specimens of Bushman Folklore*.

Janette Deacon and Thomas Dowson's *Voices From the Past:
/Xam Bushmen and the Bleek and Lloyd Collection* (Witwatersrand
University Press, Johannesburg 1996) and Pippa Skotnes's *Miscast:
Negotiating the Presence of the Bushmen* (University of Cape Town
Press, 1996), two collections of papers demonstrating the remarkable
breadth of the research inspired by the Bleek and Lloyd Collection,
are essential reading for anyone with an interest in the anthropologi-
cal and historical questions the Collection raises.

This book was already finished on the publication of *Der Mond
als Schuh: The Moon as Shoe* (Scheidegger and Spiess, Zurich 2003),

edited by Miklós Szalay, which reproduces all the paintings, drawings, maps and sculptures made by Bleek and Lloyd's informants
and gives a far more scholarly account of the ethnographical research
I have outlined here.

The following books, papers and manuscripts were useful for historical research.

Barbara Buchanan, *Natal Memories* (Shuter and Shooter, Pietermaritzburg 1941)

Luigi Luca Cavalli-Sforza, *Genes, Peoples and Languages* (Allen Lane,
London 2000)

Harriet Deacon, 'A History of the Breakwater Prison from 1859 to
1905' (unpublished BA thesis, University of Cape Town 1989)

Christopher Ehret, 'The First Spread of Food Production to
Southern Africa', in C. Ehret and M. Posnansky (eds), *The
Archeological and Linguistic Reconstruction of African History* (Univer-
sity of California Press, Berkeley 1982)

Lady Duff Gordon, *Letters from the Cape* (Oxford University Press,
Oxford 1927)

Jeff Guy, *The Heretic: A Study of the Life of John William Colenso*
(University of Natal Press, Pietermaritzburg 1983)

Sir Thomas Maclear, Diary, Cape Archives A515/72

R. Moffat, *Missionary Labours and Scenes in Southern Africa* (J. Snow,
London 1842)

Thomas Phipson (ed.), *The Natal Almanac and Yearly Register* (Pietermaritzburg 1863–1906)

L. Quintana-Murci, O. Semino, H.-J. Bandelt and K. McElreavey,
'Genetic Evidence of an Early Exit through Eastern Africa',
Nature Genetics 23 (1999): 437–41

John Reader, *Africa: A Biography* (Penguin, London 1998)

Wyn Rees (ed. L. Colenso), *Letters from Natal* (Shuter and Shooter,
Pietermaritzburg 1958)

A. W. L. Rivett, *Ten Years Church Work in Natal* (Jarrold & Sons, London 1890)

N. Worden, E. van Heyningen and V. Bickford-Smith, *Cape Town: The Making of a City* (David Philip, Cape Town 1998)

Other books, papers and manuscripts cited are included in the chapter-by-chapter notes below.

At the confluence of the Senqu and the Qaqa

!Khwa lightens . . . and *The Stars are also things* . . . were first printed in Bleek and Lloyd, *Specimens of Bushman Folklore*. The other quotes come from unpublished passages from notebooks in the Bleek and Lloyd Collection (BC151), Manuscripts and Archives Department, UCT. The site described here is entirely unprotected and is not at a confluence of either of these two rivers; the Qaqa River is not a tributary of the Senqu.

Kumm: The First at Sitting People were those who first inhabited the earth

This is a retranslation of a note from one of Bleek's notebooks (p. 3150) published in Bleek and Lloyd, *Specimens of Bushman Folklore*.

!Khwe //na s'o !kwe: The Early Race

Edith and Dorothea Bleek, 'Notes on the Bushmen'; Thornton, *This Dying Out Race* and *The Discovery of Southern African Literatures*; Guenther, *Bushman Folktales*; Theophilus Hahn, *Tsuni-//Goam:*

The Supreme Being of the Khoi-Khoi (Trübner, London 1881); Lewis-Williams: *Believing and Seeing*.

The beasts of prey were once people . . . is an unpublished fragment from Lloyd, VIII 18. *He has feet with which he is a lion* . . . is from another unpublished passage. Although *!gi:ten* were often described as lions in very similar terms, this is from a passage to do with the people of the Early Race. The story of the Quagga and her husband the Young He-Dog is based on the translation published by Dorothea Bleek in *Bantu Studies*, 'Special Speech of Animals and Moon' (1936); The story of the Anteater and the Lynx known as 'The Anteater's Laws' is a composite of versions and extracts published in Guenther's *Bushman Folktales*, D. Bleek's 'Special Speech of Animals and Moon' and unpublished passages from the notebooks in the Bleek and Lloyd Collection.

Guenther's *Bushman Folktales* discusses many of the ideas in this chapter in far greater depth and detail.

Kumm: /Kaggen, the Eland, the Meerkats and the Moon

This story owes a great deal to David Lewis-Williams' discussion of the /Xam word /a in *Believing and Seeing*, Roger Hewitt's analysis of the character and stories of /Kaggen in *Structure, Meaning and Ritual in the Narratives of the Southern San* and to Kester Thompson, who adapted versions of the story for performance at the Gate Theatre in London in the spring of 2002. Although it follows the same composite structure as the version published in L. C. Lloyd and Dorothea Bleek's *The Mantis and His Friends* (Maskew Miller, Cape Town 1924) it draws on various published and unpublished passages from the notebooks in the Bleek and Lloyd Collection. See the passage published as 'Kumm 23' in Lewis-Williams' *Stories That Float From Afar* for a complete, unabridged translation of one of the longer versions. The usage of 'eldest son' on page 59 is honorific rather than literal.

/Kaggen: The Mantis

Many of the themes in this chapter were better discussed by Roger Hewitt in his *Structure, Meaning and Ritual in the Narratives of the Southern San*. Also see W. B. Baikie, *Narrative of an Exploring Voyage up the Rivers Kwora and Binue* (John Murray, London 1856) and 'Diaries of expedition up the Niger' (manuscript in British Library add. 32448); Rev. Samuel Crowther, *Journal of an expedition up the Niger and Tshadda Rivers* (Frank Cass, London 1855); Sir Francis Galton, *The Art of Travel*, . . . (John Murray, London 1856); Alan Hattersley, *Portrait of a Colony* (Cambridge University Press, Cambridge 1940); T. J. Hutchinson, *Narrative of the Niger, Tshadda and Binue Exploration* (Frank Cass, London 1855); George Russell, *Old Durban* (Simpkin Marshall, Durban 1899); Lloyd and Bleek, *The Mantis and His Friends*; Augusta de Mist, *Diary of a Journey to the Cape of Good Hope and the Interior of Africa in 1802 and 1803* (A. A. Balkema, Cape Town 1993); Otto Spohr, *Wilhelm H. I. Bleek: A Bio-bibliographical Sketch* and *The Natal Diaries of Dr W. H. I. Bleek*; Robert Thornton, *The Discovery of Southern African Literatures*; and unpublished manuscripts in the Grey Collection at the National Library of South Africa.

Kumm: How the approach of a commando is foretold by the mist

Notebook: Lloyd, v 16, pp. 5199–205 (11 August 1875).

K'au: Commando

Fatal beating: Notebook: Lloyd v 23, p. 6872 (20 January 1876); Brody, *The Other Side of Eden*; Elphick, *Khoikhoi and the Founding of White South Africa*; Penn, 'The Northern Cape Frontier Zone 1700–c.1815' and 'Fated to Perish'.

Kumm: //Kabbo's journey in the railway train (from Mowbray to Cape Town and back)

Bleek, VIII, p. 89 (1871). A translation of this was first published in *Specimens of Bushman Folklore*.

//Xara-//kam: The Bitterpits

Unpublished passages in the notebooks; W. H. I. Bleek, *Report of Dr Bleek concerning his researches into the Bushman language and customs. Presented to the Honourable the House of Assembly by command of his Excellency the Governor* (House of Assembly, Cape Town 1873); Bleek and Lloyd, *Specimens of Bushman Folklore*; correspondence in the Bleek and Lloyd Collection, University of Cape Town.

Kumm: /Kaggen and the Ticks

Lloyd and Bleek, *The Mantis and His Friends*; unpublished passages in the notebooks. With thanks to Kester Thompson.

!Gi:xa: 'Sorcerer'

W. H. I. Bleek, *Second Report Concerning Bushman Researches* (Saul Solomon and Co., Cape Town 1875); D. Bleek, 'Customs and Belief of the /Xam Bushmen: Part III – Game Animals', 'Part IV – Omens, Windmaking and Clouds', 'Part VII – Sorcerers', *Bantu Studies*, 1932; Bleek and Lloyd, *Specimens of Bushman Folklore*; J. Deacon, 'My Place Is the Bitterpits'; correspondence in the Bleek and Lloyd Collection, University of Cape Town; R. Katz, *Boiling Energy*; G. W. Stow and D. Bleek, *Rock Paintings in South Africa* (Methuen, London 1930); unpublished passages in the notebooks.

Kumm: The man who shot the Rain

Lloyd, VIII 17, pp. 7461–72 (16 September 1878).

!Khwa: The Rain

W. H. I. Bleek, *Second Report*; Lewis-Williams, 'A Visit to the Lion's House'; D. Bleek, 'Customs and Belief of the /Xam Bushmen: Part V – The Rain', 'Part VI – Rain Making', *Bantu Studies*, 1932; Bleek and Lloyd, *Specimens of Bushman Folklore*; Stow and Bleek, *Rock Paintings in South Africa*; Bert Woodhouse, *The Rain and its Creatures* (William Waterman, Rivonia 1992); correspondence, notebooks and papers in the Bleek and Lloyd Collection, University of Cape Town.

See Lewis-Williams' *Believing and Seeing* for a far more detailed analysis of the San ethnology relating to rain. A translation of !Kweiten's story of the Maiden and the Water Child was published in *Specimens of Bushman Folklore*. 'Disgusting trespass . . .' from Thomas

Maclear's diary (Cape Archives A515/72) was first quoted (as far as I know) in Martin Hall's paper 'The Proximity of Dr Bleek's Bushmen', in *Miscast: Negotiating the Presence of the Bushmen*, edited by Pippa Skotnes. The committee member who objected to Bleek's grant was John Merriman.

Relating her story of the flood in Victoria West, /Hang≠kass'o called his wife by her other name, ≠Kuken-ang.

Kumm: The two brothers of the Early Race who hunted lions

Lloyd VIII 18, pp. 7551–88 (23 September 1878). See also D. Bleek, 'Customs and Belief of the /Xam Bushmen: Part II – The Lion', *Bantu Studies* 5 (1932).

!Khwe a tsu !kung-so: The North Wind

D. Bleek, 'Customs and Belief of the /Xam Bushmen: Part IV – Omens, Windmaking and Clouds', *Bantu Studies* 6 (1932).

Kumm: The origin of death

This story is a composite of unpublished and published versions. There are several more-or-less complete versions in the notebooks, and pages of notes, and a long translation in *Specimens of Bushman Folklore*.

The Moon spoke with a click used by no one else apart from the Anteater. Bleek, who gave it the symbol ??, wrote that this special click was made by 'curling up the tongue backwards and then with-drawing the turned up part of the tongue from the upper palate'.

/Nu !ke: The Dead

D. Bleek, 'Customs and Belief of the /Xam Bushmen: Part III –
Game Animals', 'Part IV – Omens, Windmaking and Clouds', 'Part
VII – Sorcerers', *Bantu Studies*, 1932; Deacon, 'My Place Is the
Bitterpits'; David Lewis-Williams and Thomas Dowson, *Images of
Power*; Bleek and Lloyd, *Specimens of Bushman Folklore*; Anne Solo-
mon; 'Meanings, Models and Minds', and 'The Myth of Ritual
Origins?'; correspondence in the Bleek and Lloyd Collection, Uni-
versity of Cape Town.

Kumm: The dream which Dia!kwain had before he heard of the death of his father

Notebook a2.1.64 (30 July 1875).

/Xam-ka-!ke-ta !gwe: 'The Bushman's Letters'

D. Bleek, 'Customs and Belief of the /Xam Bushmen: Part III –
Game Animals', 'Part IV – Omens, Windmaking and Clouds',
Bantu Studies 6 (1932); Edith and Dorothea Bleek, 'Notes on the
Bushmen'; Bleek and Lloyd, *Specimens of Bushman Folklore*; W. H. I.
Bleek, *Second Report*; correspondence, notebooks and papers in the
Bleek and Lloyd Collection, University of Cape Town; L. C. Lloyd,
*A Short Account of Further Bushman Material Collected. Third Report
concerning Bushman researches, presented to both Houses of Parliament of
the Cape of Good Hope, by command of His Excellency the Governor*
(Nutt, London 1889); W. C. Palgrave, *The Commissions of WC
Palgrave Special Emissary to SW Africa 1878–1885*, ed. E. L. P. Stals
(Cape Town 1991); Solomon, 'Meanings, Models and Minds,

'Myth and Ritual': Lewis-Williams, 'A Visit to the Lion's House', unpublished manuscripts in the Grey Collection, National Library of South Africa.

Kumm: The sending of the crows

Lloyd, IV, pp. 2473–86 (10 March 1874).

Kukummi: Things Told

W. H. I. Bleek, *Second Report*; Bleek and Lloyd, *Specimens of Bushman Folklore*; The Bible of King James; correspondence, papers and notebooks from the Bleek and Lloyd Collection; David Lewis-Williams, 'Introduction', in *Stories that Float from Afar*; Lloyd, *Third Report*. See also 'The Grey Collection Controversy', *Quarterly Bulletin of the SA Library* 9, 1954.

Janette Deacon first discussed the power of place and the role of the Agama lizard in the ritual culture of the /Xam-ka !ei in 'My Place Is the Bitterpits'.

Kumm: The broken string

D. Bleek, 'Customs and Belief of the /Xam Bushmen: Part VII – Sorcerers', *Bantu Studies* (1932); Bleek and Lloyd, *Specimens of Bushman Folklore*; Lewis-Williams, *Believing and Seeing*.

'This is no Bushman Painting. This is Great Art'

Shirley-Ann Pager, *A Visit to the White Lady of the Brandberg* (SAP, Windhoek 1999); H. Breuil, Mary Boyle, E. R. Scherz, and R. G. Strey, *The Rock Paintings of Southern Africa*, vol. 1, *The White Lady of the Brandberg* (Trianon Press, Clairvaux 1955); Lewis-Williams and Dowson: *Images of Power*; *Art* (Southern Book Publishers, Johannesburg 1989); Lloyd, *Third Report*; Bleek and Lloyd; *Specimens of Bushman Folklore*.

Kumm: The Bushman dies, he goes to this place

Lloyd, II 12, pp. 1173–9 (12 April 1872).

Where Is /Kaggen?

W. H. I. Bleek in Orpen, 'A Glimpse into the Mythology of the Maluti Bushmen'; D. Bleek, 'Customs and Belief of the /Xam Bushmen: Part IV – Omens, Windmaking and Clouds', 'Part VII – Sorcerers', *Bantu Studies*, 1932; Bleek and Lloyd, *Specimens of Bushman Folklore*; Deacon, 'My Place Is the Bitterpits'; Grant S. McCall, 'Why the Eland? An Analysis of the Role of Sexual Dimorphism in San Rock Art', http://rupestre.net/trace/12/eland.html; Ronald K. Siegel, *Fire in the Brain, Clinical Tales of Hallucination* (Dutton, New York 1993); Ronald K. Siegel and L. J. West (eds.), *Hallucinations, Behaviour, Existence and Theory* (Wiley, London 1975); Stow and Bleek, *Rock Paintings in South Africa*.

For a far more sophisticated analysis of the so-called *trance hypothesis* of San rock art, see Lewis-Williams and Dowson, *Images of Power*, or Lewis-Williams, *Believing and Seeing*. The rock painting of the antelope and the shaman described in this chapter is pictured and explained in the former book and the painting of the 'battle' near Beersheba is described from a reproduction in the latter.

The work of the archaeologist and rock art researcher Anne Solomon qualifies the trance hypothesis by considering the role of mythology and the importance of the representation of gender in the interpretation of the rock art of the Southern San. See her 'Meanings, Models and Minds', 'The Myth of Ritual Origins?', and 'Gender, Representation and Power in San Ethnography and Rock Art', *Journal of Anthropological Archaeology* 11 (1992). These publications were essential in writing this chapter.

Kumm: /A:kumm and the lion

This story, and the details of the behaviour of lions, comes from Dorothea Bleek's 'Customs and Belief of the /Xam Bushmen: Part II – The Lion', *Bantu Studies* 5 (1932).

!Kau-/nunu: Kenhardt

Photographs and unpublished manuscripts from the National Library of South Africa. See also Dorothea Bleek's 'Notes on the Bushman Photographs', *Bantu Studies* 10 (1936); Edith and Dorothea Bleek, 'Notes on the Bushmen'.

Index

Cape Argus, 269, 301
Cape Monthly Magazine, 172,
    173, 301–2, 305–6
Cape Thirstland, *see* Northern
    Cape
Cape Town, 6, 22–3, 98, 252,
    280, 281, 282, 283, 307,
    337
Celt, 101, 102, 103
Charlton House, 218–19, 252,
    268, 275, 282, 295, 309,
    310, 311, 312, 313, 332
Chauvet Cave, 363
chrysalids, 25, 47, 211
Church Missionary Society, 79
Clay Hand, *see* Xättin
Colenso, Frances, 91
Colenso, John William, 77,
    83–4, 91, 337
commando, 115, 119–26, 288
Committee of the South
    African Public Library,
    273–6, 281, 298, 308, 310,
    319–21
Cradock, 333
crows, 287–8
curses of the Anteater and the
    Lynx ('the Anteater's
    Laws'), 16, 19, 26, 49–51

Da, 312–15, 331–2
Dale, Dr Langham, 165, 273–7,
    298–302, 305–6, 319–20

Darwin, Charles, 107
Dassie, *see* /Huntu!katt!katten
Deacon, Janette, 295–7
death, 221, 240–43, 251–2,
    253–6, 265, 269, 272,
    277–8, 280–81, 341–2,
    351, 352–4, 359–61,
    362–3
Deception Pan, 49, 249
Devenish, Mr, 217, 281
Dia!kwain, 8, 161–5, 173, 196,
    197, 207–8, 217, 219, 233,
    269, 275, 277, 278, 283,
    292, 296, 302, 325–6, 332,
    352, 360
  appearance, 28, 209, 335
  death of, 279–80
  death of his wife, 247–51
  describes rock art, 174, 247,
    336, 346–7, 357
  dream of his father's death,
    259–61, 265
  family, 164, 166–70, 177
  is healed by a *!gi:xa*, 181–4
  letter to his sister, 270–71
  punishments at the
    Breakwater, 28, 163, 164
  return to the Northern
    Cape, 217
  watches his father make rain
    213–16
dolerite, 133, 209, 291, 370
Drakensberg, 170